THEY MAKE US
DANGEROUS

THEY MAKE US DANGEROUS

(Bolivia 1964-1980)

A MEMOIR

By Frances R. Payne, PhD

Library of Congress Control Number: 2011962968
ISBN: Hardcover   978-1-4691-4003-2
                 Softcover   978-1-4691-4002-5
                 Ebook   978-1-4691-4004-9

To order additional copies of this book, contact:
Xlibris Corporation
1-888-795-4274
www.Xlibris.com
Orders@Xlibris.com
105388

TABLE OF CONTENTS

DEDICATION

For the remarkable people with whom I was privileged to share the events described in this book, especially Rita Martin who understood.

PROLOGUE

"Bolivia" is a landlocked country in the heart of South America often portrayed in photos of picturesque indigenous Aymara women in colorful shawls and bowler derbies. It gained the world's attentions when Che Guevara was arrested and killed there during his guerrilla campaign in 1967. It made front-page news again in the nineteen eighties when it became a major player in cocaine production and trafficking. The more informed reader will know that in the year 2000, uprisings in the city of Cochabamba succeeded in pulling the Bechtel Corporation's greedy fingers out of its water supply. Bolivia has had the reputation of being the most politically unstable country in the world. In the first century and a half, after winning independence from Spain, it chalked up no fewer than 188 revolutions; in other words it has had more violent government changes than any other country in history!

However, these are not the only remarkable things about Bolivia. In fact, it is impossible to write about Bolivia without a generous use of superlatives; here are just a few of the records it has held or continues to hold:

> The world's biggest tin mine, the world's highest navigable lake, the highest capital city, Latin America's largest indigenous population, widest variety of musical folklore, smallest number of paved roads, world's highest ski-run, oldest mint in Latin America, the world's most nutritious grain (*quinoa*), the most dangerous road in the world, and the only legal labor union made up of producers of a narcotic plant, the first to rebel against the Spanish Crown, the first to gain its independence from Spain and the first in Latin America to implement agrarian reform and university autonomy. In recent times, it boasts of the world's largest deposit of lithium used in the production of modern day batteries.

Sad to say, global warming done away with the glaciers on Mt. Chacaltaya and Bolivia can no longer boast of the world's highest ski slopes. The powerful Bolivian Workers' Central (COB) has almost gone the way of the snow; this due to a shift in the economic climate called neoliberalism

In most vital statistics, i.e. in infant mortality and morbidity rates, illiteracy, life expectancy unemployment, Bolivia has historically followed closely behind Haiti at the bottom of the charts. This is the result, of course of the ever-present and all-reaching tentacles of foreign interests, for hardly a single aspect of Bolivian life escapes their reach, directly or indirectly. And, as with so many other nations at the bottom of the capitalist pyramid, its rich mineral deposits (gold, silver, tin and much more) have created immense wealth for a few, and desperate poverty for the many. The largest percentage of the population is deprived of basic needs and scratches out a miserable existence in subhuman conditions. That is how it has been ever since the first ray of sunlight skipped off the conquistador's helmet.

Bolivians are admirable for their unrelenting pursuit of freedom and dignity against all odds. They have done so in the midst of grim poverty caused largely by the sacking of the country's natural resources during five centuries. Chronically infected with political corruption and battered by foreign, "interests," life in Bolivia can be bleak and especially harsh in the mountainous regions, but remarkably, it does go on. Presidents come and go from the government palace, babies are born, students pass exams, poetry is written and young people fall in love. Music and laughter, drinking and dancing and acts of decent humanity keep it rich at its deepest roots. And beyond the poetic simplicity, there is an epic struggle for sovereignty that few people know or read about except when the situation suddenly boils over in such proportion as to merit a few column inches in the New York Times.

For years, friends and family and especially my three older brothers suggested that I write about Bolivia and I've even made several attempts, keeping notes and old publications. It was only after losing my job of sixteen years that I finally began working in earnest. At last, with some quality time on my hands, I delved into a stack of yellowed letters that I had written to my family from 1964 to 1983, while in Bolivia. My brother John had kept most of them and with a final word of encouragement he returned them to me in February 2000. He died of Lou Gehrig's disease in September of that same year, and I'm sure he'd be pleased to know that I followed up on his suggestion. My brother Ed also helped by digging through his "archives" for things I had sent him. In addition, conversations with friends from that period in my life have helped me recall many things that I had forgotten and reconstruct some of them here for the reader.

This, then, is the story of a political struggle that was and is, of a people who refuse to be crushed under the boot of military dictators who too often have been financed, coached and manipulated by the government of the United States. It is the story of a people who pledge in their national anthem to, "Die rather than live as slaves." What follows tells of one of the most convulsive periods in their history and how I saw it unfold.

CHAPTER 1

TIME FOR CHANGE

A mid morning breeze crisp with the scent of autumn leaves drifted in off Lake Michigan and the gray-yellow brick walls of St. Catherine's convent glowed in the sunlight. The bespectacled Mr.Canfield squinted as he stood waiting to open the door of the convent car, a sleek black limousine, which the sisters amusingly referred to as "the hearse." In minutes and with no further fanfare, I would be on my way to South America. It was October 1964.

First, however, I will back up a bit to describe how this all began. In the spring of 1962, I was a Dominican sister, twenty-seven years old, and assigned to teach fourth grade at Sacred Heart Elementary School in Racine, Wisconsin. My name in the order was Sister Ruth.

I had left home in 1952 when religious life was steeped in the tradition of ascetic monasticism, a basic framework that had changed very little over the centuries. My religious home, the convent of Saint Catherine of Siena was no exception. During those years of preparation for religious life, my companions and I followed a rigorous schedule of prayer and study, isolated from events outside the convent walls. We were imbued with a profound sense of mission that was reinforced by sharing it in common with others who held the same ideals. Above all a religious vocation was a divine call to a life of contemplation and service. During our formation years, we were put through a series of hurdles, rigid practices in self-denial. We were told that there was a "right" and a "wrong" way to do just about everything: drying dishes, dusting a stairway and folding a sheet. What is more important, we also learned the value of silence, reflection and study. We were taught to search for truth and to be uncompromising in our determination to go after what was right. We accepted all of this with eagerness and sincerity. And we were very young and very innocent.

As serene and sheltered as were the formation years, they were also filled with many lighter moments of laughter and good humor. Fortunately, there were strong, intelligent and very dedicated women, who patiently put up with our exuberance and guided us through those early years and somehow we survived and thrived and finally, professed our vows.

By 1962, I had matured in this way of life. The community was my family, and I was exactly where I wanted to be by choice, by vocation and by the grace of God.

Thus, one fine spring day after showing sixty-four nine and ten-year olds how to identify rivers and mountains on a map and how to use basic study skills, I had no reason to suspect anything would interrupt my predictable routine. I gathered up a stack of papers to correct, closed the classroom door behind me and crossed the schoolyard to the two-story wooden frame house that served as our convent.

I was tired and lost in thought when I opened the kitchen door, quite oblivious to what was about to happen.

I jolted to attention when I realized that Sister Marjorie, the Superior, was waiting for me. She said, "Sister Mary Magdalen is here to see you." A visit from the Director of Studies could not be taken lightly. I was both delighted and intimidated, because of all the superiors, she was the one I most admired. She oversaw the professional development of the sisters and decided who would study what, where and when. "But," I wondered, "I already have my degree in elementary education, so why would she want to see me?"

There was a note of urgency, even anxiety in Sister Mary Magdalen's voice when she said we needed to speak alone. She explained that plans were being made to open a mission somewhere in South America, maybe Bolivia. She was concerned: "Our community knows nothing about Latin America. We've no experience in foreign mission work, and I think we need someone to study in this area for us. I'd like you to apply for a scholarship for the doctoral program in Latin American Studies at Saint Louis University."

A wave of objections rushed through my mind. Me? South America? This is really crazy! A doctorate in Latin American Studies? I hadn't the least interest in Latin America or missionary work, not to mention that I couldn't speak a word of Spanish.

Before I could voice my objections, Sister Mary Magdalen added, "Well, we think you probably can do it but you'll have to study Spanish this summer."

Truthfully, I was frightened. After all, I was very comfortable in the protective surroundings of community life. Going to graduate school would mean being out on my own and facing the uncertainty of a new challenge. Other members of the community had even collapsed under the strain of doctoral studies. Could I really do this? As for working in a foreign country, it was something I wasn't able to imagine. And Spanish! I had studied enough French and Latin to convince me that I had no foreign language ability whatsoever.

She handed me a scholarship application form to sign with the admonition that the plan had to be shrouded in confidentiality. "Don't say anything to anyone about this." Then, almost as an afterthought, she pulled a small booklet out of a black bag and said, "Here, in the meantime you should read this." She left quickly before I had a chance to react. The other sisters were curious about the visit but assuming that it had something to do with a summer study program, they said nothing.

I took the booklet to chapel that evening. It was Msgr. Ivan Illich's essay called, "Missionary Poverty", a scathing account of the Catholic Church's failure to identify with the poor in Latin America. In it he laid out the need for a change in the attitudes and practices that had for centuries put the Catholic Church in the same camp with the rich and powerful oppressors. As I read Illich's words that evening and re-read them in the following days, I gradually began to feel a tug at my heart. Yes, this would be a challenge but also an opportunity to do something more. I began to understand that the "mission" was to learn about another culture, to respect it and value it. The poverty I had professed would take on a new dimension. It would be an invitation to detach myself from my comfortable ways of thinking and being. I wasn't so sure I could do that but there would be time enough to find out.

That summer I immersed myself in Spanish 101 and when the more curious sisters inquired, I became pretty adept at creative explanations for studying a new language.

In the fall, after one last heartfelt, but unsuccessful, attempt to dissuade Sister Mary Magdalen from sending me to St. Louis, I reluctantly left friends and familiar surroundings to begin graduate studies. Her dispassionate response was ringing in my mind as I boarded the old North Shore commuter train in Racine, "Well, we feel that you just might be able to do it. Even though you are an overachiever, we think you have the emotional stability to handle it. And if you can't, you can just come back."

I had a sick feeling in the pit of my stomach. Surely I was doomed for failure. I switched trains at Union Station in Chicago and was on my way to graduate school. I took in every detail along the way, straining in vain to see something interesting, but there were only bushes and flatland and the dull backside of an occasional small town. By the time we crossed the Mississippi and pulled into St. Louis the car was filled with soot and grime. I arrived on campus with just enough time to drop my suitcase at Notre Dame residence hall before beginning the complicated enrollment process.

My separation anxiety lasted about three hours. That was when a Sister of Mercy offered much needed advice and friendship. Her room was next to mine at Notre Dame Hall, the residence for religious women on the Saint Louis University Campus. She told me that she had been there working on her doctoral thesis in English for five years already and despaired of ever finishing it. She had an affinity for Snoopy cartoons and knew anything I needed to know about the university and the city. I was horrified by the thought of being there for so long but the prospect of new friends made the transition almost tolerable.

Notre Dame Hall housed about sixty nuns; mostly graduate students, representing nearly that many different communities and major academic fields. During my stay there I learned as much, if not more, in conversations with them as I did from classes. There were sisters from Uruguay, Honduras, Guatemala, Spain, several who had worked in Third World countries, and even a Dominican who had been exiled from Castro's Cuba. All were serious students creating a kind of on-call reference library bound in flowing garments.

For the next two years all of my classes were focused on Latin America. I became acquainted, though superficially, with its literature, history, geography and politics. As I read about the coup against Arbenz in Guatemala, the U.S. occupation of the Dominican Republic, Betancourt's Venezuela, I wondered why I had never learned anything at all about Latin America, not even the Spanish Conquest, in school. I realized that my knowledge of the rest of the world was woefully deficient.

Sister Mary Magdalen regularly provided me with "confidential" and somewhat scandalous reports sent to superiors about the church in Latin America and more material from Ivan Illich and his missionary training center in Cuernavaca, Mexico. There were more reports of missionaries living in lavish comfort in the midst of misery, and of the alliance of church officials with the arrogant ruling elites. His earlier essay on poverty had just hinted at the insensitivity of some missionaries, and now this new flow of information clearly documented the flaws and failures of the Catholic Church in Latin America.

Meanwhile, back in Racine, Mother Albertine, the major superior, planned a visit to several South American countries in search of a place to send her first group of foreign missionaries. She went to Venezuela, Colombia and Peru; then and at the invitation of two Dominican priests from the Chicago Province, to Bolivia. The Racine Community had close ties to the Chicago Dominicans; for years the sisters had been cooks at their seminary. Now two of the Dominican priests were stationed in Bolivia. Dan Roach and Chris Gaerets had been chaplains and teachers for the sisters in Racine, and they both offered to be of help in getting the community established in Bolivia. It was very likely that this played a major part in Mother Albertine's plan to open the mission in La Paz.

Sister Mary Magdalen wrote me immediately about the decision, and I charged off to the local libraries to borrow everything I could find on Bolivia, which was practically nothing. I found a lone recording of Bolivian music at the St. Louis Public Library and only two books. In desperation, I subscribed to Presencia, a daily newspaper from La Paz. The newspaper's circulation manager agreed to mail me the "best" papers once a week. How or why he chose the particular issues I do not know, but my excitement grew with the arrival of each bulky packet.

During those two years, the Saint Louis campus was host to a group of Peace Corps trainees. Wherever they went, through the halls or up and down the elevators, ripples of admiration followed them. They were already seen as young heroes, an elite of idealistic men and women whose motivation and genuine desire to help others were contagious. Without a doubt, I was very much influenced by their presence and by the politics of the moment.

The civil rights movement was at its peak and opposition to the war in Vietnam was getting very heated. Sisters from Racine marched in Selma and others began leaving traditional teaching in schools to work in what they felt were more socially significant ministries. University campuses overflowed with a generation of young people who would question this nation's policies, and shake it at its roots. The Berrigan brothers and others were preparing to challenge the power structures and take radical steps. We added new words to our vocabulary: teach-ins, sit-ins and civil disobedience. We were paralyzed with fear during the Cuban missile crisis and had our innocence and sense of security shattered with President Kennedy's assassination. The wave of protest rumbling beneath the surface would soon erupt in a new sense of reality and social responsibility and a general mistrust of authority.

After two semesters, I received a Masters in Education. After another year, I passed comprehensive and oral exams for my doctorate and my advisors approved a very loosely structured proposal for my dissertation. It would be a study of Bolivian university women and their cultural values. Thus, by the summer of 1964, equipped with a cursory knowledge of Bolivia and halting Spanish, I was ready to begin field research in La Paz.

I emerged from those two years keenly aware of how little I really knew about Latin America. I knew that from now on I would take a back seat and listen and learn and absorb a new culture in a foreign land. There would be no proselytizing, no preaching, only respectful observation in hopes that a framework for analysis might emerge from the experience. Finally in May, I was awarded a research scholarship from the Organization of American States (OAS), and I returned to Racine for the summer and final preparations for Bolivia.

Those months, however, would not go smoothly. A new administration was at the helm of the community. Mother Albertine's term as Mother General had come to an end, and Sister Mary Magdalen was elected to replace her. She and her new assistants began voicing concerns about the Bolivian venture that they had inherited from their predecessors. The old objections persisted: the Community was not prepared for work in a foreign country and things had been rushed into prematurely. Instead of enthusiasm and support from the superiors, the atmosphere was filled with doubts as thick and suffocating as the steamy Lake Michigan summer fog. So intense were the objections we were certain that the whole project would be scrapped.

The uncertainty was made even more unbearable by the rigid authoritarian structure still in place in the community. Although many rules and regulations would soon be swept away, in 1964, they were still the law, and compliance with them became the source of many small crises and misunderstandings. Who was in charge of what and who could make which decisions? Who could make the small purchases required for the trip? Who would give us permission to leave the premises for necessary errands? Who could make phone calls to make appointments for visas, immunizations and shipping arrangements?

With or without support, the wheels were spinning. The previous administration had already selected four of us to open the new house in Bolivia. Sister Marie Joseph was to head the group as superior. She had been my tough-as-nails high school history teacher when I was a freshman in Detroit. She and Sister Julianne, a much-respected young superior, were to leave Racine first, traveling by train to New York. From there they would embark on a freight ship to Arica, Chile, supposedly keeping an eye on our baggage at each port making absolutely sure that not a single object (sacred or profane) would be pilfered along the way. Their plan was to see the cargo through to La Paz, Bolivia. Then they were to fly to Lima, Peru to study Spanish for six months at a special language school for missionaries. I would travel directly to La Paz on my own and Sister Giovanni would be the last to leave, going directly to language school in Lima. In March we would all be reunited in La Paz, and the Sisters of St. Dominic of St. Catherine of Siena of Racine, Wisconsin, would begin a totally new and different type of work in a part of the world they had barely dreamed about.

We spent the better part of July and August sweltering in an empty classroom at St. Catherine's High School, sorting and packing piles of trivial articles that had been donated by well-intentioned friends. Everything had to be counted meticulously for customs, we were told. I've kept the numbers safely in my mind all these years: 7,000 holy cards with sacred images, 5,000 medals of the Virgin and other saints of Holy Mother Church, 3,000 rosaries and 1,000 miscellaneous religious trinkets (small statues, key chains, holy water fonts and such). Those extremely tedious hours in the muggy Racine heat rivaled the medieval penance devised by our 13th century founding fathers for their early monks. The highest point of the summer finally came the afternoon when we hauled three steamer trunks and four huge barrels to the Kenosha railroad station and, with a surge of triumph and relief, sent them off to New York.

As a final touch, the superiors decided we should officially use the Spanish form of our names, so Marie Joseph became Madre Maria José, Julianne, Madre Juliana, and Giovanni was translated to Madre Juanita. Since my name was the same in both languages, I simply became "Madre" Ruth.

So it was that in between immunizations and dodging disapproving stares from superiors, we moved ahead with plans for La Paz. Pope John XXIII's request would be fulfilled. After all, that was what had set this in motion in the first place. The Pope had called for ten percent of all U.S. religious personnel to serve in South America.

In mid-September, the four of us made a trip to Detroit and Assumption Grotto parish, where I had taught second grade for three years in the fifties. The pastor arranged a formal sendoff with a special Sunday morning liturgy in which we were each given a small missionary cross to remind us of the sacrifices we would have to make. Actually, I remember nothing of that day, except that it happened and that when it was over, there was no turning back. It was final.

The following morning we packed for our flight back to Racine, but as it turned out, my trip would have to wait. My father stopped by to say a final farewell, and I hurried down the convent hall to meet him. I opened the parlor door expecting a bear hug, but instead found him slumped forward in a chair, his bifocals on the floor. He had suffered a stroke. The next hours and days were devastating, and I do remember each detail. I stayed at his side as much as possible and wanted to be sure he was out of danger, and that he would recover. I seriously considered not traveling to South America, but my three brothers Ed, Chuck and John, convinced me they would take good care of him. Several days later, I hugged him good-bye and left him in his hospital room in the company of friends. I looked back from the doorway and still unable to speak, he smiled a big Irish grin and waved. I returned to Racine with a very heavy heart. Mom had died when I was five years old and he had always been the most important person in my life.

By the time I got back to Racine, Sisters Marie Joseph and Julianne had already left for Bolivia. The next day I received a phone call assuring me that my ticket to La Paz would be waiting for me at the Pan Am desk at Milwaukee's Mitchell Field on Friday. I would be on my way to Bolivia, courtesy of an Organization of American States (OAS) scholarship to do doctoral research in Education and Latin American Studies.

On October 3, 1964, I said my last good-byes in the front entrance of the convent, and as I viewed its polished black tile floor and the winding spiral staircase, I recalled cleaning them as a novice, often not to the satisfaction of Sister Eunice, the novice mistress. She would call the cobwebs I neglected to remove, "Good Friday curtains." My very last memory of the old convent was the potpourri aroma of fresh coffee, incense and newly waxed floors.

I gathered my long skirts into the back seat of the "hearse" and Mr. Canfield politely closed the door. I looked long at the small group of sisters standing silently in the sunlight. This was a life, a place and a time that I would never know again.

CHAPTER 2

BOLIVIA AND THE CATHOLIC CHURCH IN 1964

I was on my way to Bolivia to become part of the history of a country and a church, both poised on the brink of revolution. Change may have been centuries overdue for the Catholic Church, but for Bolivia, it was nothing new. The years leading up to 1964 made the time of my arrival in La Paz especially ripe for another violent explosion. In order to understand that moment, it is worthwhile to retrace some of those events.

In 1951, Victor Paz Estenssoro, economics professor at the University of San Andres in La Paz and head of the National Revolutionary Movement (MNR) party won the presidential election in Bolivia. However, before he could be sworn into office, the military supporting the old state oligarchy, intervened, occupied the presidential palace and forced the leaders of the party into exile. However, Hernan Siles Zuazo, an energetic young militant and co-founder of the MNR, returned to the country in secret. From a clandestine hideout, he was able to organize and mobilize the opposition, and by April 9, 1952, the major cities and mining centers exploded in a popular uprising. After nine days of intense fighting in the streets, Siles' followers defeated the military.

Paz Estenssoro victoriously returned from exile in Argentina and was sworn in as President. Having led the uprising, Hernan Siles Zuazo was named the Vice President. A third co-founder of the party, a strong and popular labor leader named Juan Lechin Oquendo, completed the top leadership of the MNR. These three men were able to unite workers, students and campesinos to defeat the famed, "tin Barons", the Hoschild, Patino and Aramayo families who owned the tin mines and personified the Bolivian oligarchy that had ruled and exploited Bolivia's mineral wealth and its miners for decades.

Under enormous pressure from the masses, especially the campesinos and the Labor Movement, Paz Estenssoro implemented far-reaching nationalist reforms. These included: the near dissolution of the military, the nationalization of the mines, agrarian reform, universal suffrage and an educational reform based on an all-reaching code that some herald today as one of the most farsighted pieces of social literature ever produced in Latin America.

Siles Zuazo succeeded Paz Estenssoro as President from 1956 to 1960. During that time, he gradually re-established the military, mostly for agricultural work and road building. By then Bolivia had nationalized its mines, but it was still impoverished. The U.S. State Department opportunistically took advantage of Bolivia's poverty to make inroads into its policies, and dependence on US aid grew rapidly. Moreover, a serious thorn in Siles side was the infamous "Stabilization Commission" he had inherited from Paz. The Commission had been formed at the recommendation of the IMF (International Monetary Fund) and George Jackson Eder, a U.S. citizen directly employed by Washington, was named director. In his case history of Bolivia, Eder traces with luxury of detail his part in the Commission, conversations with Presidents Paz and Siles and his unprecedented intrusion as an active participant in cabinet meetings. He blames U.S. aid for Bolivia's corruption, calling it, "the most potent source of illegal enrichment in the history of that nation," and adds not too kindly, that it has turned Bolivia into a "master moocher."

Miners, factory workers, students and the general populace took their opposition to Eder and the IMF recommendations to the streets. However, in spite of the upheavals it was creating, the Stabilization Commission and Eder were able to impose a rigid austerity plan. Among the measures forced on the country were cuts in government subsidies and social spending, a wage freeze and, of course, the devaluation of the peso. The plan was accepted by Siles only after the IMF threatened to discontinue financial aid altogether. In the wake of these unpopular measures, and foreign meddling in the affairs of the country, support for the MNR began to erode. To be sure, Siles held the country together, but with great difficulty.

By now it is generally believed that in 1952, the three leaders of the MNR had made an agreement that each would take his turn running for president in succeeding electoral campaigns. However, Paz Estenssoro did not keep his part of the bargain. He edged out the next in line, Lechin, campaigned again and returned to the presidential palace in 1960.

During Paz's second term in office, the split emerging within the MNR widened. His policies became increasingly repressive, alienating the campesinos and the miners. The teachers' union and factory workers protested. High school and university students took to the streets. Under pressure from the U.S. in its anticommunist, anti-Castro struggle, the military budget was almost tripled and some 1200 members of the Bolivian military were sent for training to the School of the Americas, which was located in Panama then.

By the end of his term, Paz Estenssoro was accused of betraying the ideals of the 1952 Revolution and Lechin, as well as other leaders of the MNR, formed other political parties. It became increasingly difficult for Paz to maintain his position without bloody repression. Opposition members were hunted down and sent into exile. Others were tortured and executed at the hands of Victor San Roman, his infamous henchman.

In 1964, after a visit to Washington where were strings were most surely attached, Paz announced his candidacy again. This was in direct violation of the Bolivian constitution, which prohibited a president from serving two consecutive terms in office. He was re-elected in a process that was anything but clean.

As his third term began, he knew he had lost the support of the campesinos and workers who held him responsible for massacres of the very miners who had fought to bring him into power in 1952. Now he was almost wholly dependent on his friends in the armed forces. It is significant that when he was sworn in on August 6th, 1964 his Vice President was not chosen from his MNR party, but rather from the ranks of the military. Allegedly, General Rene Barrientos Ortuño, head of the Air Force, was the handpicked choice of the U.S. State Department.

By October 1964, at the time when I was on my way to Bolivia, a brutal repressive apparatus was up and running. Dissenters who organized in opposition to the regime suffered bloody consequences. During this period, Washington was devoting time and effort and resources in an all-out war against communism. Soon it would turn its full attention to the southern cone of Latin America and Bolivia and intensify its activities there and that, with disastrous results. I, of course, was for the moment blithely unaware of these events.

In that autumn of 1964, changes were about to occur in the Catholic Church, as well. Its leaders were in the midst of a Council, only the second of its kind in history. By then, some of the first documents of the sessions were already being published. As news of their contents became public, there were rumblings of change and questioning, with dogmas and tradition coming under close scrutiny. Theologians were re-examining centuries old traditions and teachings and setting a new course for the church, one that would emphasize and promote the personal dignity of each human being. Moreover, this would be a movement that would eventually cause great division within the church. The new focus would define religion as a celebration of life and a commitment to living, rather than an exercise in self-denial; a search for fulfillment in community rather than morbid self-preoccupation; and an alignment with the impoverished and oppressed of the world instead of a courtship of the powerful. The crust of cumbersome, unnecessary traditions was beginning to crumble and there was every promise of new life. There were new causes and new issues and new commitments to be made. For many in the church, it was a time of great enthusiasm and exhilaration but for others it was a time of fear and anxiety; some even believed, of excesses. For me, it was a time of hope and optimism that the church could really make a difference.

In Latin America, the sixties heralded the influx of a large group of North American religious women and men. This was in response to the call from the Vatican to send missionaries to Latin America. They went into the jungles and cities with varying degrees of preparation; some were quite ready to plunge into the work and others were not at all acquainted with the culture, history, language or political problems of the countries where they were sent.

Many were sent for cross-cultural training first, to schools that were already a few steps ahead of the Vatican Council. These were centers where the traditional role of the Catholic Church, especially in Latin America, was being seriously questioned and openly criticized, and they became focal points for disseminating the new ideas of the Vatican Council. Possibly, the greatest lesson taught in these centers was that the failure of foreign missionaries to adapt would make them agents of cultural alienation, and that it was they, not the Latin Americans, who needed to change.

CHAPTER 3

ON TOP OF THE WORLD

But back to Racine and my mission: As promised by the OAS, my ticket was waiting for me at the airport and, after checking my small black suitcase, a high school graduation gift from my father, I boarded the plane. I settled in to my seat for the short flight to O'Hare. Any feelings of excitement or expectation were numbed by the summer's tensions and my father's illness. At Chicago's O'Hare field I changed planes and continued on to Miami where I checked in at the Pan Am desk for the midnight flight to La Paz. Everything was in order; I had the required immunizations: yellow fever, dyptheria, typhoid/paratyphoid, hepatitis, small pox and cholera.

I was not a veteran flyer by any means, but I felt safe and secure as we lifted off from Miami in a small turbo jet. We floated into a velvety darkness until a stopover in Panama, where the door opened to allow passengers to exit and the cabin filled with the delicious sweet aroma of tropical air. The trance-like atmosphere was interrupted momentarily by shouts of *"cucaracha!"* An enormous insect as large as the sole of a man's size eleven shoe was clinging to the back of one of the passengers. Man and roach were ushered off the craft midst screams and panic. Soon after, the doors were shut and we again were lifted into a sea of darkness. With only the purr of the engines in the cabin; I felt enveloped by a protective silence and as the distance from loved ones grew, tensions and misgivings melted away. I fell into a deep, deep sleep.

I awoke to the aroma of coffee and piercing rays of sunlight flitting through the aircraft. My long white habit was twisted and bunched up underneath me. Even though the convent seamstress had narrowed the long sleeves for convenience, there was still just too much cloth all around and I spent my first waking moments sorting out the layers and putting each in its proper place. I sported a newly designed black veil, which allowed a small clump of unruly hair to show at the forehead, a tribute to modernization (and poor taste) but a harbinger of things to come.

We touched down briefly in Lima, Peru, and then began the last leg of the journey. We left the Pacific coastline and *Atacama* Desert in a matter of minutes and ascended over enormous mounds of gray earth, like a herd of giant elephants grazing under the tropical sun. As we continued to climb, the gray mountains below gave way to the snow-capped western range of the Andes. Still over Peru, the pilot treated us to a breathtaking dip into the volcano *"El Misti."* Soon, in the distance, there shimmered the teal blue crystal of Lake *Titicaca*, from whose sacred waters, according to the legend, the gods drew the first Inca Prince and Princess. Then to the left in all of its glory and with passengers straining to get a better view, was the aptly named Royal Cordillera, the magnificent eastern range of the Andes, stretching from horizon to horizon. The plane glided lightly and effortlessly, and then touched down in the alluringly barren *Altiplano,* the high tableland that stretches for 500 miles in between the eastern and western Andes mountain ranges. At 13,000 feet above sea level, this was Bolivia!

In 1964, the Pan Am airport was one of several in the Altiplano. The airlines shared the landing strip but located about a mile apart, each had a small house that served to receive and dispatch passengers. The Pan Am airport must have been the smallest international airport in the world; a neat little one-room stucco building out in the middle of nowhere. The entire area included a desk where passports were stamped, a baggage claim counter, a snack bar seating five or six people, and a large, welcoming fireplace. Friends and relatives greeted each other and embraced by the fireside. With my passport stamped and suitcase in hand, I stepped outside to admire the Cordillera. Off to one side, llamas were grazing, and children with brown and cracked cheeks, offered to shine shoes and carry luggage. Others were hawking souvenirs. The staccato of their voices echoed across the open plain. I breathed in deeply and waited for Brother Kevin to pick me up.

I waited. The small crowd slowly disappeared into the chilly afternoon. It was 4 p.m. I had memorized the names of the mountains and I recited them to myself, *"Illampu, Huayna-Potosí, Mururata, Illimani . . . ."*

Minutes later: *"Madre!"* A friendly *"gringo"* approached me.

"Do you have a ride to the city?"

"Yes", I said, "I'm expecting someone to pick me up."

It was official; he called me, *"Madre."*

I waited a while longer and the airport door locked behind me. The children and the llamas left. I was alone but still confidant that my ride would be there. I waited.

"*Madre*, are you sure someone is coming to meet you?"

It was the same American. He had circled around in his jeep and returned to where I was standing.

"*Madre*, the airport is closed now and we're the last car going to the city. We can give you a lift."

It was beginning to cloud over a little and the air was beginning to feel chilly.

"I'm Padre Roberto from St. Louis and I just came to meet two lay volunteers who were on vacation in the States."

"I'm Sister Ruth. Racine Dominican. A Dominican Brother was supposed to meet me, but I guess the telegram didn't get through." I accepted the ride.

I climbed into the jeep, and was introduced to the lay missionaries. We drove down a narrow road lined with an adobe wall on one side and open fields on the other. It was the upper part of the city of La Paz called "El Alto." Today this settlement is a city of half a million with its own mayor and city council, but in 1964, it was just a stark, cold, windswept no-man's land.

We passed a row of one-room adobe houses. Padre Roberto explained that the tin roofs were "a sign of progress." Indian women hurried alongside the road, on their backs, babies wrapped in bright colored shawls.

We made a turn to the left and drove under a white cement arch. It read, "*Bienvenido a La Paz*," Welcome to La Paz. And there it was! Defying superlatives, La Paz - 2000 feet below! Since then the city has climbed upwards all the way to the top of the gorge and beyond but in 1964 it was pressed into the very bottom of the canyon. At the southern rim, exposed in its entirety with nothing to obstruct its splendor, was Mt. *Illimani:* a snowy deity that lights up with the first rays of the morning sun and catches the last glow of each sunset, standing as sentinel and silent witness to the centuries. That afternoon it was thrust against an icy gray sky, huge, white and majestic, completely worthy of the worship given it by the Incas.

Slowly, we began to spiral downward and became immersed in unfamiliar smells and sounds. As far as I could see, everything was shabby and poor; the air was dusty and stuck in my throat. The children's faces were cracked by the cold. Indian women selling fruit and bread along the roadside were brush strokes of color on this canvas of beige adobe and dust. I had expected poverty, but the magnitude of it was overwhelming.

I had seen slums in the inner cities of Detroit, my hometown, and had worked a summer in a depressed neighborhood in Chicago; I was familiar with pockets of poverty, but this was not an isolated "pocket" of poverty. This was a whole city. Neighborhood after neighborhood – one long seamless ragged garment stretched across the horizon dotted by doorways revealing small stores with baskets of bread and flour sacks of grains. Roadside ditches filled with raw sewage soured the air.

Although there must have been words of welcome and laughter and joking as we drove along in the jeep, I mostly remember the unending ribbon of human need unrolling along the road. Nothing was shielded: barefoot children in the cold, raw meat hanging in the open air, women nursing babies and cleaning their bottoms and Indian women squatting and urinating along the side of the road. In the pit of my stomach I felt old doubts return. Would I be up to the challenge?

We followed a narrow street along the west wall of the canyon to the parish of Cristo Rey where the two lay missionaries worked. They bundled themselves and their luggage out of the jeep, and Padre Roberto and I continued the descent, now at last through several blocks with cobbled streets, sidewalks and streetlights. Here, there were larger homes barricaded behind high walls topped with broken glass or barbed wire. It was an upper middle class neighborhood called *Sopocachi*. Closer to the bottom of the canyon, I looked up and around at the sides of this deep gully, walled in by misery. I wondered how so much need could exist in one place.

"Here, the wealthy families live at the lower level of the city, where the weather is a little warmer. The poor live higher up where it's colder," explained the priest from St. Louis.

Padre Roberto was a very kind person and I was forever grateful for his having rescued me that Saturday afternoon. Only later did I realize what my plight might have been had he not been there. There were no taxis, no busses, no way of getting to the city except by foot. And not another flight would be coming in for three days. I met Padre Roberto occasionally after that and when I did it was always a reason to remember his kindness and my naiveté.

I hadn't come with any illusions about adventure. I was there to learn. And there was so much to learn! Books about this country in English were very scarce, as though it had been deliberately ignored. Or maybe no one knew that it was here. If others found little to interest them here, I was not among them. On the contrary, I was undeniably seduced.

My plan was to stay only one year, collect the data for research and then return to Saint Louis University to write my dissertation. It was not clear what would happen after that. In the meantime, I was to stay with the Sisters of Loretto from Saint Louis, Missouri and wait for the other sisters to arrive from language school in Lima.

Five years earlier the Sisters of Loretto had bought a drafty 19th century mansion, a giant mausoleum of a structure with twenty-foot ceilings and walls a yard thick. At 11,000 feet above sea level, La Paz is very cold and there was no central heating anywhere in those days. Adding to the discomfort were the rough wood floors. The sisters used kerosene heaters, and carried them from chapel to dining room to recreation room barely cutting the worst bite off the chill. Surprisingly though, there was one luxury - each bed was supplied with an electric blanket! The sisters even made the rounds early in the evening to turn them on, thereby sparing themselves and their guests the risk of death by shivering during the night.

The Saturday I arrived, floors and furniture had been freshly polished and the heaters dutifully filled, so the air was thick and pungent with kerosene. The wonderful Sister Stephen, rozy-cheeked, blue-eyed and unmistakably Irish, showed me to a large room on the top floor with a wide window overlooking the *Avenida Arce* and the Plaza Isabel la Catolica with its ceramic tile walkways, manicured trees and flowers. This was the doorway to embassy row. Across the street behind a high wooden fence, a car mechanic repaired autos. Over to the right, was the Hotel Crillon and girding the rest of the Plaza were the homes of foreign diplomats from Paraguay, Peru and Czechoslovakia. I could see nannies with long braids and starched aprons playing with the children in the cold *Altiplano* afternoon. My head was light and I wondered if I would always feel like this. Everyone else seemed to be functioning normally. I welcomed the advice to go to bed until suppertime

CHAPTER 4

BLISSFUL BEGINNING

I spent the first two or three weeks completely involved in the life of the Loretto house, getting unpacked, helping in the kitchen and trying to keep warm. Behind the school, I discovered a laundry area and a small garden, where the sun was glorious and I could actually thaw out for an hour or two each day. I spent that time reading or writing letters.

Those first days were almost idyllic. I became acquainted with Andean flute music, rode to the top of Mt. *Chacaltaya*, the world's highest ski run, and basked in the sun. Best of all, I received news that my Father had been released from the hospital. Sadly, however, he would not be able to manage for himself any longer and had gone to San Francisco to live with my brother, John. I was assured that there was nothing I could do for the moment and that he was in very good hands. Even the days finally began to warm up a little.

The Loretto house where I was temporarily staying was a hub of activity in those days. It served as a stopover for many women missionaries passing through La Paz. Some of the guests were old-timers who came up from the rain forest to buy supplies or just to rest. Others were recent arrivals, like myself, on their way to language school or about to open brand new missions at the behest of the Vatican.

The Loretto Sisters had plenty of room and lots of good advice for newcomers. They were admirably warm and considerate and always ready with names of doctors and dentists who spoke some English, carpenters who could drive a straight nail and shoemakers who could measure and make a comfortable shoe for a non-Bolivian foot. The house was under constant renovation: salons had been turned into classrooms, the dining room was moved five times while I was there and even stairways were rearranged.

During my six-month stay at Loretto I became somewhat of a permanent fixture helping with the cooking and tending to visitors as well as new arrivals, who were usually announced via short wave radio to the Franciscan friars who would pass the message on to us. Beds would be prepared and an extra plate or two would be placed on the table. During the rainy season it was common for people from the "*monte*" (mountain jungle) to get stranded in La Paz for days due to washed out roads and landing strips. A Maryknoll sister, who was trying to return to her parish in Riberalta by a "stopwatch" flight on a meat cargo plane, held the record. For six weeks, she left the house each morning with her suitcase, a brown bag lunch and a book, hoping the clouds would open up enough for a plane to get through. Every evening she would return. Finally, when she failed to return one evening, we assumed she had made it to her destination. Dodging the freshly slaughtered cows swinging from side to side in the little plane, she must have prayed fervently for the pilot who had to plunge blindly through the mountain passes with only a stopwatch to calculate turns and changes in altitude.

One of the most memorable characters that passed through Loretto was Madre Gabriel or "Ma Gabe," as she was dubbed for her pioneer-style service to a remote community in the North *Yungas* mountain jungle. Ma Gabe had trooped into the jungle town of Apolo, with her handful of companions and set about her work with all the gusto of a cowboy in a rodeo. She was an ex New Yorker who feared nothing and attempted everything. A woman in her fifties and an elementary school teacher, "Gabe" rode the mountain trails on a mule, delivering babies, pulling teeth, giving injections and burying the dead. She wielded a firm pick and shovel when it came to building roads and planted crops alongside the people in the fields. Necessity had transformed this woman into the Marjorie Main of Apolo, while her companions quietly taught the children how to read, write and do sums. Never had the townspeople seen such an impassioned insistence on order and righteousness. I don't know where Gabe is today, but I am sure that somewhere deep in the rainforest some father is telling his son, or grandson, all about Ma Gabe.

Most, if not all of the religious men and women in Latin America in the 1960's were there to run a school, a clinic or work unquestioningly within the parish structure of the Catholic Church. Our mission would be different. I was there to do research in order to lay some kind of groundwork for the future of the Racine Dominicans in Bolivia. I was not tied to any expectations except those imposed by my research. I set to work reading, organizing my notes and designing a questionnaire.

On one Saturday afternoon, all of the religious women in La Paz were invited to a very formal event at *Inglés Católica*, a private girls'school in the center of the city. I jumped at the chance to go since it would be a great opportunity to meet all of the religious communities working in La Paz. Once there, we were shepherded into a long dining room filled with an assortment of religious garbs in blacks, grays and browns with rosaries and crosses dangling from waistlines or necks. Most of the sisters were from European communities and Spanish was spoken in German, French, Italian and other accents. This event was the celebration of the archbishop's birthday!

Cups of tea were already served and plates of cookies graced the great tables. Sister Marius told me that these events were pretty frequent. I felt eyes staring at me and concluded that it was the patch of hair showing from my veil. I could see that it didn't sit too well with the crowd, and I did my best to be quiet and unobtrusive. Finally, the assembled nuns began taking their places on very long benches each one seating about a dozen. Careful not to call attention to myself, I waited until last to slide into my place at the table. Just as I settled my weight on the rustic wooden bench, there was a loud crack and a crash, sending table, tea, cookies, veils, legs and habits flying in every direction. Oh what a mess! After that, I no longer needed an introduction in any crowd of nuns. I was "*ella*," "her!"

In those first weeks, I had few opportunities to get out of the house to explore the city. The Loretto superior was very protective and concerned about my being on the streets by myself. Understandably, she felt responsible for me as long as I was a boarder and so my only trips were in one of the school vans to buy food in the Indian Market or to mail letters. However, I knew that would have to change, for after all, I had work to do, contacts to make and a thesis to write.

The time for restrictions lasted only three weeks, although it seemed much longer. My liberation came with the arrival of Sisters Marie Joseph and Julianne, who had traveled by boat with the cargo

The sisters came through immigration and customs without problems, but the same could not be said for the cargo. It was to remain in customs and would be tangled in paperwork for an indefinite length of time, possibly days, weeks or even months. But since my companions were scheduled to start Spanish classes in Lima, they couldn't stay behind long enough to handle the red tape. Fortunately, the Dominican priests came to the rescue and offered their services in the person of Brother Kevin.

With nothing more to do with the customs situation, we visited and caught up on news and stories of the ports of call where they had stopped along the way. Their job of watching over the trunks and barrels had been impossible.

Only once did they catch a glimpse of the cargo area and there were so many boxes and crates piled up on one another that they couldn't identify anything that looked like ours. So they sat back in their deck chairs enjoyed the trip and didn't worry until they docked in Arica, Chile, where they boarded the plane for La Paz and left the baggage on its own.

With her background as a Spanish teacher, Sister Marie Joseph was determined to start an English language laboratory in Bolivia. I felt this would be an example of the "cultural alienation" I had been reading about, but I kept my opinion to myself for the time being. I liked Sister Julianne immediately. She was good-natured and open. We were happily setting out on a new venture, optimistic and motivated, but hardly aware of what was happening right under our noses.

Our introduction to reality came on October 28. We had just finished supper and were settling down to our usual evening of exchanging stories and planning. It was about 7 o'clock and Sister Brideen was playing Harry Belafonte's "Day O" on the record player. We tried to keep warm around a space heater as we talked.

Suddenly there was a series of "pop, pop, pops." I thought at first that someone was making popcorn, but Sister Steven knew better and dove for the radio. We stopped the music and listened. The same popping noise echoed over the airwaves. We then realized that it was machine-gun fire. Sister Steven explained: the government militia was attacking the main building at the University of San Andres, three blocks away. Protesting students had run inside for refuge. We watched from the window in silence, as the shooting became heavier. Sister Steven spotted two jeeps and some crates on the street below behind the Czech Embassy. "They're loading arms in those jeeps," someone said. The vehicles drove off taking a back street to the University. The exchange of fire became more intense. It lasted for three hours, until about 10 o'clock when the last of the students had been routed from the fourteen-story building and the small garden area surrounding it.

We retired to our rooms that night lost in a very sober mood. My companions were suddenly anxious to leave for Lima and language school. I began to understand that the University of San Andres, where I would be doing my research, was not very safe.

The following day's newspaper said that the Ministry of Health, located a block north of the university, had been dynamited and all of the records were destroyed in the fire. It also reported that several students had been killed in the shootout. A few days later, priests from the city parishes told us they had officiated at funerals for more than fifty university students.

Often embroiled in political struggles and acting as a training ground for revolutionaries, the universities had been guaranteed autonomy in 1952. They were given the freedom to manage their own budgets, determine their curriculum and hire professors without interference from the government. That night, all of this was about to change. The United States, intent on protecting its interests abroad and making the world safe for its investments, was waging a cold war throughout the third world. Bolivia was about to become another battlefield of U.S. imperialism and I, along with my companions, would have something more than a ringside seat.

When some calm returned again to the city, we were finally able to go out and do things that the Loretto superior hesitated to let me do on my own. We took taxis (about a nickel a ride), walked to bookstores and the post office. Then we paid the Church authorities an official visit. We introduced ourselves to Archbishop Abel Antezana, a crusty church leader, whose great concern was the need for money to complete the spire of his cathedral, and who, to our disappointment, mentioned nothing of the needs of the people.

We also spent time exchanging ideas with other religious groups, especially the Chicago Dominican priests. We visited their residence, which was set in a maze of lush gardens and small buildings in the southern and warmer part of the city. At that time the grounds were used as a seminary for initiating young Bolivian men to the priesthood. There was a greenhouse, a small glass-enclosed swimming pool and even a chicken coop in this peaceful setting. A llama and a friendly Irish setter roamed the grounds freely while a more menacing German shepherd was tied up near the entrance. A bright green parrot in residence cocked his head and observed us from a tree.

Conversations with the Chicago Dominican priests were helpful. They knew a great deal about Bolivia: the customs, the social problems, and seemed to me to have great insight and experience. On one of our visits, I walked the gardens with the respected and venerable Father Van Noenan, an Austrian priest who had preached the ten-day retreat in preparation for my class's reception of the habit in 1953. I was sure I was as close to a saint as ever I could be. Schooled in European mysticism and having a flare for the dramatic, he asked me if I was going to stay in Bolivia. I replied that I would love to, but that for now, I was just supposed to collect data for my doctoral thesis. With a theatrical gesture heavenward, he prophesied, "You are destined for Bolivia!"

The Dominicans had recently opened a social research center in the city of La Paz and were planning to do a case study in each geographical region of Bolivia to gain experience and knowledge of the people, their problems and organization. They had already finished a study in Ancoraimes, two hours north of La Paz.

Surprisingly, the survey of aspirations in this cold, wind-swept town revealed that the most-desired improvement by townspeople was an outdoor swimming pool! Following sound community development theory the research team helped them build one though they knew that it had no practical use. Later, they organized a cultural center, more valuable in the eyes of the research team.

Padre Dan Roach invited us to the opening celebration. He borrowed a jeep from the U.S. Embassy's Point Four Program. "A relic," he said, "and the tires are in bad shape."

It was our first trip to the Altiplano, the flatland high in the Andes Mountains. We drove along a corrugated dirt road and searched the horizon for something to see besides dry hills, clumps of sagebrush and lichen-covered rocks. There was only an occasional *campesino* dwelling made of adobe walls and thatched roof. The well-off *campesinos* had sheep and a pig or two and their dwellings had a roof of corrugated tin. Along the way, we noticed a two-story structure with painted walls. It bore the sign *"Le Petit Hotel Andino."* As we bounced along, we learned more about Bolivia from Padre Dan. The Methodist Church had been doing admirable work in the area for several years, "Where the Methodists go, progress follows. The rich *campesinos* live around Lake Titicaca where the soil is fertile and fish are plentiful."

We learned that the transistor radio and the bicycle had recently been introduced into the *campo,* causing something of a small revolution. They brought the *campesino* closer to the city and its values and commerce. Padre Dan added, however, that there were still very primitive areas in Bolivia, where oxen were still used to till the soil and others where even the wheel was still unknown. We passed through the town of Achacachi, whose *campesinos* had played a key combative role in the 1952 revolution.

We arrived at Ancoraimes without any difficulty and in less than fifteen minutes we completed a tour of the town and saw its lack of a sewage disposal system. We also visited the cemetery where each grave was a miniature house-like structure formed from mud. The little cave-like mounds were topped with crosses giving the impression of small rustic shrines. Over time, though, the wind and rain had taken their toll on these "tombstones. Bones and skulls lay exposed as a gruesome and somber reminder of the passage of life. Those who had been afforded so little respect in life were, even in death, robbed of their dignity.

Soon after our arrival, we crowded into the cultural center along with about a hundred people. The room was mostly stocked with booklets and pamphlets, donated by various embassies, covering subjects like nutrition, hygiene and agriculture. Almost everything I saw, chairs, tables, dishes and booklets bore the stamp, "Alliance for Progress," lest anyone forget the benefactor to the North. "An Alliance," I thought, "for whose Progress?"

The rough wooden floor swayed beneath the weight of the villagers. I couldn't understand the speeches, then I, too, began to sway. On the verge of fainting dead away I bent over to tie my shoe, and regained my equilibrium. An elderly man, seeing my pallid face, ushered me to the door. I sat on the steps outside breathing deeply until I completely recovered.

The campesinos invited us to drink generous quantities of Coca Quina, a local soft drink and soon we were in serious need of a restroom. One of the town officials showed the way. Sr. Julianne and I were led behind one of the houses where a three-foot adobe wall extended out about 8 yards. We were told that the bathroom was at the far end of that wall. Indeed, there was an open-air latrine built for two. There were two holes in the ground side by side, separated only by a knee-high row of adobes. Squatting over one of the holes was one of the locals. Holding his pants around his knees with one hand and tipping his hat with the other, he stood up politely when he saw us. With a little bow he motioned to the hole next to him and said, "*Buenas tardes, Madrecitas! Pase, no mas, hay uno mas aquí.*" Good afternoon, Sisters. Come right in; there's another hole right here. Nature has a way of making us all equal in the basic necessities. The gentleman so rudely interrupted handled the situation with perfect poise. Although finding a decent bathroom in Bolivia would prove to be one of our greatest challenges, none of our experiences ever equaled this one in charm.

We joined the others in making simple conversation with the people, drank more Coca Quina and soon it was time to start for home. It was about 5 p.m. and we expected to be back in the city by 7. We started off at dusk, and picked up a couple of passengers along the way. Then, without warning, it happened. We popped a rear tire on the washboard road. Dan Roach had to patch the tire because there was no spare. We started out again, but after a mile or so, we popped another tire. Then after a while on the road again, we had another flat. By that time it was dark and VERY cold and we had no more patches. We waited for an hour on an abandoned road, not even a moon in the sky, until another vehicle finally came along and Padre Dan was able to bum a patch from the driver. It was so cold and windy that the matches wouldn't burn long enough to galvanize the patch. By the time we finished, we had used the last match on the only patch. Miraculously, we did not blow another tire until we reached the arch overlooking the city, where there was a gas pump. Just as we rolled up to the pump, we blew a tire for the fourth time. The attendant emerged from a little candle-lit room, a patch in one hand and in the other a match. With a mixture of Spanish and Aymara and scuffling sounds on the gravel road, the flat was repaired and there was time to gaze enthralled into the starlit canyon below - La Paz by night! This time all four tires held out until we reached the mechanic's garage across the street from Loretto. We were at our doorstep. But the priests, fed up with changing flat tires, left the jeep there and went the rest of the way on foot.

We were covered with dust, very tired and cold, and finally and sadly, unimpressed with the quality of foreign aid Bolivia was receiving from the Point Four Program. If the vehicle was any indication of the success of the program, it was sure to be doomed to failure. And it was.

In the days that followed I visited the Instituto Boliviano de Estudio y Acción Sociales, (IBEAS), the Dominicans' Social Study and Action Institute. Someone from the Institute would oversee my research. I was eager to get started on plans. I had known for more than two years that I would very likely be going to South America, and for more than a year, I was quite certain that it would be Bolivia. My interest was cultural values, and I had read and researched everything I could about value theory and formation, which in those days before the Internet, was a long and painstaking task.

The Director of IBEAS was Jaime Otero, a former cabinet member. He introduced me to Eduardo Bracamonte, a very likeable lawyer from Potosí, who had a gentle and persuasive manner about him and an innate respect for others, no matter what their social condition. And I met a factory worker, a labor union leader, who had narrowly escaped death several times. He had actually been a militant member of the Communist Party, which was legal and able to carry on its program freely in Bolivia at that time. He relished talking about that phase of his life, and claimed that once he had been ordered to put a bomb under the car of a wealthy businessman, but that the night the bombing was to take place, the businessman left his four-year-old son sitting in the front seat. He remembered with emotion, how he came out of the shadows with the bomb in his hands. He recalled that at seeing the innocent face of the little boy smiling at him, he disappeared into the night, shaken and terrified, with the bomb still in his hands and tears in his eyes. He told us that he was expelled from the party for failing to set off the bomb

It was not long before I went to the Panamerican Union office and pick up my first check. With my OAS stipend in hand, I went shopping and bought a kerosene heater for my room, a portable typewriter, paper, a typing table and my first installment of books in Spanish. After buying all that I still had enough left over to pay my rent (*pensión*) at Loretto, an amount that served to support the whole house.

On Friday of that same week, I attempted to make my first contacts at the University of San Andres (UMSA), whose students would be the subject of my research. After a pleasant five-minute walk uphill in the sharp midday sun, I found the main door open, but there was absolutely no one inside. I walked through the first floor hall and out to the garden behind. There were a few students sitting by a small pond. They told me that a state of emergency had been declared and that classes had been cancelled. Before I left the building again, I heard the crack of sniper shots nearby and realized it was not safe enough for me to begin my work just yet.

Back at Loretto, kittens had been born. They became an amusing distraction in between reading and writing.

CHAPTER 5

REVOLUTION

Early on the morning of November 4, before the arrival of the children for classes, we gathered as usual, around the table for breakfast: the menu was coffee, fresh bread and a slice of papaya seasoned with limejuice, sugar and cinnamon. The placid morning routine was interrupted by an alarming phone call from one of the parents.

"Cancel classes. " There were serious political problems. He advised us not to go out and to "be careful."

Just minutes later as Sister Marius locked the front gate, army trucks filled with soldiers in combat gear rumbled menacingly past the house on their way to the center of the city. She counted. "About twenty," she said breathlessly. We forgot whatever plans we had for the day and gathered around the radio. My vocabulary was limited but I knew enough to understand the frantic orders alternating with triumphant military march music.

They reported, "The official government station has been taken over and is now being used as central command."

We were terrified to find ourselves in the middle of a revolution. The government station's announcer shouted instructions to various civic groups. "Go to the Ministry of Mines and take it over! Go to the Ministry of Defense and seize it!" The people were being called to arms. "Take to the streets and defend the nation against its enemies: Paz Estenssoro and San Roman!"

I imagined the announcer clutching the microphone, red-faced and defiant. Then the shooting started with a constant barrage of strafing from above, with explosions and heavy artillery fire. We were right in the crossfire between the Ministry of Defense to the front and the hill of Laicacota to the rear, where Paz

Estenssoro's *milicianos* were entrenched. These were Special Forces organized by Paz Estenssoro to replace the disbanded military in 1952. They remained loyal to the government.

After a while, it sounded as if bullets were ricocheting off the school. Every shot was echoed and amplified by the surrounding buildings. Explosions shook the building and we crowded into a room with no windows, still listening to the radio. The rebels were seizing and blacking out radio transmissions, station by station. First, there would be a shout that the radio was under siege and then a calmer voice would announce, "We are having *technical* difficulties." Then the station would go off the air. Finally, the only two radios broadcasting were Batallon Colorados operated by the armed forces and Illimani, the official government station. I was so terrified that I could barely breathe.

The steady exchange of fire lasted for an agonizingly long two hours, and then, suddenly as a summer storm, it stopped. Immediately, the cook, a young Indian woman, appeared in the doorway and announced that lunch was ready. Amazingly, she had continued cooking through all the shooting and bombing, demonstrating an astounding sense of duty but not a very clear idea of what happens to a stomach unaccustomed to revolution.

All of us emerged from the interior hallway where we had hidden and set up chairs in the ample entranceway under a skylight. We sat with trays on our laps and tried hard to swallow. Halfway through the salad, a loud blast bolted us out of our chairs. Several trays crashed to the floor. Mine slid the entire length of the hall. Once recovered from the shock, we managed to eat as best we could, clutching trays and chairs, flinching from the intermittent shooting and sporadic explosions. There were ten of us that morning: two Canadians, three Dominicans, and five Sisters of Loretto. Luckily, everyone was present and accounted for. Not a single one of us had been caught out on the street.

Gradually, the shooting and the blasts subsided. General Jose Ovando Candia, Commander in Chief of the Armed Forces, addressed the nation. Paz Estenssoro had been defeated and had left the country. Bolivia would now have a military government. Much to my relief, Bolivia would maintain friendly relations with the U.S. and all the countries of the world. My very active imagination had been working overtime, and I was relieved to know we would not be arrested and executed, after all.

The revolution was over! Trucks loaded with young people careened around the Plaza Isabela la Catolica. Shouts of, "Victory," and "long live the revolutionary government!" rang out. Other vehicles with white flags with red crosses painted on them picked up the dead and wounded from the streets. Some of them drove around in official vehicles that had just been confiscated from seized government buildings. The whole scene was as spirited as a college homecoming game. The men and women on the trucks hugged and kissed and sang and there was great jubilation even as the bodies were being counted. The carnival atmosphere was very unnerving.

Although the radio reported that Paz Estenssoro had escaped the country dressed as a woman, the truth was that General Ovando had escorted him to the airport and allowed him to go into exile. The next day there was talk of a Barrientos-Ovando co-presidency, but in the end, Rene Barrientos Ortuño, head of the Air Force, was named President of Bolivia. Although Ovando had led the takeover, he was, in the end edged out of the presidency for letting Paz Estenssoro leave the country unharmed.

Although the MNR had fallen and all points of resistance were under control, shooting continued sporadically through several days and nights. One night a particularly heavy exchange of gunshots broke out. My huge bedroom window was right in the line of fire or so I thought. I was so terrified that I tore out of my room and jumped into bed with a very startled Madre Juliana and I stayed there until the shooting stopped. Heroism doesn't come easily.

Gradually an icy calm settled over the city, and as soon as the airport was open to traffic, Madres Maria José and Juliana left for Lima and language school. They made no secret of their relief at leaving the country. Returning from the airport, I thought or hoped, "Surely, the worst of the violence is over." Well, almost.

On the Saturday after the coup, while I was studying in my room, I was jolted out of my chair by the blare of a loudspeaker in the Plaza below "*Que muera San Roman!*" (Death to San Roman!) Like menacing storm clouds, a crowd began to gather. They joined in the chant, "Death to San Roman! We want San Roman's blood! San Roman Assassin!" In a short time the mob grew to about 2000. Phone calls informed us that the Avenida Arce was blocked and that Paz Estenssoro's hated henchman, General Claudio San Roman, was hiding out in the Paraguayan Embassy next to the Hotel Crillon directly across from my window. Family members of the victims he tortured and killed were threatening to raid the embassy and drag him into the street to rip him to pieces.

I sat frozen the better part of the day, unable to think of anything else. The chanting lasted all afternoon and into early evening, broken only occasionally by the arrival of someone trying to mediate between the embassy and the mob. By nightfall, President Barrientos had convinced most of the crowd to leave the Plaza. Finally, as I prepared to go to bed, a sudden rainstorm forced the last stragglers to withdraw.

I lay in bed unable to sleep. The chanting of the frenzied mob calling for the blood of another human being still seemed to echo on the wet pavement below. This was, indeed, very far from the convent halls, where the only chants I knew began, *"Gloria Patri. . . ."*

On Sunday, things were quiet and by evening the Paraguayan Embassy gave San Roman safe passage into exile. The next day's newspapers were filled with photos of the torture chambers of the MNR. Reporters recounted horror stories of San Roman's ten-year reign of terror as head of the infamous *control político*, repressive organism known for unspeakable Nazi-style interrogations.

In the following days I saw more alarming evidence of the brutality of the coup, of how the opposition forces had ravaged and ransacked the homes of ousted Bolivian government officials. We drove past President Paz Estenssoro's residence in Calacoto were shocked to see how it had been stripped of everything, even the electrical wiring, leaving no more than a gutted hollow shell visible through the broken windows. My introduction to Bolivia was becoming a frightening and sobering awakening to reality but this was only the beginning. My real education in Latin American Studies was about to begin in earnest.

The US Ambassador at that time was Douglas Henderson who in 1963 had replaced Ben Stephansky (known for not only sitting in on but also actually officiating at Bolivian cabinet meetings). The official U.S. response to the coup was to suspend foreign aid and withhold recognition of the new regime. This alarmed a group of American priests and religious who found that the suspension of aid directly affected people in rural communities where they worked. Their projects came to a standstill, the distribution of food products was stopped and *campesinos,* ready to plant, were without the seeds they had been promised. At the request of this Church group, Ambassador Henderson agreed to a Sunday evening meeting at his residence to give a briefing on the status of U.S. – Bolivia relations. About twenty-five guests assembled to view charts and slides showing the triumphs of the USAID programs in Bolivia: roads, bridges, schools and clinics had been funded and built thanks to the generosity of US foreign aid. It was a real "snow job." Even with my cursory knowledge of the country, I recognized flaws in the presentation. I challenged the value of the work of USAID. Did the Ambassador know that only 4 of the 70 schools allegedly built by the US were actually functioning? Did he know that 66 were abandoned and falling apart?

Finally, one of the priests brought the meeting around to its objective and questioned the morality of cutting off humanitarian aid for political reasons. The ambassador explained that since Bolivia had not promised democratic elections yet, it had not complied with international law and, therefore, relations could not be normalized.

The objections continued, "Why should Bolivian *campesinos* be deprived of food and seeds?"

Henderson answered, "I say this to you in strict confidence as Americans: we can never put the welfare of people of another country above US interests. We are taught that as diplomats, and that is our first obligation: to **protect America's interests.**"

"Even when that causes suffering for a lot of innocent people?" Someone shot back.

"Yes," he answered without hesitation.

I added, "Just what", Mr. Ambassador, "are America's interests?" There was no answer

That was a something I would have to find out for myself.

CHAPTER 6

CHRISTMAS, 1964

After the coup, I put the political events out of my mind as best I could and turned to my research. I managed to write a draft of the first chapter of my thesis but most of the time I was busy getting to know the many visitors to the Loretto house. A month slipped by and I already felt very much at home and probably had met most of the North American missionaries stationed in and around La Paz, as well as a few from Santa Cruz and Cochabamba.

In addition to getting acquainted with a kaleidoscope of personalities, I was at last trusted to go out on my own and I became familiar with the city and its shops. My daily outings would take me up past the university and to the center of La Paz with its street of bricks and cobblestones and assortment of office buildings, shops and colonial buildings.

In spite of the oddity of a nun in a white habit appearing in unusual places, people were respectful to a fault. Grown men bowed reverently when I passed them on the street; I wondered what they were really thinking. Some asked me for a blessing or a "*medallita*" or "*estampita*" (medal or holy card). Embarrassed, I'd smile and return the greeting politely. The habit afforded me instant trust, if nothing else, and if there were negative connotations, I was oblivious to them.

On the day before Christmas I set out to find a present for the Loretto Sisters. It was the beginning of summer and the sun was brilliant and warm. Storeowners were only then decorating windows with tinsel. There were no trees or lights or ornaments. Christmas card vendors blocked the narrow sidewalks, and the streets were filled with passers-by. Indian women flounced their *polleras* (skirts) and worried parents looked for something affordable.

Children stood motionless in front of the few shop windows that displayed imported toys. Although some commerce was done in small stores in the center of town, most of it was in the open Indian markets in the northwest part of the city. The narrow brick streets vibrated with repressed excitement as the few people who could afford to, prepared to celebrate Christmas. I returned to Loretto with a gift for the sisters, a box of imported chocolates.

Later in the afternoon, Sister Marius invited me to visit an orphanage just a few doors away. The *"hogar,"* as it was called, was reached through a small manicured park with a steep descent down an embankment overlooking the river *Choqueyapu* that runs through and under the city of La Paz and serves for sewage and garbage disposal. Luckily, the *hogar* was still sufficiently above the river so as to escape the smell most of the time. But that was about all that could be said in its favor.

There were several old barracks-like buildings on the premises: a dormitory, dining room, chapel, hall and laundry, all in need of repair. The girls were sitting outside on cement benches, combing their hair, playing with stones or flowers and teasing each other. An orphanage employee came to greet us. She explained that she was alone that day since her co-workers had gone home to spend Christmas with their families. She told us about the girls, explaining that no effort was made to separate them according to their needs. This meant there were physically and mentally disabled children alongside runaways, throwaways and the emotionally disturbed. Then, of course, there were genuine orphans who had no family. All were herded together in one depressing and pitiful place. The girls giggled and took our hands. Hungry for affection, they clung to us as we walked and talked with the woman in charge.

They needed so much. Some had no shoes; their dresses were torn. They needed books, better food and more blankets for the cold La Paz nights. What did they do all day?

"Nothing", we were told. "They get very bored, *Madrecitas*. Maybe you could come and play games with them or give them classes?"

There were about forty girls from ages 3 to 15, she said, "some were rebellious and hard to work with and the parents send them here because they can't do anything with them."

The dormitory had two rows of beds, no nightstands, no closets, no chairs, nothing on the walls. "But," we were told, "it is better than sleeping in a cardboard box on the street." And that it was.

By now it was dusk and very cold. We crossed the path to a building that had just one large empty room. Under a dim bare light bulb, was a big table with some branches on it. There the children had prepared the *nacimiento* - a *creche*. Except for the traditional plaster figures of Mary, Joseph and child and a paper star, it bore no resemblance to anything I had ever seen at Christmas. The girls had gathered the greens from the riverbank and spread them on the rough table. Then each one brought something to give to the Christ Child: barrettes, pieces of broken toys, a chipped ceramic dog, a little pig, a ping pong ball, even pencil stubs and bottle caps. It was the most heartfelt display of generosity I could imagine.

The girls bounced up and down with pride, clapping their hands to their faces. We noticed they had sores on their cheeks and their hair was matted. They crowded into a corner of the room and sang *villancicos* (Christmas carols). Then they recited poetry with words they didn't understand, written by some adult who probably never meant the rhymes for surroundings such as these. We stayed with them and listened to their chatter until it was time for them to go to bed. This was Christmas Eve. We left in silence, each drawing private lessons from the wretched little celebration.

Then there was a celebration of another kind. Next door to the *Colegio Loretto*, was a five-story clinic, a private hospital staffed by another group of religious women from St. Louis, Missouri. We were invited to Midnight Mass in their chapel and for refreshments afterwards in their living quarters on the top floor penthouse. I was unprepared for what came next. Inside the apartment, there was a real pine tree with lights, a fireplace with burning logs and luxuriously soft alpaca rugs on the floor. They had wine and candy and beautifully wrapped gifts from wealthy patients or the doctors who staffed the clinic. We sang Christmas carols and laughed at the main attraction, a large toy dog on wheels that barked as it rolled along. In another setting, this all might have been lovely. But as the cups were filled and good cheer reigned, I felt that something was grotesquely inappropriate.

I swallowed hard as I thought of the forty little girls sleeping in their cold, hard beds just a few doors away. Sister Marius smiled and I knew she shared my discomfort.

CHAPTER 7

EXPLORING BOLIVIAN VALUES

By January, with the onslaught of summer rains and penetrating cold, I learned that the keep and care of the kerosene heater was both tricky and time-consuming. Kerosene had to be bought from a special dealer who measured it into containers provided by the buyer. The heavy ten-liter container had to be transported home and lugged up three flights of stairs to my room. Filling the heater was a clumsy task, and the kerosene almost always ran over on the floor. Regulating the wick was even more problematic; when cut too long, it spewed out a sticky black smoke that coated the walls and furniture. Once, when I sat too closely to it, my habit caught on fire. The lack of oxygen at the high altitude saved me from the flames, and luckily, my clothes smoldered only briefly. I suddenly felt that I was wasting precious time on keeping warm, and besides, I wasn't finding any adequate theory of values in my books to guide my research, so I snuffed out the heater and headed for the University of San Andres to begin my work in earnest.

The front of the building was riddled with gaping holes from the October 28 shootout and windows were still broken. It was ominous, but I turned my thoughts to the task at hand. I wanted to know what was important to the young women studying in the University. Who were they? What were they like? What were their dreams and aspirations? What kind of role were they going to play in Bolivia?

First, I needed to make official contact with the university authorities, and easily got an interview with the rector (equivalent of president). I explained that I wanted to do a study of the values of the young women enrolled in the University. I needed permission to interview them and use written questionnaires, as well as to make a general background study of the university, its organization, budget and history. He was pleased and polite to an extreme, as are Bolivians as a rule. It was the first time that a nun had ever sat in his office. He was a distinguished looking engineer in a gray suit, had tinted glasses and silver hair. He thanked me for my interest in his university and, with what seemed to me a tinge of sadness, said that it was the first time a foreigner had come to study it. More than anything, he must have been very weighed down by worry, having gone through the attack on his students and then the coup. My request was simple enough to oblige. I left with a letter of presentation in my hand. Now the doors of San Andres were open to me and I had his permission to do whatever was needed.

I began my work by going over the available student records. Since the University had not compiled data, I began by doing my own student survey: place of origin, age, income and major field. I visited all of the faculties (departments) and conversed with students and professors, in classrooms, cafeterias and offices. Classes frequently were cancelled because of political unrest, but that gave me more opportunity to chat with students. I was often approached out of curiosity, and while the habit may have been a barrier to any real communication, it didn't seem to be a deterrent to getting the information I needed. The students explained the concepts of autonomy and co-government to me until I had them perfectly clear and could explain them myself in unhesitating Spanish. They were probably amused by my presence, but they treated me with unquestioning respect.

Finally, I decided it was time to get some real information on values. At IBEAS I formulated a questionnaire, and had it corrected and mimeographed. I went to each university department to leave questionnaires with student leaders. "This will be easy," I thought, because each group of students was assigned a fixed classroom similar to a "homeroom," and the professors went to their rooms. In two days I had distributed them to most of the departments where women were enrolled, and a date was set for picking them up. "At last I have begun!" At least it seemed that way.

Then unexpectedly, because of continued political unrest, classes were cancelled for weeks, all of my contacts were lost and so were the questionnaires. That was my first lesson in Bolivian social research. When the students returned to classes, I tried various other methods, but always, always there was an interruption. Nothing worked except for the many conversations on the benches in the garden.

Although politics was never discussed specifically, it ran like an undercurrent through every encounter. Whenever fellow students and professors were mentioned, it was always by party affiliation. Events were dated as "before" or "after" the coup. Many criticized the students who participated in the takeover. I spent the most time with the students in the Faculty (Department) of Social Work. I did this partly because it was an all female department but also because the students there insisted I observe all of their classes and participate in their activities: fiestas, study sessions and house meetings.

One afternoon, a law student, convinced me to go with her to a political party meeting of "the opposition." At first I hesitated, but she felt that if I wanted to understand what was going on, I had to do this, "Even if they don't like it, you should go!"

That night, we took the elevator to the top floor of the empty *monoblock*. From there another student ushered me into a clandestine meeting room. Recalling the violent exchange of fire there in October, I was apprehensive. At first the students were uncomfortable with my being there, but as things heated up, they all but forgot my presence. Their initial objection was not my being a nun, but rather my being an American. I sat back and took mental notes. With my limited Spanish, I understood that they wanted to protect autonomy and that they were bitterly opposed to the military dictatorship.

During that January and February I continued experimenting with written questionnaires and interview schedules but had little success. I jotted down every piece of information about the university, the strikes and continuous street blockades and states of emergency. This was a particularly unsettled time for the country and the university. The military dictatorship said it would guarantee rights, but in reality it was bent on eliminating all opposition. Workers, students, teachers, *campesinos* were all frequently arrested and beaten. I kept a journal of events and learned to be very careful when speaking to Barrientos supporters and even more wary when conversing with those who were not.

During the following months, I attended meetings and events and often ate in the university dining room. Some professors approached me and invited me to observe their classes.

I questioned and observed and questioned again. I listened and learned and tried not to impose any pre-conceived and artificial techniques of analysis on what they said. I read and conversed and took notes. I collected piles of information about the universities in Bolivia, their history, organization, budgets and teacher preparation. I walked in and out of classrooms and offices easily and never once had to use the letter prepared for me by the rector. On the whole, the students and professors appeared flattered to have someone show an interest in them. It is possible that they were more comfortable with my presence than I was with theirs.

It was about then that for the first, but not the last time, I had to flee with a mass of students with government troops in hot pursuit of us and shooting teargas *cartuchos* and scattering us in several directions. The advice given me as I gathered my long skirts around me and sprinted down the stairs, out the back door and through the garden, was, "Keep running, *Madre*, and don't look back. Don't stop running until you get home." And run I did, all the way home.

I was out of breath and out of place; something was definitely happening to my religious decorum.

CHAPTER 8

COPACABANA

The next month I was invited to go on a trip with a group of North American religious women who had planned a special weekend to the National Shrine to the Virgin of Copacabana on the shores of Lake Titicaca. This would not be my only trip there, but it was among the most memorable. The Loretto Sisters chartered a bus and packed an assortment of necessary articles, among them toilet paper and flea powder. They also told us we were going to stay at the best hotel in town.

It was a gloriously sunny day and emotions were high. We were especially excited as we began to skirt the shores of the deep blue-green Lake Titicaca. Finally, we reached the straits of Tiquina, where small ferryboats carry vehicles and passengers across the Lake. The bus fit compactly on one ferry and we on another. The water was calm and the light waves clapped against the side of the boat. In this land where nothing goes to waste, the sails on the boats were made of flour and "Gasser y Cia." sugar sacks sewn together. We gazed at the breathlessly beautiful snow-capped Cordillera that stretched across the horizon. Once on the other side of the lake, we boarded the bus. My eyes were fixed on the Cordillera until it disappeared from view behind the hills. Our bus then climbed up into the mountains and down again to the lake and the town of Copacabana. We checked into a hotel, which had no hot water, terrible beds and a swarm of hungry fleas in waiting. I envied the ease with which everyone applied the flea powder to the mattresses and were able to take the deprivations in stride.

We then visited the Shrine, where I took out the three dollars given to me by my dear sister-in-law, Marge, to light a candle for her in Bolivia. The money bought me exactly three hundred candles and I spent the better part of an hour setting them up in their own drippings and lighting them. That should have covered Marge's needs for a good while.

We admired the lake and made the traditional climb up the Calvario, but not on our knees, as is the custom. In the evening we returned to the shrine. Built by the Spanish conquistadors, its miraculous Virgin presides, bedecked in jewels and gold. I remember the droning hymns and the thick cloud of incense and the bowed heads of the Aymara Indian women draped in black shawls, hats removed out of respect. The moaning and the sorrow were so distant from what I was accustomed to. These religious symbols and expressions were unfamiliar to me. I would need to find a new meaning in this unfamiliar religion. "here," I thought, "In Copacabana, the political turmoil did not seem to filter in."

Back at the hotel, I choked on the flea powder in the air. It was surely more harmful to us than the insect bites!

The following morning, after much haggling with the local police officials, we were allowed to cross over into Peru to visit Franciscan Sisters from Wisconsin. They had just moved into a brand new convent that rivaled any I had seen in the States and it was grossly out of place in this impoverished rural setting. After lunch, we said our "*hasta luegos*," and set out across the border back into Bolivia and continued on the ride back to La Paz.

After having circled a few mountain roads up and out of Copacabana, the bus suddenly wheezed, and the wheels crunched to a stop. The bus driver said that it would take at least an hour before we would be on the road again. The gas tank was clogged with dirt and needed cleaning. It had to be taken apart and reassembled. At first the interruption was annoying, but while the other sisters stayed on the bus to rest, I quickly welcomed the time to set out alone and climb a slope and drink in the stark and barren hills. I sat there in the afternoon sun, looking down at the parched valley and up to the gigantic sun-baked Andean foothills. From the distance I could see a little boy, maybe twelve years old, coming over the hill playing his *quena*, a native reed instrument. He sat on the horizon, close to me but unaware of my presence and played his plaintive music. It was a moment designed for poetry, a perfect time, a time to be drawn in wonder and prayer. In the midst of poverty and misery, there was this little boy making sounds that might have been mistaken for the wind in the mountains, rising and falling in spellbinding magic. He played only for himself and the hills and a mesmerized roadside observer.

As are most Bolivian chauffeurs, our driver was a good mechanic, but it took a little longer than expected to put the tank back together. Once it was, we were pressed for time. We had to cross the straits before the late afternoon winds came up, and the aura of the peaceful interlude came to an abrupt end.

The bus flew up and down the mountain roads, all of us clutching the seats in front of us, leaving a trail of fervent prayers in the dust. We were screaming here and jolting there, rounding curves on a narrow dirt road, skirting bumps and ruts and grabbing at flying veils at 13,000 ft above sea level. Much to our relief, at sunset we came to a final jolt at the straits. No amusement park ride was this return trip.

There was a bit of arguing between the driver and the ferryboat operator about taking us across so late, but the ferryboat owner finally lowered his head in resignation. He took us aboard at the guarantee given by the bus driver: "Nothing will happen. They're *madrecitas*. They'll pray." That may also have been the bus driver's justification for the breakneck ride through the mountains.

The crossing was rough, but the ferry made it safely to the other side at nightfall. There were no boats on the lake, no moon and just one little hut nearby with a candle burning. After a short delay, we boarded the bus again and began a lumbering upward climb from the lake. We sat back and relaxed, relieved to have made it through the hurdles safe and sound. Then, in an instant, we were plunged into total darkness. The headlights on the bus had burned out. We inched along the road for four more hours in complete blackness. The driver's helper, a small boy, hung outside the front door feeling the edge of the mountain with a stick and telling the driver when to turn his wheels to the left or the right every time we came to a curve. Three or four times we terrified an oncoming vehicle and were saved only by the agility of the other driver who picked up our image in the night. And somewhere along the way, another very little boy who had hitched a ride with us hopped off the bus and was swallowed up by the inky night.

I slept happily in my bed that night, thankful that we had made it back safely. The shrine of the Virgin was impressive but more than anything else, it was the magical beauty of a solitary little boy playing his *quena* high in the Andes that warmed my heart.

CHAPTER 9

——∘∘⊶⧓⊷∘∘——

COMMUNITY

Before the Sisters had left for Lima, they had asked Brother Kevin to find a place where we could live when they returned from language school. By February he located a few apartments for rent and since I was the interested party, I had to accompany him on an inspection tour. We made more than one head turn as we knocked on doors and climbed stairways, checking kitchens and bathrooms and ohhing and ahhing – all this in our medieval Dominican habits. Red-faced and uneasy, we made the most unlikely of couples. We tried to make it look like we did this all the time, as if there were nothing unusual about it but, to ourselves, we howled with laughter. Finally we made a pre-selection that would have to be approved by Sister Marie Joseph when she returned from Lima.

At last on March 7, Madres Juliana, Maria José and Juanita arrived from language school in Lima and we were finally ready to settle in. Madre Maria José accompanied Kevin to the apartments, causing more heads to turn as he appeared with a second woman, older and plumper, at his side. She decided on a second-floor apartment in an old building on the 20 de Octubre Street, just a block from the University of San Andres.

Brother Kevin, who had heroically retrieved the cargo from customs, brought over the barrels and trunks and we unpacked. We bought used furniture and had a few things made by a carpenter recommended by Madre Pedro Miguel from Loretto. Then we set to work on the apartment. It looked as though no one had lived there for some time, for it needed cleaning and painting. Wallpaper was peeling off the walls and the doors hung loose at the hinges. It was very spacious, except for the kitchen which measured about 3' x

4' and was reached by crossing over an outdoor walkway. It was an effort to fit two people in it at the same time. A glassed-in corridor ran the whole length along the back of the apartment. Except for that hallway, the sun did not penetrate any corner of the apartment. There was a tub in the bathroom that ran scalding hot water or none at all. Usually it was none at all. We scraped paint off 500 windowpanes of varying sizes, painted the rooms, polished floors and shopped for pots and pans.

We moved in on a national holiday and, we discovered, we were right on the parade route. So we stood on the balcony and felt welcomed by marching bands, cheering crowds and confetti.

We set up a small chapel in the apartment and Bishop Gutierrez came to celebrate mass with us weekly. We suspected that he showed us this special attention because we served him corn flakes for breakfast after mass. Someone had told us that he had acquired a taste for the cereal while studying in the U.S so we made sure we had an extra supply on hand. He also dipped into the barrels for the little religious trinkets we had brought and I, for one, was happy to see the supply put to use.

Slowly, we began to get involved in some work. Juliana and Juanita made contacts with high school students. They took on religion classes in the public schools and tried organizing meetings and groups among the young people. The students readily made many promises to show up for meetings, but they rarely followed through. Always ready to quantify information, I calculated a 20% success rate for their efforts.

At that time electricity was regularly and not so regularly rationed in La Paz. Without warning, the lights would go off and stay off for several hours. Juliana spent the afternoons at home without light and just as they went back on, she would leave to teach an evening class for students who had to work during the day as bootblacks, servants and nannies. The school was two blocks away, and the lights would be off there by the time she arrived. She had to adjust to teaching by candlelight. Visual aids were useless and might even catch fire. Students brought their own candles and the more impish ones would entertain themselves trying to singe the braids of the servant girls sitting in front.

For us these were days and nights of exploration and discovery: We bought a VW bus from the Dominicans and were now able to really set out on our own. One Saturday, we decided to explore the Valley of the Moon, a barren area south of the city, which was named for the land formations that gives it a non-earthly look. Surprisingly, we discovered a large area of green grass. A lovely spot for a picnic lunch! We spread out a blanket, opened our sacks and as we were about to bite into the first sandwich, a golf ball whizzed past Madre Juliana's head missing it by an inch. So there were rich people here who played golf! This was the one and only golf course in La Paz frequented by embassy types and their cronies. We packed up the sandwiches and headed for safer, humbler surroundings.

Whenever the U.S. Embassy had information about a pending political upheaval, Americans were called and told to stay at home. The Embassy had an inside track on events, but it seemed to me that it grossly exaggerated the risks. Rather than deter me, the call would be my signal to take off and see what was going on at the university.

Occasionally at night we would drive to some place in the hills overlooking La Paz to admire the view and say our evening prayers. The most astounding view was along a back road to the south of La Paz, at a lower altitude, where we could see the city above us. Looking up into the night sky the cluster of city lights formed a spectacular seamless jeweled canopy with the stars. And for one brief silent moment one might be fooled into thinking that the misery and poverty were bedecked with diamonds. That was all before the developers began building homes there for the wealthy.

The barrage of new images and information and events kept me so busy that I had little time for books. The impact of sights and sounds was overwhelming, and I needed more time to process it all. I requested and fortunately, received a short extension to my scholarship.

It wasn't long before Sister Mary Magdalen visited us and we enthusiastically shared ideas. She agreed that we should not be quick to structure anything or impose our ways on the Bolivians, and that we should take time to learn. She brought news from home of many sisters leaving the community and of an unsettling stressful period.

She was satisfied that we were adapting and that we were taking our time before making any permanent commitments. Why not accompany the Dominican priests while they did their second case study in Suapi? Madre Maria José would go and lend a woman's touch to the endeavor. The Chicago priests had formed a team of researchers including an anthropologist, a sociologist, an agronomist and a social worker to document and promote development projects in the *Yungas* mountain jungle area. Madre Maria José joined them. In March, we all made the trip to the jungle town. Madre Juliana and I returned to spend the week before Easter.

Suapi is a village located in the North *Yungas*, mountain jungle area. At the time we were there, there was no electricity, no drinking water, and even the ruts called roads ended there. It was carved out at the edge of a dense jungle where coffee, bananas and oranges grew in the wild. There were maybe 15 or 20 one-room adobe houses with dirt floors in the town. We slept in a two-story building, on a hard floor. Life there was reduced to the bare bone necessities.

On Holy Thursday, along with a couple of townspeople and a social worker, Madre Juliana and I helped stake out fourteen locations for shrines, the Stations of the Cross, along a narrow ten-mile stretch of mountain road. Markers were set in place where people would come the next morning and arrange shrines. We walked the entire day along the mountain path and picked oranges to quench our thirst.

On the way back, it started to rain. There was no place to seek shelter. We had no choice but to continue on in the downpour until we returned to Suapi. The only habit we had was the one we had on. It was so humid and hot that we feared it wouldn't dry out for days. The social workers offered to lend us some old clothes so our soaking wet habits could dry by the kerosene stove in the makeshift kitchen. However, I went to supper in my damp habit and Juliana sported coulats, a credit to her common sense and my lack of it.

The next day we repeated the trek along with the townspeople, this time under a blazing sun. We joined them in a long procession along the same road with prayers at the shrines marking events along the *Via Crucis*.

Back at the town, in the evening tired but content, we gathered around a kerosene lamp on an old splintered table to discuss the problems and needs of the town. Those included a schoolteacher, running water and a road wide enough to transport coffee and fruit to the city. I was able to follow the conversation in Spanish, but not quick enough to make any intelligent contribution.

The next day we took an unforgettable side trip with the research team to buy dynamite to be used to blast a new road through the jungle. I sat in the back of the jeep wedged in between various crates of explosives. For two tense hours we labored along a narrow road full of ruts and half washed out by the rains the day before. The wheels skidded to the edge at each curve and I was almost grateful that the dynamite blocked my view of the precipice down the side of the mountain. If I were to go out with a blast, it would at least be quick!

That week was a lesson in doing without and not really needing anything. We climbed the hills, washed in the river and observed coffee beans drying in the sun. It was as glorious as it was primitive.

Finally, on Easter Sunday, we began the trip home. We stopped in Coroico and prepared for the second part of the trip, the road to La Paz. It is a four-hour trip on a one-lane dirt road that clings to the mountainsides. It is called the "most dangerous road in the world" for its many hairpin curves overlooking 2000-foot drop-offs. That alone would have been enough to make it a memorable Easter Sunday, but there was to be more. As luck would have it, the jeep broke down just as we headed out of town where the most spectacularly hair-raising length of the road begins. Padre Jaime (Jim Burke) the Dominican priest at the wheel convinced a truck driver to tow us all the way up and around the mountains. Much to our dismay, he accepted, and off we went. At each curve, we were whip lashed toward the outer side of the road, threateningly close to the edge. For four hours we ate the dust of the vehicle towing us and expected at any minute to be hurled into eternity. At last, we reached the highest peak in the road, and were then cut loose to coast down the rest of the mountain for about an hour. Padre Jaime rolled the jeep slowly down into the city, carefully gauging some traffic lights but bullying his way through more than a few. We finally arrived exhausted and forever grateful for the technology that brought us the electric light bulb and running water.

While the three of us in La Paz went on with planning, Madre Maria José was spending much of her time in Suapi, brushing her teeth using the local soda pop, Coca Quina, for lack of water and suffering from the food and lack of minimum necessities. Eventually, she found the adjustment too hard and requested to return to Racine. A young Madre Felicia came to replace her. She joined us in La Paz helping with religion classes in the public schools and an occasional *jornada* or daylong retreat for young people. In contrast to most religious groups, we did not establish a school or clinic or program of our own. We were a kind of freelance community searching for a non-invasive way of serving the people.

One evening Madre Juanita and I squeezed two chairs into that tiniest of all kitchens in the world, and we began a conversation about what the community's role in Bolivia should be. We had been tossed together by this mission and had spent some time together the summer before departure, but it was not until then that our ideas began to take form. I listened as she told me about the orientation classes they had had in Lima and how they coincided with the reading I had been doing. I was delighted that I could say what I had been thinking without offending her. We talked about the failure of the Catholic Church to meet the needs of the poor in South America, and even more, of the inability of many missionaries to adapt to the culture. We understood the contradiction of living at a level so far above that of the people they served. We shared the conviction that our presence there couldn't be justified if we were not willing to identify with the conditions, the poverty and the culture. We accepted the fact that we would have do without many of the comforts we had taken for granted. I recalled the comment of one of the more dedicated Franciscan Friars, "If I've already given up living with a woman; I guess I can live without a stereo." We would not become instruments of U.S. foreign policy. We would not impose our way of living and thinking; and we would try to learn new ways. An implicit pact was sealed in that most unlikely of settings: a true meeting of mind and spirit and the formation of a lifelong friendship.

CHAPTER 10

THE UNIVERSITY OF SAN ANDRES

During the week in Suapi, I had met an American anthropologist who came through the village and we had had a chance to compare research notes. He advised me to completely change my methodology. "Try to remember entire conversations and later record them word for word." As soon as I was back in La Paz, I put his suggestion into practice and began to have good results.

With each passing month, I became more and more familiar with the university's campuses and organization. In 1965, there were three campuses. The main one was located near the center of the city and housed law, philosophy, and economics. It consisted of a fourteen-story building called the *monoblok* and several smaller ones, including a former military academy, all occupying about the equivalent of a city block. There were also a number of single room dwellings where university service employees lived in conditions similar to those found in the campo with roosters and chickens running freely in the yard. (One thing I noticed from the start was that no matter where I was in Bolivia, even in a hospital or the presidential palace, if I stopped and listened long enough, I would hear a rooster crow.)

One block away from the *monoblok* was the school of social service, where the students, all women, attended classes in a large colonial house. Social service was unique because it had a modest residence, which was overseen by the Teresians, Spanish nuns in secular dress with eyes that never drifted off their charges.

A second campus was in the *barrio* of Miraflores, a neat and mostly middle class part of the city. Biological sciences (the schools of medicine, dentistry and pharmacy) were located there. The buildings there were new and impressive but behind the School of Medicine stood a couple of rooms used as a morgue. They had wide window frames with no glass in them, and a doorway with no door. Exposed in plain view were the cadavers for the following day's "anatomy lesson." I was startled enough to make this discovery, but it was made even more gruesome because I was led there, by the hand, by three little children no more than seven years old. This was where they played, along a narrow strip of ground, cadavers on one side and a steep precipice overlooking the Choqueapu River on the other. Safety and precautions were low priorities and, indeed, within the week, I returned home saddened and shaken after learning that the little boy, who led me there, had fallen over the edge to his death.

The Exact Sciences building was located in the heart of the city. It had been newly built with funds from the U.S. government. Not surprisingly, along with the funding, came the imposition of a program of studies designed in the U.S.A. This change was received with bitter resentment and indignation on the part of the Bolivian students and professors and created a fierce resistance to anything northamerican. In the days following the November 4 revolution, it became a political football, and finally, the "gringo" curriculum was thrown out and the school again implemented its traditional Bolivian program. In the heat of this controversy, I chose to spend as little time as possible there.

The highest administrative body in the university was the "Honorable University Council," consisting of an equal number of elected representatives from among students and professors. This was co-government in its purest form and the members participated in all university decisions and policies. The official student organizations were FUL (Local University Student Federation), which was mandatory in each university, and CUB (Bolivian University Student Confederation), which functioned at the national level. According to its statutes, it is a political organization whose objective is "the protection of the oppressed and exploited and the promotion of freedom and peace." The offices of CUB and FUL issued all declarations of strikes and demonstrations and public denunciations of the government.

This system of co-government grew out of the struggle for university autonomy, which began after World War I as an effort to throw off a repressive, archaic medieval system in Cordoba, Argentina. The struggle spread to all of Latin America within a decade. In 1924, the University of San Francisco Xavier in Sucre, Bolivia issued a manifesto declaring itself independent, and in 1931, autonomy was officially recognized by the Bolivian constitution. However, the struggle did not end there because succeeding governments continued to put limits on the universities, until the revolution of 1952, which fully restored the university's rights.

During that year of research, I came to understand the power of the university students, that they had participated directly in the November, 1964 revolution, something the government radio station reminded us of periodically in the days after the coup by praising them for their courage.

Latin American universities were born out of the political necessity to prepare governors and teachers from among the ranks of and for the ruling elite. Later, revolutionary literature from Europe and the United States found its way to the universities of Latin America, and a new governing class rose up to throw off the old order and claim power for itself. Indeed, the independence movement in Latin America began in the University of San Xavier in Bolivia.

CHAPTER 11

LAST PROJECT AND FIRST FAREWELL

With many lessons of the year well in mind and documented, I was ready to go back to the U.S. However, before leaving. I had one more project to complete: a visit to the other universities in the country to get a better perspective on the University of San Andres. The rector of San Andres provided me with a letter of presentation to all of his fellow rectors, asking them to tally up the data on their students and submit a report to his office of statistics immediately. I was to interview each one and deliver his personal message.

The first university we visited was in the city of Oruro. Madre Felicia and I set off for Oruro in a train that was no more than a little yellow tin can of a bus mounted on tracks. Four hours on this fiercely vibrating Toonerville Trolley made not only conversation or reading out of the question but it was even a feat to retain a thought in one's head. We rattled into the station in Oruro where a Dominican priest, whose sister was a fellow Racine Dominican, met us. He gave us a quick orientation to Oruro and the university. There, the rector was also the uncle of a student I knew in La Paz and I presented him with a letter from his niece. So the door was wide open, I think, for us. He was a member of the Communist Party but that didn't seem to matter. He graciously gave us a tour of the school and promised he would promptly send the data we requested for the office of statistics in La Paz.

After a frigid night in a convent in Oruro, Madre Felicia and I boarded an early morning train to Cochabamba. By comparison to the ride from La Paz, this was smoother. Only by comparison. When we arrived, we were welcomed by the Dominican Sisters from Sinsinawa, Wisconsin, and they kept us entertained for hours with stories of their misadventures and cultural mishaps. Cochabamba is a favorite city, especially with foreigners. Known as the "the city of flowers," it boasts of a perfect climate with warm days and cool, comfortable nights. In the sixties it was still famous for Quechua Indian women wearing tall white stovepipe hats and there were more bicycles than cars on the narrow, dusty streets. On balmy evenings students from the University of San Simon studied by the lamplight in the city's parks.

I was not able to meet with the rector of the university to deliver the message from La Paz, but I did leave the letter with his secretary. It must have been received because I learned later that the needed information was dutifully dispatched to the data office at San Andres in La Paz.

Our next stop was Santa Cruz, at that time still just a frontier outpost located in the eastern lowlands or "*Oriente*." We arrived on the heels of a torrential tropical downpour that turned the city streets into rivers of muddy water. To handle such storms, the wooden sidewalks in the center of town were built on stilts as high as three or four feet above the ground. Jeeps and ox carts were the vehicles of choice. Nothing else could make it through the streets. Again, it was the Sinsinawa Dominican Sisters who received us. They staffed a parish school and taught religion classes in outlying rural areas on weekends.

I continued my quest for university officials and information but to no avail. I could only peer at the university archives through mud-encrusted windows. The records were obviously in a shambles. Loose and yellowed papers were crammed into dusty shelves and stacked on the floor and tables. Doors were locked and it looked like there hadn't been any activity there for quite a while, except for the spiders weaving their webs..

From Santa Cruz we flew to Sucre, the official political capitol of Bolivia and the cradle of the independence movement in Latin America. It was the University of San Xavier that ignited the sparks of rebellion against the Spanish crown. It was the proud site of *the Casa de la Libertad* where Bolivia held its First Congressional Assembly. Neat, clean and elegant, Sucre is affectionately called "*la ciudad blanca*" for its many whitewashed colonial homes and buildings. The entire city was an impressive, well-preserved, historical monument. I easily collected the information I needed there.

We had two more universities to visit: Tarija and Potosí. In my pocket I had a piece of paper with the name of our next contact in Potosí, a name I couldn't seem to remember when anyone asked me. Mostly because it wasn't a Spanish surname, "Bachinelo," head of the FUL (Local University Students Federation). We were to present our letter of introduction to him at the University of Santo Tomás in Potosí, and he would help us with whatever we needed. We planned to go there by bus, but heavy rains had washed out the road and the trains were suspended until further notice. We considered a flight to Tarija, but there were no planes leaving for another week. After waiting in Sucre a couple of days hoping that the road might be cleared, it was clear that the rainy season had trumped our plans and we decided to return to La Paz. One day I would meet Señor Bachinelo, but not just yet.

As soon as the clouds parted and flights were allowed to depart from the airport, we boarded a small cargo plane with seats for only four passengers at the rear. We were told that this type of plane was not built to fly above 10,000 feet and since the airport was at that altitude, the first fifteen minutes of the trip would be crucial. Passengers and cargo were weighed carefully before boarding. We prepared for takeoff.

There was nothing to hold on to, so each time the plane changed altitude or turned, we were unexpectedly propelled out of our seats. Still in a sitting position and feeling and looking quite foolish, we shuffled the length of the plane towards the pilot, and, as the plane leveled off, back to our seats again. We spent those crucial fifteen minutes like subjects in some weird scientific experiment in centrifugal force. Eventually we got to stay seated and enjoyed a spectacular flight over the gleaming snow capped Andes.

I reported back to the rector of San Andres that I had delivered his message to his fellow-administrators, but I did not make it to Tarija or to Potosí and Enrique Bachinelo.

This was the end of my field research in Bolivia. I had learned a lot about the University of San Andres and its students. I had recorded their problems, aspirations, complaints and fears. I had begun to understand the price they were paying due to U.S. foreign policy. They hated American imperialism, yet were obliged to study the English language and American ways in order to survive in the world economy. They regularly tore the stones from the streets and blocked traffic not only to shout out against their own government but also against U.S. policies: the bloody war in Vietnam, exploitation by foreign corporations and the School of the Americas in Panama. They understood the source of their underdevelopment. They experienced repression and violence and had little hope for the future. Even the high school students, who frequently took to the streets demanding desks or the release of fellow students and teachers who, had been arrested knew how and why they were being exploited. They understood that the rules of the game were written by the powerful elites and by the transnational corporations, and they resisted. The lesson of the 1952 revolution taught them that victory could only be won in the streets. When we spoke of the United States in conversations, what most dumbfounded the students was its shocking and incomprehensible record of racial discrimination.

Study by candlelight and kerosene heater, the slight discomforts of the high altitude and many trips on crowded and flea-infested city buses were among the minor inconveniences of doing research in Bolivia. However, through these experiences I felt I most surely had learned more about myself, my own values than I did about those of the Bolivian women I came to study. Now it was time to pull all of this together and make some sense of it.

As a religious woman in 1965 I was not free to decide what I did or where I would work. I had hoped to return to St. Louis for at least another year, doing more coursework and finishing my dissertation at a leisurely pace. However, in May, I had been told there would be a change in plans for me. I was named to the new "Motherhouse," to be in charge of the community's newcomers or "postulants," as they were called. Instead of going to St. Louis, I would return to Racine. It was a vote of confidence from Sister Mary Magdalen but a disappointment for me.

To complicate matters, the postulants had already arrived in Racine two months earlier, so at the end of November, when I couldn't delay my departure any longer, I reluctantly packed my notes and books into a small olive green steamer trunk. As I did so, I realized that the early doubts about being able to adapt to Bolivia had been quite foolish and unfounded. I had in fact thrived as never before in this place that made constant demands on my heart. Here I was needed. Here I could make a difference. I did not want to leave. I was at home as never before in my life.

The ride up the winding road to the airport was routine by then. I had often watched Pan Am take off and gradually become a little speck in the sky before disappearing completely from view. Now it was my turn not knowing if I would ever return. I dreaded the work with the postulants, and wondered how in the world I would ever write a doctoral dissertation while doing a full time job.

There was a flurry of good-bye hugs, good wishes and messages to take back to Racine and then I too became no more than a speck on the horizon.

CHAPTER 12

ASSIGNMENT RACINE

The trip back to the States included a stopover in Lima. In those days, airlines would pay to lodge travelers if there were a layover on a long trip, and so when we landed in Lima, I was put in a taxi with other passengers and taken to a hotel. Anyone who has spent any time in Lima will know that I am not exaggerating when I say that the cab driver was maniacal. So impatient with the slow traffic on his side of the highway, he crossed over the center divide and wove his way at breakneck speed, through the oncoming traffic all the way to center of the city. Taxi drivers in Lima have a reputation: some say they are suicidal, and they may even be homicidal.

At the hotel, I found out that the airline did not arrange for a room and I, along with the other passengers in transit, had to wait until one was available. I tried to sleep in an armchair in the strange, plush lobby but the Pan Am employees frequently interrupted what few snatches of sleep I was able to get to assure me that they were "working on it." It turned out to be a sleepless right at the door to the cocktail lounge. From where I sat, I could see a telephone on the bar. I toyed with the idea of calling friends in Lima, but history wasn't ready for a nun in a bar, nor was I.

The rest of the trip was uneventful, and I arrived back in Racine to a new Motherhouse, which was still under construction. All 32 postulants, mostly first year college students came out to meet me. After a whirlwind welcome with introductions, hugs and good-natured teasing because they all towered over my 4'11", I made a quick trip to see my Father in Detroit. He had recovered from the stroke, but not completely. Amazingly, he had somehow managed to drive on his own all the way from California to Michigan to see me. But he was changed: in the past we often had long and lively conversations. He had been an avid reader and always loved to talk about books. Now we spoke only of simple things. The stroke had left him somewhat impaired, but I was glad he was still there to hug, and I was relieved when he said he was happy to be living with John in San Francisco.

Back in Racine with the postulants, I did my best to take on my new role. I had to figure out how to initiate new members to religious life at a time when everything was being analyzed under a microscope and possibly "up for grabs." The community was in the process of building a new "Motherhouse" on the shores of Lake Michigan. Two wings were near completion and the novices and postulants moved in to the building before the sisters. This was, in part, to help with the cleaning.

The circumstances were considerably less than convent-like. There was no permanent chapel and construction noise, confusion and workmen were everywhere. The rules that had marked my own initiation to the community some thirteen years earlier did not apply in this situation. On one of my first evenings, I found the postulants' little black rulebook in the bottom drawer of my desk. I read through the pages hoping to get a clear idea of what I was supposed to be doing. Most of the regulations had to do with places and times of silence signaled by a bell. Bells? Silence corridors? We were dodging under and around scaffolds none more sacred than any other. I certainly wasn't going to invent new rules just for the sake of having rules. There were other regulations about the postulant garb, but they were not wearing the traditional long black dress and veil. Keeping hands under the cape was difficult if there was no cape. We were all caught in between tradition and the full-blown changes that were beginning to sweep the church. I carefully deposited the rulebook way in the back of the drawer and tried applying common sense. Moreover, my own ideas were redefined from the perspective of the year I had spent in Bolivia. I cared little about details such as construction dust on a staircase or the length of a skirt. I had my priorities: toilet paper in the restrooms was one. I was later told quite firmly that I should have been watching the dust more closely.

The "formation program," as it was called, consisted of four levels of preparation with a director for each. We were a close-knit team of four young sisters. Following the cues of very strong and wise women leaders, we weighed everything we did and searched for the meaning behind the external practices and traditions and questioned everything. It was a time of change in the Racine community, as it was in many others. Doors were opened to experimentation in life styles and work. The church's mission to the poor and needy was finally to be taken very seriously. I had learned that many of our traditional practices had little to do with what we were about, whatever that might have been. We carefully studied each Vatican II document as it came off the press and made it our own.

The old Motherhouse, the yellow brick structure located on Park Avenue in Racine, was destined for the wrecking ball. It was a treasure of happy memories, young dreams of monasticism and saintly illusions, a cradle of idealism, but unfortunately, it was also firetrap. The Sisters had approached the Racine city officials in hopes of rescuing the building and preserving it as an historic monument, but its importance was not understood. So, significantly, at this time in church history, when great many myths were being torn down, this lovely old relic would have to go as well.

The new Motherhouse hadn't even been named yet - it was simply called the "new Motherhouse." It came into existence thanks to the foresight of an early treasurer, Sister Sabina, who years ago had purchased the land and understood the value of a beautiful piece of property on the shores of Lake Michigan. She had purchased the land to the dismay of many, for no one knew why. In the end, it was just what was needed to relocate the sisters. And it turned out to be a very valuable stretch of undeveloped lakeshore property, indeed. It was a pristine site, with birch trees, a beach and wildlife. Today the city of Racine has grown out to the area and the property is surrounded by housing developments. In spite of that, it still stands as a beautiful retreat and a hub of spiritual, artistic and community involvement.

This was 1966, a time of transition, and all of us, young and old alike could only "hold on tight and let the winds of change rip." This was particularly obvious on moving day. The construction work was finally completed and it was time to welcome the most senior members to their new quarters. In former days, the older Sisters were on hand to welcome new members into the community, but on this day, it was the youngest among them who stood at the door and took them by the hand to steady their faltering steps and guide their wheelchairs along the corridors. The novices and postulants carried their suitcases, showed them to their rooms and helped them settle in.

That year passed quickly and I grew to admire the young women under my charge. I loved their enthusiasm for life and wholehearted generosity. Still Bolivia was never far from my mind. At first, I had regular short wave radio contacts with La Paz, by crossing the city to the home of a friend who had a powerful transmitter. Later, the communications tapered off and only on rare occasions would news trickle up to Racine by way of a letter or visitors.

In July, the postulants went home for a final visit before receiving the habit. I took advantage of the time to complete my dissertation. I finished the draft in two weeks and sent it off to the typist.

That month there was also a contest to name the new Motherhouse. When

"Siena Center" was decided on after Saint Catherine of Siena, the community's patron, one of the elders, a bit hard of hearing, misunderstood. "My dear, that's a bit disrespectful! Why are they calling it "Senile Center?"

In August the postulants moved on to the novitiate and the new group arrived in September. By then the construction had been completed. The house was organized and I had a better handle on things. I thoroughly enjoyed my second year and resigned myself to staying in the U.S. It was then that Sister Julianne returned from Bolivia and we knew someone was needed to replace her. Sister Miriam was selected in January and we sent her on her way with hugs. I was surprised that I still felt a twinge of nostalgia and wished it were I who was going.

Right after that, I made a trip to St. Louis to successfully defend my dissertation. It was a subject that no one knew anything about, and the examining panel concentrated on the methodology. They congratulated me, and with all due respect to the judges, I probably could have said most anything and they would have had no way of proving or disproving it.

Quite unexpectedly, on a chilly afternoon in April, Sister Mary Magdalen, major superior and mentor (the one who had visited me at Sacred Heart four years earlier), asked me to take a walk with her around the convent grounds. I recall the exact spot where she asked me, "How would you like to go back to Bolivia?" The moment still evokes tears of joy when I recall it.

"Did I?" How could I not want to return? There was no doubt in my mind. Of course, I understood there would be criticism - the community had prepared me for academic and spiritual leadership and now my talents would be used elsewhere. Also why send someone with a doctorate to work among poor Indians? But Sister Mary Magdalen made it clear that I was needed to guide the work in Bolivia and if necessary, receive and prepare new members. Her trust in me and in my judgment was complete. It was the kind of confidence that was a great source of strength and very humbling.

Not surprisingly, my last two weeks in the U.S. were hectic. First, I was fitted for a suit since the Sisters in Bolivia were no longer using a habit. Then I flew to St. Louis for the final defense of my dissertation, and then on to San Francisco to visit my Father and brother, John who was taking care of him with his usual sensitivity and devotion. The summer of love was in full bloom and in full religious garb, I mingled with the hippies on Haight St. and fit right in! On the way back, I stopped in St. Louis again, this time for graduation. Finally, with diploma in hand, I flew back to Racine and to all the details that went into preparing the postulants for the novitiate and the reception of the habit. They were keenly aware of the incongruity of their putting on the habit while I was setting it aside. Although they made it known loudly that they did not want to wear a habit, they went through the traditional ceremony. At last, my duties screeched to a halt and I said my tearful good-byes. With hardly time to catch my breath, I was on my way to Bolivia the very next day.

Looking back on my experience with them, I realize that I had received more from the postulants, by far, than they had from me. Preparing for their classes, I had to hone my own thinking about the social mission of the Church and re-examine many traditional practices and ideas. My own training had been a regimen of discipline and stoic acceptance of life, and in traditional monastic spirit, a denial of friendship. But the time I had spent with these beautiful young women touched me deeply. They had won my heart and I believe I became a bit more human for the experience. I would miss them.

CHAPTER 13

BOLIVIA ENGULFED IN TURMOIL

In the old rule of convent law, friendships were not to be cultivated and a culture of secrecy prevailed. But now it was a time for openness and clarity. Many traditions were finally abandoned and ways more in keeping with the historical times were adopted. Celibacy was under serious scrutiny, as were other practices. This led many religious women and men to rethink their own decisions, and it marked the beginning of a mass exodus from religious life and the priesthood. Everything was under question, and there was no clear idea as to where or how it would end. It was against this backdrop that I set out for Bolivia for the second time.

It was June 1967 and I was indeed, following my heart. I was ecstatic with expectation and even presumed that I knew what was ahead. This time I was not traveling alone for Pat Downs, a tall redhead, very funny, and very smart and a good friend was now going with me.

The three members of the formation team and the house superior accompanied us to O'Hare Field. By then I had closed out the Postulant Department checking account, and, with all the distractions, I completely forgot about money for Pat and myself. So, there we were, ready to fly off to a foreign country without a cent. Pockets and purses were pulled out of folds of white habits and every last penny was quickly emptied onto a table for our trip. We thereby won the dubious distinction of having "screwed up" in one quick swoop, every account at the Motherhouse.

The sweet dark flight from Miami to Lima was almost a carbon copy of the first one, minus the *cucaracha*, thank goodness! But the arrival in La Paz was very different from my first one. We were met by a bubbling group of

Sisters in civilian clothes and with much chatter about their move from the apartment on 20 de *Octubre,* and how they were again staying with the Loretto Sisters. I renewed my friendships at Loretto and re-installed myself in my old room overlooking the Plaza. The very next day we left for Cochabamba where I would have a chance to rest and reflect for a couple of weeks, and Pat would enroll in the Maryknoll language school.

The Bolivia I returned to was still governed by Rene Barrientos, who had assumed power after ousting Paz Estenssoro in the violent coup of November 4, 1964. At first, he had been widely supported by the people, even hailed as a hero by the workers' union. But COB, the powerful national confederation of labor unions, immediately regretted backing Barrientos and withdrew its support. The day after the 1964 coup the workers hoisted their leader, Juan Lechin Oquendo, on their shoulders and began to march triumphantly to the Government Palace to show their solidarity with the new regime. However, the army met them with a barrage of bullets and stopped them in their tracks. In no uncertain terms, Barrientos let them know who was in charge, and that they would not be a part of his government.

So violent were Barrientos' attacks on labor unions that Juan Lechin was arrested and exiled in May 1965. A few days later, the army occupied the mining centers. By September, labor unions were declared illegal. Foreign mining companies were given leave to extract minerals for a song, and the miners were forced to accept a 50% wage cut which they could only overcome by working seven days a week. It was a cruel and cynical move forced on a sector of the population already coughing out its lungs to maximize profits for COMIBOL, the government owned mining company.

In July 1966, democratic elections had been held. Surprisingly or not, Barrientos won 63% of the vote, possibly because the repression had not yet reached the wide population and because he still had the unwavering support of the *campesinos.* Barrientos charmed the rural sector with his open personality and fluent Quechua and then formalized this support in a special pact between the military and the *campesinos.*

However, Barrientos' treatment of workers, especially the miners, worsened. In spite of this, the miners continued in their efforts to organize and protest. He arrested and exiled their leaders and waged a campaign to buy off other labor leaders. The brutality came to a head in the pre-dawn hours of June 24 when the miners were gathered in the Llallagua/Siglo XX mining camps to hold a two-day meeting. However, before the work began, they planned to celebrate the traditional fiesta of San Juan and combat the chill of "the coldest night of the year." According to the union leader, Simon Reyes, the delegates arrived with enthusiasm and were confident that the meeting would be productive.

Bonfires were lit throughout the camp and it came alive with music. Spirits were warmed with drinking and dancing long into the night. Finally, trouble came just before daybreak as the last embers were smoldering. On most streets, the fires were out and it was quiet, except for an occasional barking dog and the crunch of the lone footsteps of a straggler. That is when the army marched into the camp with the force of lightening. Armed with bazookas, machine guns and mortars they aimed at the last revelers and opened fire. They burst into homes and brutally massacred women and children, some even as they slept.

News of the attack on the mining camps of *Siglo* XX and Llallagua was sketchy at first and the number of victims was unconfirmed. The operation was painted as an effort to wipe out supporters for the Che Guevara guerrillas and other undesirable agitators. In reality, there had been sharp division among the miners over the question of guerrilla support. The action was obviously meant to put an end to labor organizing in the mines.

That is also when Che Guevara's guerrilla "*foco*" in Ñancahuasu was causing alarm at the Pentagon with fears that a Cuban style revolution would take hold and spread like wildfire. For its part, the Barrientos government was trying to maintain an image of stability and security for foreign capitol, and Che Guevara's ELN (National Liberation Army) was scaring away serious investors. U.S. Colonel Joseph Rice and Robert Shelton were sent to Bolivia to train 600 Rangers. Some 20 Green Berets were sent as support, making for an almost entirely CIA-run operation. News about the ELN was confusing and alarming. Among the people on the street, there was resistance to the ELN, since no one wanted guerrilla warfare or terrorism on Bolivian soil. On the other hand, the U.S. operation was also repudiated as "foreign intervention." Barrientos used the threat of the guerrillas to garner support for his repressive measures.

So while Che, weakened by asthma, was trudging through the jungle some 500 miles to the east and 30,000 miners marched in a funeral procession to the west, I waited in Cochabamba for travel restrictions to be lifted. A few days later, with Bolivia under a somber cloud of fear and tension, I returned to La Paz, aware of events but for the moment, focused on the course we would now set for our work.

CHAPTER 14

OLD STONES

Back at Loretto, we were sheltered from disturbing events in the country, and we turned our attention to finding a place where we could live and work. Madre Felicia and I spent the next two months house-hunting. We drove and walked through every barrio in the city and knocked on a hundred narrow double doors on adobe houses with rooms painted in bright blues, greens or pinks. We followed leads in the *"comerciales"* (real estate offices) that advertised rentals, sales and *anticrético*.

As far as I know, *anticrético* is a system that exists only in Bolivia. The tenant gives the owner a lump sum of money, from two or three or twenty thousand pesos, depending on the location and size of the property. The tenant can then occupy the house or apartment for as long as the contract states- usually one or two years- at the end of which time, the owner returns the money or increases the amount of *anticrético*. The tenant is free to re-locate or come up with more money and stay on for another year or two. We thought about doing this but in the end decided to buy.

We settled on a place in the barrio of Achachicala, an Aymara word meaning "old stones." It is an industrial area that at that time had most of the city's factories: a flourmill, a plastics plant, a textile mill, a distillery and a blanket factory. These factories, we were told, sounded their sirens to signal strikes, walkouts and to mobilize workers for protest marches. We were also told that it was at the far edge of a large parish run by the Canadian Oblate priests and that no women missionaries were working there.

Achachicala's landmark feature was the municipal slaughterhouse, which is located at the entrance of the barrio where two main roads, Chacaltaya and Ramos Gavilan, begin their long parallel ascents straight to the snowy top of Mt. Chacaltaya. Our first visit to the barrio was on a warm and sunny morning. We had no idea that during the rainy season the intersection would be transformed into a wide, muddy lake.

The house we picked out was two blocks up from the slaughterhouse. It had four adobe rooms with cement floors. The ceilings were made of burlap dipped in plaster and hung from the corners on nails. Their narrow double doors opened onto a common patio. Directly across the street was the Industrial School, Pedro Domingo Murillo, a sprawling two-story factory-like building, with a program of studies patterned, coincidentally, after a technical school in St. Louis, Missouri.

We had no legal authority to make the purchase of property, so the community treasurer made a trip all the way from Racine just to sign the contract. Purchasing a house is not simple anywhere, but in this case the snags were all due to an intercultural standoff when the Aymara couple who owned the house refused to sign any document until we gave them the money in cash. The Racine community treasurer would not give them the money until a contract was signed. It was a two-week cliffhanger, with meetings in and out of offices, several street corner encounters and many anxiety-charged conversations. In the end the treasurer, exhausted by the ordeal and resigned to Bolivian idiosyncrasies, signed a blank sheet of paper and told us we could write whatever we wanted on it and left for Racine.

That same afternoon we paid the Aymara couple; they put the wads of money in a shopping bag, and with a customary Bolivian *abrazo*, a handshake, a hug and another handshake, gave us the deed. Eduardo Bracamonte, a calmly bemused lawyer from IBEAS, presided at the event. He was the only one who knew from the start just how it would turn out.

Construction work had to be done, but we were too excited to wait and we moved in immediately. There was electricity but no water and no bathroom. We occupied the two rooms that had a window and stored the barrels and trunks in another. At night as soon as we slid into our sleeping bags, unsettling sounds came from the darkened street. Against the constant chorus of barking dogs, there were voices too close to the front door in conversations we couldn't distinguish and an assortment of unfamiliar noises. The knocks at the gate and footsteps of passers-by sent my vivid imagination into overdrive and I was certain that we were about to be robbed and assaulted. The other *madres* sleepily but kindly, I think, tolerated my paranoia.

One night, we were awakened by a male voice calling insistently at the patio door, "Serafina! Serafina!" That was the name of the Aymara Indian woman who sold us the house.

When it was obvious he wouldn't stop, Miriam shouted back, "*Quién es?* "Who are you?"

"I am Serafina's brother." Miriam had done especially well at language school and was able to convince him in Spanish that his sister had moved.

The following day we discovered that the Aymara couple who sold us the house also owned the property right behind us. When his head popped up over the adobe wall that separated the properties, Miriam dutifully explained that his wife's brother had been looking for her the night before. Lowering his chin to his chest, he murmured, "Serafina doesn't have a brother." It was probably better not to deliver messages taken in the middle of the night.

CHAPTER 15

SETTLING IN

With an address of our own, we could finally turn to sorting out our work. Felice took on the project of remodeling the house. It would be no palace. She planned seven small bedrooms (or cells), a dining room, a kitchen, a chapel and a laundry room, a living room and an entrance arranged around a central patio. Juanita continued her work with youth groups in the city while Miriam and Patricia still had classes to finish at the Maryknoll language school in Cochabamba. I accepted a short-term contract with the Dominican priests at IBEAS's newly built research center. It involved gathering and organizing information on technical and professional education in the country. The subject matter was dry and matter-of-fact; the best part was knocking on the doors of officials at the military and technical schools and the ministry of education.

Just before Christmas, Pat and Miriam returned from language school, but the house was still unlivable even by our newly acquired minimal standards. After the holidays, we decided to leave it in the hands of the construction workers for a couple of weeks so that they could hammer, saw, mix cement and kick up all the dust they needed to without interference. We had been invited to visit the North American sisters who were working in the jungle town of Caranavi and we jumped at the chance to take a break.

We set out again on "the most dangerous road in the world." Once we crossed the *cumbre* (peak) we began to circle the mountains up and down around agonizingly sharp hairpin curves on the narrow dirt road. Occasionally, sporadic waterfalls washed over the rocks above and pelted the jeep. After three or four hours of churning stomachs, we descended into musty, mountain jungle air, rich with the scent of tropical vegetation and bananas, citrus fruit and coffee plants along the road. Dusty and grateful for surviving the trip, we finally arrived at our destination: a pleasant and simple convent in the gold mining center of Caranavi.

The beauty of the mountain jungle was spellbinding. There were enormous metallic blue and green tropical butterflies and wild orchids, even a secluded waterfall for bathing. This was definitely not the Altiplano. The soothing setting was in stark contrast to the harsh terrain and climate of La Paz. However, not all was lovely and idyllic; the Caranavi sisters warned us that this peaceful town was a hotbed of political tension and that the garrison just down the road from us was used to keep the townspeople and *campesinos* in check.

We returned to La Paz refreshed but were dismayed to see that the work on the house had not progressed much. The workers had taken an unauthorized vacation and we had to resign ourselves to more delay.

Focusing on a work schedule, Pat signed on to teach mathematics at Colegio Loretto, a job she held until she left in 1970. Miriam was especially enterprising, having been invited to do a variety of jobs and was always in demand. Over the years she would teach English classes at the University and work as counselor in a number of places; she was principal of a public high school, and at one point even administered psychological tests to the Bolivian military, which gave her a unique appreciation of the military mind. Juanita chose to work full time in Achachicala, walking the hills and making contacts with neighbors. I continued my work on the Vocational Guide for IBEAS.

In addition we helped the Dominican priests with high school and university youth groups. There were weekly meetings, daylong courses or *jornadas* and weekend retreats. There were occasional religious functions and celebrations at the city convents, and while we attended them, it was with less and less frequency and waning enthusiasm. I sensed a growing awareness that we did not fit the traditional mold and began to feel very much out of place. I renewed old contacts at the University of San Andres and presented a "career day" in the main auditorium, complete with a slide lecture and information for the hopefuls who were taking the entrance exam and aspiring to study there.

Felice continued the remodeling project, and was appointed Superior. I was to coordinate the work and train any new members that might want to join our community.

CHAPTER 16

BARRIO DAYS

It wasn't long before we began reaching a broad spectrum of people. However, closest to my heart was the time spent in Achachicala. Thursday was declared "*Barrio* Day." It began with a reflection in the morning and then time to walk and talk and make new friends. We discovered the *barrio* was not even on the city map, so we drew our own large plan locating every little room and hovel tucked into unsuspecting corners. From there we pooled our information about who was who, what the needs were and what might be done about it. We had no plan except that Juanita would stay in the *barrio* and follow-up on whatever we had picked up from our conversations with the people.

It was about then that we met Pierre, a French priest from the parish of Espiritu Santo, run by an order of Canadian Oblates. The parish house was located closer to the city but Pierre helped out part-time in a little chapel in Achachicala. I don't know if he discovered us or if we discovered him, but one day he climbed up the two rugged rocks that served as steps and knocked at the patio door. He offered to celebrate mass once a week in our all-in-one room (kitchen, dining room, chapel, study hall, etc.) He eyed us with suspicion, for we were Americans and not to be trusted. On the other hand, we were doing something no one else was doing: we were asking the people what they wanted and needed; maybe we were harmless.

Then one day, Madre Juanita located a defunct medical clinic and resourceful as always, succeeded in reopening it. University students and even secretaries from IBEAS became interested in volunteering in Achachicala. Medical students helped by tending to the sick, and others worked with the children in a street corner educational program. We celebrated birthdays and baptisms with our neighbors. For the fiesta of Achachicala, we were covered with serpentine and confetti and watched them drink themselves into a stupor. The rooms of their homes were sparsely furnished, a table, straight back wooden chairs, walls painted in the preferred bright greens, blues or pink. At the barrio *junta* meetings, we sat stiff and shivering on splintered benches while the *dirigentes* (leaders) debated in the dim shadows of a bare light bulb. On rainy nights we slipped and slid down the muddy hills in the pitch dark. Our voices were heard at the assemblies and wakes and Juanita went with the leaders to request a bulldozer or medicines from city authorities. By the end of the first year we were part of the life of the barrio, sharing the difficulties and discomforts of Achachicala, no longer fearing noises in the dark.

One of the volunteers who visited the sick with Juanita was Nestor Paz Zamora, an ex-seminarian and a medical student. He was one of the few who came from a privileged background and who had come to get firsthand experience of poverty in his own country. As is more common that we might think, the rich do not know the plight of the poor in their own country. Even in a small nation such as Bolivia where poverty is everywhere, the wealthy live in an isolated bubble, sheltered from reality.

On the night when Nestor made the rounds with Juanita, he followed her into the hut of an elderly woman who was dying. He was so overcome with the stench and the squalor that he suddenly darted out into the cold and vomited in the street. Nestor's dedication and idealism radicalized him profoundly and he later joined the guerrilla movement, ELN. He took the *nom de guerre* of Francisco for St. Francis. He died of starvation because he chose to give his rations to his companions in the movement. Although he left behind an inspiring journal of his days as a guerrilla, outside of Bolivia his story is practically unknown. To Bolivian youth he is a hero, an example to admire if not to emulate.

Eventually our house was finished, and what a monument to discomfort and austerity it was! Each bedroom held only a very small bed and a chair; the dining room was bare and cold and the floors were of cement. However unadorned and harsh, it was still a notch up from our neighbors' homes. Most families were crammed into one room with a dirt floor. Some had no electricity. Even though we had installed indoor plumbing with shower stalls and toilets, water came through the pipes only once or twice in the three years we lived there, and we hauled water from the spigot on the street half a block away. And always, always the rooms were as cold as dungeons. Not a crack of sunlight ever graced the interior.

Our presence in the barrio became widely known and the *vecinos*, neighbors, came to our door with all sorts of problems. On one occasion, we were awakened in the middle of the night by a man pounding frantically on the door. He needed help with his wife who had just given birth. He had come on foot to find us. Juanita and I felt an icy blast from Mt. Chacaltaya as we quickly threw on ponchos and backed the VW out of the driveway. We flew over the dirt road and up to a one-room dwelling in and among the eucalyptus trees in the neighboring *barrio* of Pura Pura. Sadly, to the side of the doorway on the dirt floor was the body of the tiny newborn, cold and lifeless. We turned our attention to the mother who was in need of help. She had not expelled the afterbirth and was hemorrhaging. She sobbed in heartbreak and physical pain. She needed medical attention. Nothing could be done for the baby.

We helped carry her into the VW and rushed her over ruts and cobblestones down into the city and to the General Hospital. Once satisfied that she was out of danger and being cared for, and with a promise to return later, we started for home. Just as we passed the Plaza San Francisco, a slit of daylight opened over Mt. Illimani, and *cholitas* in the Plaza Perez Velasco were serving piping hot *Api*, a sweet purple corn brew seasoned with cinnamon and cloves. Steam from the cauldron rose in the semi-darkness and we stopped for an early-morning drink. There, as daylight slowly cut through the freezing La Paz morning we clutched our hot cups and looked at each other. Only then did we notice that we were still in our pajamas.

Later that morning Juanita returned to the side of the woman to make sure that she received adequate medical attention.

In Achachicala, we hosted many visitors, among them some young students from Brazil who were curious about the American nuns living with the poor. During their stay with us, they told us about a literacy program they were using in poor barrios in San Pablo. It was a new method developed by their teacher, Pablo Freire. They explained that they tried to reach the people through the issues that meant the most to them: bread, jobs and children. We were privileged to have Pablo Freire's Brazilian assistants stay with us for a few days and during that time, describe in simple and practical words the theory of *Educación Liberadora*. Except for an afternoon spent with Pablo Freire and his wife, Ilza, years later at Stanford University, my encounter with his first students taught me the most about *concientización*.

All the while we were moving and getting acclimated to our new surroundings, one of the most important events burst out onto the international scene. All that year the newspapers were filled with reports of guerrilla fighting in Ñancahausu, in southeastern Bolivia. The presence of Che Guevara was no longer just a rumor. There were casualties that could not be denied. There were reports of Che's men in Camiri, but no one really knew what was happening and it was hard to distinguish between rumor and fact. This created a constant undercurrent of tension in the whole the population. The thought of guerrilla warfare on Bolivian soil was frightening. I knew of no one who supported the guerrilla campaign, certainly not openly. Then, suddenly and tragically, it was over. In October, Che was captured, interrogated and then executed. The details of what and how it happened were sketchy. But rumors flew: Who actually executed him? What happened to his diary? Was it true that his hands were severed? And who gave the order to kill him? There was little doubt that the order came from the North. There were many questions without answers. Reactions varied; some bishops and priests even celebrated mass giving thanks that the guerrilla warfare was over. Our barrio was very far from the action but we all shared the relief that the fighting had ended, and had little understanding of what it was all about.

CHAPTER 17

IBEAS, SICUNAI AND THE CAMPO

Early in 1968, I signed a contract to work full time as Director of the Education Department at IBEAS. Now it was located in a new three-story structure with a garden, one of the few places in the middle of the city with green grass and flowers. In the rear in separate quarters, it housed the residence for the Dominican priests. It had just won the distinction of "building of the year" for its modern architectural design.

My first project there was a *diagnóstico* (survey) of Bolivian Education. Although I had a good idea of what the universities were doing, I knew nothing about the rest of the educational system. So, by day I put together a description of Bolivian schools and plowed through studies done by the Ministry of Education and U.S. Government agencies. After hours and on weekends, I slopped through the mud in Achachicala, froze when the sky was overcast and alternately baked in the tropical sun. I delighted in the scattering of nasturtiums blooming at the far end of the patio amid the construction material and piles of dirt left behind by the men who had worked on the house.

That same year I also worked on a study of religious women with Jaime Ponce, a Bolivian sociologist, and Oscar Uzin, a Bolivian Dominican priest trained in the U.S. We met almost daily for nearly a year to analyze the results and to write the final report. Besides being one of the most rewarding projects I ever worked on, it was an excellent opportunity to learn Spanish. We would all give our ideas, interpreting the data, and Jaime and Oscar would record into a dictaphone. Each chapter was typed and we edited and re-edited until we were satisfied with the final draft.

However energizing the process, the results of the study were disappointing. We hoped that the religious women in Bolivia were reacting positively to the changes recommended by the Second Vatican Council. To our surprise, many had not even heard of the Council, much less read the documents. Others were still engaged in quite medieval practices like corporal penance and had jansenistic attitudes of self-denial. The spectrum ran from some with no formal schooling whatsoever to others with college degrees and a fair amount of social awareness. I left the follow-up in other hands and moved on to another study.

In April, I was assigned to a research project in Sicuani, Peru, where a group of North American missionaries invited us to help them figure out why they were not having any success at attracting young women to their newly built high school. On a moment's notice, Padre Miguel, a Massachusetts priest who had been working in Sicuani for a few years, whisked me off across the Altiplano to Peru. He was something of a wheeler-dealer, who took charge of any situation and made it work. With typical gringo impatience, he couldn't wait until morning to travel. There was no transportation to Sicuani? Easy! Call a cab. At about eight o'clock in the evening and for what must have cost a fortune, we started out and rode all the way across the Altiplano in pitch darkness, around Lake Titicaca to Puno in Peru. It seemed surrealistic taking a cab across the Altiplano but what surprised me most was to see that rural Peru enjoyed the wonders of electricity. No such electrification project had come to Bolivia's *campo*.

I was deposited with the Maryknoll Sisters in Puno for the night, and early the next morning, we boarded the train to Sicuani, traveling a favorite route of tourists on their way to Cuzco and Machu Pichu.

We reached Sicuani and received a quick briefing on the problem we had been called to examine. Five years earlier a group of sisters from Chicago had built a beautiful new school that even had a modern Home Economics department and business school. The enrollment dropped with each successive year and after three years, they had more teachers on their staff than students enrolled in classes. Meanwhile, in the center of town, there were Carmelite nuns who ran another high school in an old building that was falling apart. The physical conditions in this school were abominable: cement floors, sagging ceilings, and cold air whipping through broken windows. The classrooms were so small and crowded that several students attended classes standing and had to use the walls for a desk. In addition, the Carmelite nuns ran a rigid medieval-style operation. The Americans were disappointed and mystified by the town's rejection of their school. I returned to La Paz with a mystery to solve.

A month later with questionnaires and an assistant, Teresa Valdivia, I made a return trip to Sicuani to conduct a census, an attitude study and an educational survey. We recruited teachers as interviewers and visited all of the schools and educational facilities in town. Two weeks later we returned to La Paz with a couple of trunks filled with data.

A highlight of the trip, which I made several times before the project was completed, was the overnight sail on a small antique English ferry that ran across Lake Titicaca between Guaqui and Puno. The ship's interior has been heralded in travel books for its polished brass and fine woodwork. In the evening a full dinner was served in a dimly lit dining room. After a short time on deck and admiring the moonlit lake, we retired to our cabin and comfortable bunks for a good night's sleep. The next morning after a tasty breakfast of hot coffee, jam and fresh bread, passports were collected and we awakened from our serenity by immigration red tape. I was anxious that our documents would be forever lost in the heap of papers on the table where an officious agent took his job much too seriously.

Back in La Paz again, we organized the mass of data we had collected and analyzed the results. Six months later, we were ready to present a draft of our conclusions and recommendations. The Publication Department at IBEAS was late in binding the study and it was handed to me on my way out the door to catch the train to Guaqui, where the little British ferry would take us across the lake to Peru. Finally settled back in my seat with several hours to kill, I began to look over the report. I flipped the pages to the appendix with all of the statistical tables. To my surprise, pieces of pages flew out on the floor. I gathered them up and concluded that in an effort to even up the edges of the study, the publication department at IBEAS had chopped the pages with a paper cutter severing all of the statistical tables that had been folded. Then, I saw the final work of the typist, who evidently had never seen or typed a table in her life. Wherever there was a 0%, she deleted it and rearranged the columns so that every slot had a value. The tables were meaningless but we were already on our way, and nothing could be done.

Once we arrived in Sicuani, I discovered that the presentation of the results of our study was a major civic event. It seemed like half of the city turned out to the local theater to hear abut what we had found out. The study showed us that Sicuani took great pride in its educational tradition. It boasted of several educational institutions: a school of agriculture, a normal school, a military academy, and more. It was a town where the parents trusted the older school run by teachers they had known for years, even if the conditions were far from optimal. In fact, the townspeople were frankly offended by the intrusion of the foreigners and not very receptive to modern ways. A lesser concern was that the new school was not conveniently located, as it was near the edge of town.

Actually, it was fairly easy to find a solution. With mixed feelings and to the credit of the Chicago Sisters, they turned the new school over to the Carmelites and returned to the U.S. Everyone seemed satisfied.

Through this evaluation process, the American missionaries began to understand that their presence was not only seen as intrusive by the people of Sicuani, but the resistance they encountered was part of Sicuanians' rejection of U.S. foreign policy in Latin America. They returned to Chicago with a new awareness and were determined to make a difference by trying to influence U.S. foreign policy. Two of their members went on to found the Washington Office on Latin America, WOLA dedicated to informing the American public and lobbying legislators about Latin American issues.

The first thing I did when I resumed my work at IBEAS was to carefully show the secretary how to type tables and point out to the publishing department that folded pages needed to be left uncut. I had learned not to take anything for granted, and the erring secretary became an expert and was in demand by all the researchers after that.

About that time, a Spanish Jesuit, Pedro Negre, came to work for IBEAS. He and two other Jesuits moved into an apartment on Buenos Aires Street in the crowded market area of the city of La Paz. While he taught Sociology at the University of San Andres, one of his companions, Luis Espinal, was a film critic who ran weekly reviews that were often politically charged. Luis had a sharp wit and was very well received, even by those he exposed. A third priest taught classes at the Jesuit secondary school, San Calixto.

Pedro and I continued the Sicuani research project and worked together with Miriam and Pat in the Young Catholic Student movement. Besides the overland trips to Peru, we initiated a project to introduce the students to the social realities of their own country. That involved many weekend trips to the campo and provided a new set of experiences.

Once a week we met before sunup on one of the cold cobbled side streets in the Indian Market where open trucks lined up to take passengers to the campo. Indian women sat on the corners behind low tables topped with steaming coffeepots. The shivering travelers, mostly Aymara campesinos, huddled close to the kerosene burner and sipped from laminated tin cups clasped in both hands. The passengers spoke quietly, mostly in Aymara punctuated with grunts as they heaped cargo and bundles on top of the truck. Then we all climbed up and found comfortable perches on top of the bundles. Wrapped in blankets or ponchos and fingers stiff with cold, we settled in to survive until the sun came out. The truck would finally jerk to a start and creak and groan as it slowly climbed out of La Paz with passengers under covers and in complete silence. It would lurch from side to side up the road to the Altiplano. The first stop would be El Alto, where children with unruly hair and cheeks cracked by the Altiplano climate, sold fresh bread out of flour sacks. The women in braids and bowler hats sat behind their tables brewing coffee in the pre-dawn light. At their feet were carefully arranged piles of oranges and cheese. One or two passengers would crawl out from underneath their wraps and hang over the side of the truck to buy some bread. After about another half-hour into the trip, when the sun came up, the covers would be peeled back and smiling faces would appear. Babies would be fed and sometimes food and jokes would be shared.

We traveled regularly starting out from Buenos Aires Street and headed for Tambillo or some other rural community to help build a school or start some project. The *campesinos* were happy for the help and once they sent mules to meet us at the road. I learned that adobe bricks are very heavy and what it was like to walk for hours across the barren terrain. If it rained, we got soaked. If it hailed, we were pelted with hail. If it was sunny, we burned. We walked and walked across the Altiplano for hours and I thought of how the early explorers went on foot everywhere and I understood that it was, in fact, quite possible.

Around that same time Flora Arias and I organized classes for rural schoolteachers at IBEAS. Flora was a former teacher who had an Aymara language radio program for *campesinos,* and with her assistance, the response to our classes was overwhelming. We had prepared for around 100 rural teachers, but more than 500, many of them *campesinos,* came to the city by truck, mule, boat, bicycle and bus. With a flurry of last minute changes, we reorganized and spent two weeks helping the teachers learn how to teach with the few materials available to them in the campo. Stones and grains could be used for arithmetic. A stick could be used to write in the dirt. Reading could be taught from labels on products bought at the local *feria* or farmers market (sardine cans, powdered milk, etc.) Before long, the classes grew in popularity. A thousand teachers registered the following year and the year after that, two thousand. They returned to their schools with a modest stock of supplies and a few new ideas. I was invited to visit their schools in the remotest of locations to encourage and work with the rural teachers.

During two years, I continued trips to the campo for classes with rural schoolteachers. I would start out alone but along the way there would always be familiar faces, someone who recognized me and offered me a piece of cheese or an orange.

The rural schoolteachers I worked with were mostly indigenous men from the campo themselves. They had studied at rural normal (teacher-training) schools. They laughed at me when I insisted on washing my face each morning in ice-cold water. They were respectful and smiled approvingly when they discovered new ways to help their students learn. In the evening we danced in the open air to the plunking of a *charango* and the puffing of the *zampoña*. Afterwards, each teacher lit a bonfire to keep warm and when the embers faded, the darkness and silence swallowed a day well spent.

CHAPTER 18

GROWING AND QUESTIONING

By the beginning of 1969, Juanita had the clinic in Achachicala up and running, with dental care, an immunization program and pre-and peri-natal care. The staff now included a doctor, a dentist and two nurses, who joined us daily for lunch. Meals were lively affairs with discussions and plans for the *barrio* and even fantasies about a new hospital.

It was about that time that Sister Felice returned to Racine and Sister Helen (Madre Elena), a librarian, came to replace her. The Dominicans at IBEAS had invited her to organize a social science library. Quiet and reserved, she was an unlikely choice for Bolivia but she plunged into her work with surprising ease and adapted almost effortlessly. As if her job at IBEAS were not enough, she organized a modest one-room library above he chapel in Achachicala. Since then a new building has been built, and the children continue using it to this very day.

A young Bolivian woman, Elsa, also joined our little community at that time. Her mother, whom I had met and interviewed in 1964 for part of my thesis, was the first woman to graduate in Economics from the University of San Andres. Her family lived comfortably in an upper middle class neighborhood in La Paz. Whatever their thoughts may have been, her parents were politely silent about their daughter's spartan surroundings when she moved in with us in Achachicala.

Elsa wanted to be a Racine Dominican at a time of great exodus from religious life, when we were trying to sort things out for ourselves mid the many questions about the validity of religious life. Because of this, her initiation into the group reflected our doubts. We could only offer her a simple and honest lifestyle and some guidance. However, we could give her little assurance that there would be a religious community there for her in the future. Elsa enrolled in social service classes at the University of San Andres and stayed with us for more than a year. She was always a joy to be with and endeared herself to us.

It was not long before Sister Mary Magdalen visited us again, and we continued fleshing out our role and the role of religious women in the social mission of the Church. They were truly days of soul-searching questions and unflinching determination to do the right thing by God and fellow human being. As always, she was warmly supportive and trusting.

In November, I took a day off to reflect and pray. There was no better place than a tiny chapel set in a quaint old-fashioned plaza called Montículo high up in the *barrio* of Sopocachi. The Montículo is a little park with picturesque lampposts and tree-lined paths and is a world away from Achachicala's smells, dirt streets and adobe houses - it was truly a breath of serenity and greenery. From my perch on the hillside, I could see the Loretto School below and I recalled my first days there and how little I knew when I first walked through their doorway. Padre Van Noenan's dramatic prediction came to mind, too. Whether it was "*destino*" or not, I was very glad to be a part of Bolivia.

I took time to ask myself some serious questions about the many changes in religious life. What did I really think? Even though I had been in the vanguard of some innovations, I had to admit that I was uneasy about other changes. Earrings, makeup, movies, parties and not wearing a habit were all rather insignificant, but they could easily lead to no restrictions at all. I reflected on other issues, as well: many religious women were requesting dispensations from their vows. In both North and South America, priests and nuns were leaving in great numbers, some marrying. Racine was no exception. Some of my own classmates had already gone down that road. I had no particular difficulty in accepting that. These were good people making honest decisions in good faith.

In some ways it was much easier in this setting to distinguish between petty, arbitrary rules and genuine commitment to the poor. I wondered if religious life as we knew it, with all of its rules and trappings, might not eventually become a thing of the past. I wondered, with surprising frankness, "What would I do if I fell in love with someone? How would I react?" If the winds of change were ready to sweep us away from this secure world of religious service, would I be prepared? I could only answer honestly that, "Life evolves and I need to be open to change." Who could know what we would be thrust into next? Then, on the horizon, Illimani's snowy crest glowed with the soft golden hues of sunset and it was time to descend from "Montículo" and face reality again.

CHAPTER 19

CARNAVAL

What a delightful reality it was! Before the Lenten season of penitence begins, many Catholic countries celebrate with a day or even days of dancing and reveling. The most famous of the celebrations is *Carnaval* in Rio de Janeiro, Brazil, but Bolivia is not far behind in its partying. *Carnaval* in the city of Oruro is less well known in the United States, than that of Brazil, but it is very well known in Europe and other Latin American countries. In Oruro the whole town practices all year for the dances, and during those few days before Lent, the city throbs with the beat of drums. Thousands fill the streets with spectacularly colorful costumes and reach into a rich folklore treasure of music and dance to perform the *diablada*, the *morenada, saya, cueca, huayno*, and more. Tourists arrive from all over the world and Oruro becomes one immense party.

That year we were lucky to have an invitation to celebrate together with the Castro family. Dr. Castro worked in our clinic in Achachicala and he made all the arrangements with his parents who lived in Oruro. We gladly accepted the invitation and set off for a weekend of folkloric delights. All day Saturday, hundreds of groups or *comparsas* paraded through the main plaza, performing for the exuberant crowd. At night the *diablada*, or hordes of devil dancers, sporting enormous horned masks and bulging eyes, leapt across the stadium. St. Michael the Archangel appeared to admonish them and banish them to eternal damnation. The devils faltered momentarily, but they rose again to the shouts of the audience and invigorated, leapt tirelessly into the night. The next day every side street became a battleground for children and adults alike, hurling water at each other with a total lack of respect for age, sex or condition. We passed through the madness unscathed until it was time to return to La Paz.

A Bolivian Dominican priest was also in Oruro for the celebration and was accompanied by his maiden aunt who was visiting from Europe. He did not want her to make the trip back to La Paz by herself, so he asked me to stay for one more day and be her companion. I agreed not to leave for La Paz with the other sisters and said I would meet him the next day at 1 p.m. at the front door of the Castro's home.

After waking the next morning, I discovered that *Carnaval* was still in full swing. I had barely swallowed my breakfast of bread and coffee, when the Castros appeared and dragged me out of the house and down the street to *"challar"* (bless) the neighboring stores and houses to keep away the evil spirits. At each stop, we were covered with serpentine and confetti and invited to drink a deceptively sweet, seemingly mild drink, careful to pour a share on the ground for the *pachamama*, mother earth. After having a few of these, I was actually drunk - there was no denying it. We kept going from house to house and I tried to refuse the drinks, but my feeble protests were useless. The word "no" had disappeared from Bolivian vocabulary. At our final destination, we were invited to have lunch. By that time I could barely bring my wristwatch into focus but I did manage to see that there were only fifteen minutes before the padre and his aunt would come to take me back to La Paz. I panicked and stood up to leave. At that point, I got scooped up and dunked head first into a barrel of water. No one escaped playing with water during *Carnaval*, not even a nun! It is an essential part of the celebration everywhere! Then, with only ten minutes to spare and without even excusing myself to my hosts (they would not have known the difference), I left the patio, still dripping and trying to maintain some sense of direction and balance. As I staggered back down the street on the way to the house, I was doused by buckets of water from all sides. It made no difference. I couldn't have been any wetter.

Stumbling and tripping, I somehow got into dry clothes, packed a small bundle and propped myself up like a broom just inside the gate to wait for my ride. When the jeep appeared, I needed reassurance and asked, "Am I here?" I insisted, "Am I here? Am I really here?" Then climbed into the back of the vehicle and immediately fell asleep. I did not wake up until the padre let me know I was home. I had been a total failure as a companion. I could only manage a shame-faced *Adios* and wondered when my hosts back in Oruro would realize that I was gone. There was a lot of partying in Bolivia and life can be very carefree but not always.

CHAPTER 20

INDIGNATION

Not everything in Bolivia is parties and celebrations. Achachicala in the sixties was grim. No one had running water; there was no sewage system. The streets with dangerously few streetlights were not paved and garbage was left in a heap for dogs and children to scavenge through. We could not help but feel indignation at the sharp differences with those who lived at the far and southern end of La Paz. Life was very different there. This was where the wealthy lived in their comfortable homes protected by high walls. They had lush gardens and late model cars. Their children went to music lessons and dance classes and were enrolled in the best private schools. They sent little servant girls with long braids and crisp starched aprons to carry their children's books to school for them. Later on they would send their children to Europe or the United States for further studies. This was where the politicians, bankers, entrepreneurs and diplomats met for cocktails and weekend barbecues and where the powerful met to form alliances. The women shopped for Christmas presents in New York or Paris, and knew more about foreign cities than they did about their own country. They had benefited from the sweat and labor of those who lived in the Achachicalas of Bolivia.

Where we lived and where most Bolivians lived, the children tied strings to sardine cans and pulled them along the dirt streets, pretending they were little cars. Many did not even have the luxury of going to school. And often, those who did merely went through the motions of getting an education without textbooks or materials, sometimes without a desk. Each day they would trek down the hill in their white smocks called, *"guardapolvos,"* literally "to guard against the dust," often only to learn that classes were suspended. It might be because of a teachers' strike, or maybe because there was no chalk, or no light bulb or for of any one of a hundred reasons. Teaching was done by dictation; the children copied word-for-word into a notebook whatever the teacher told them to write. It was teaching at its simplest, but it was the best that could be done under the circumstances. In hindsight, it may not have been as bad as it seemed to me then.

In the 60's and 70's when I was in Achachicala, the required number of schooldays was never completed in any one year. Students passed on to the next grade by presidential decree. In other words, most Bolivians were deprived of a good education, as well as adequate health care and decent nutrition and housing.

As the months passed, we slowly became even more involved in our Bolivian life, and gradually lost contact with our North American friends. Our weekends and holidays were spent in the *barrio* with our neighbors. More and more we went to their parties and meetings and less and less to the teas and events arranged by the local religious groups. Increasingly, Achachicala began to absorb our lives.

The barrio had a local junta, elected leaders who saw to the needs of the area, petitioning water, roads, transportation, sewage and electricity. Some Sundays were spent in a*cción communal* (community activity), digging a ditch or working for some type of improvement project. Every local community, rural and urban, in Bolivia has a local governing body or *junta*. The *junta* president is responsible for making improvements in the locality: getting heavy machinery to move dirt or pour cement or clear a road. He or she also serves on a board of *junta* presidents, a politically powerful arm that flexes its muscle in many a political battle. Often the local juntas are the movers and shakers who can bring progress to the barrios and mobilize protests on the spur of the moment. Someone once observed that Bolivia is the most organized country in the world.

Achachicala was no exception. We attended the regular junta meetings, which were held at night in an empty room, except for straight back chairs or rustic benches. The space was dimly lit by a bare light bulb, which I have often considered to be as much a symbol of Bolivia as is the bowler derby and the llama. Light fixtures and lamps were rare commodities. In the cold night everyone sat bundled up in overcoats with collars and scarves pulled up around their ears. There was no notion of how to move a discussion along. Each member would stare ahead without making eye contact with anyone else and respectfully repeat almost word-for-word what the first speaker said. Beneath this apparent inaction, however, an important process was taking place. It included information, affirmation and agreement. Action and planning had to be done at another level. The following day over a cup of tea or a bottle of beer, the logistics were crystallized. And so it was that the clinic re-opened, a library was organized, medical students organized a smallpox and polio immunization campaign and volunteers began a series of creative experiences for the children.

We watched, accompanied, at times prodded gently, and gradually came to understand how they talked and worked with each other and after a while we became a part of their lives. The neighbors in Achachicala had welcomed our presence and invited us to become a part of their celebrations and community projects. After all, we stood in line with them for water in the bitter cold morning air, carried our buckets of water down their streets and just as they did, we swore when the spigot was turned off without notice. We waited patiently at their side to buy bread from the corner oven. We jammed into the rickety buses with them and we swallowed the same dust from the road. We prayed silently that the brakes wouldn't give out on the steep incline and not so silently when a wheel fell off and we skidded crazily to a stop against the hillside.

What we had read about marginality and underdevelopment we now talked about in the first person. It was our reality. These were not simply deplorable and unfortunate conditions, but the result of exploitation and oppression. So there had to be exploiters and oppressors who served very unjust societal structures. The policies of governments and multinational corporations were skewed in favor of the powerful and rich, and unresponsive to the needs of the majority. The theories took on life: they were etched in the lines drawn on people's faces, on the tiny bare feet in the cold and a table set with a meal made of only flour and water. These intolerable conditions filled my eyes with sadness and my spirit with indignation and a desire to find a solution.

CHAPTER 21

BEYOND INDIGNATION

At IBEAS, a Dominican priest-economist did a study of the Gulf Oil Company in Bolivia. He invited both Gulf Oil and government officials to a presentation of his findings. Miriam, Pat and I sat in the back row of a large classroom at the Institute and watched as he showed charts of Gulf Oil's double accounting. The barrels of oil reported to the market in Wall Street far exceeded what was reported to the Bolivian government, which translated into a theft of taxes. The Gulf Oil officials, red-faced with anger, stormed out of the meeting. Not too long after that the Bolivian Director of IBEAS, Jaime Otero, was found hanged in a print shop he owned in the center of town. It was spine chilling. The timing may have been coincidental, but there was never a satisfactory investigation of the killing.

While we were settling in and finding our way, the country was embroiled in great political turmoil. The Barrientos regime brutally repressed the miners and the mines remained under military occupation. The number of political detainees grew. The university students and factory workers were on the front line of opposition in La Paz and students rioted almost daily. In contrast to Barrientos' repression of the miners, were his friendlier relations with the campesinos. He sealed his commitment to them with a signed agreement giving them special benefits that at the end of the day remained largely on paper.

Suddenly, in April of 1969, there was a news flash that President Barrientos had been killed when his helicopter crashed after takeoff from a town he was visiting in rural Cochabamba. Mystery surrounded the event. Rumors were circulated that it had not been an accident. Even though he had many enemies, he was considered a popular president, a likeable figure and a nice person. The joke was, "He had many women, but he was a good man - he treated them all equally." At any rate, the official version of his sudden death was that the aircraft became entangled in high voltage wires, even though some locals claim that there were no such wires in that area. On an unusually hot afternoon, as we watched the long cortege passed on its way to the cemetery, the country was in mourning. In keeping with the national mood, radio stations cancelled all programming and filled in with classical music.

The mild-mannered Vice-President Luis Adolfo Siles Salinas, my acquaintance from the University of San Andres, was then sworn in as president. It is said that he had few friends among the military and that he was something of a solitary figure. If, indeed, it were true that he was uncomfortable with the job, relief would soon arrive.

Just six months later whether by intent or by chance, Siles was out of town, and General Alfredo Ovando Candia simply marched in and occupied the government palace. Ever since the day of the November 4, 1964, coup, when the crowd booed him off the balcony for allowing Paz Estenssoro to escape from the country, Ovando had wanted to reclaim what he felt was rightfully his. Now, under a military dictatorship, one of the most unsettled and stormy political periods in Bolivian history began.

Ovando was a militant nationalist whose term in office was characterized by deep contradictions. This was a period during which the left re-organized, but it was also a time of repression. Although a military man, Ovando openly opposed U.S. intervention, and he assembled a cabinet of young radicals: Mariano Baptista, admirer of Ivan Illich's de-schooling theory, as Minister of Education, Oscar Bonifaz, Minister of Mines, and most notably, Marcelo Quiroga Santa Cruz, brilliant and articulate Socialist Party leader, was named Minister of Hydrocarbons. Ovando was pressured by these and other progressive cabinet members to reinstate labor unions and political parties: also, he lifted censorship and renewed relations with the nations of the Soviet Bloc, but not with Cuba. He allowed open protest to USA's interference in national affairs, and he did nothing to stop progressive leaders in all sectors from clamoring for reforms.

Soon Marcelo Quiroga Santa Cruz nationalized Gulf Oil, a bitter blow to "American interests." Movie theatres ran commercials depicting lavish outdoor barbecues that the Gulf Oil employees enjoyed while the poor had nothing. Mariano Baptista, Education Minister, invited Ivan Illich to speak to the teachers' union, and they practically ran him out of town for suggesting that the first step in an educational reform should be to "hang all the teachers." That year the May Day rally was one of the biggest in Bolivian History. Miriam and I joined the march and noticed that cameras were often aimed at us.

Reactionary factions in the Bolivian armed forces were furious with Ovando's liberal young cabinet members and with the openly leftist rhetoric and activities. Along with, and most certainly because of this climate of freedom in Bolivia, the United States stepped up military aid and CIA activity in the country. To further show its displeasure with the progressive decisions and policies of the Ovando government, Washington tightened its grip on Bolivia and cut non-military aid by almost a third.

Yet another thorn in Ovando's side was the ELN guerrilla movement that had scattered and gone into hiding after Che Guevara's defeat and killing. Their members now reappeared and tried to organize in La Paz. Many students had elevated Che to martyr status and revered him as a hero. His guns were silenced but his ideals echoed in the halls of the universities giving rise to a generation of new recruits..

The rumors of plans for an urban guerrilla movement must have caused particular alarm in the U.S. State Department. High on its list of priorities was an intensified hunt for these remnants of Che Guevara's band of followers, the *Ejército Nacional de Liberación* (ELN). A price was put on their heads, and their photos and descriptions appeared in the daily newspapers. Along with the majority of people, we feared the violence and knew that random bombings might take place. The threat was all too real.

It was just then that a university student, acting as go-between, asked Juanita if we would be willing to provide refuge for three members of the ELN who needed a safe place to hide out. Simply stated, they were in grave danger. Their lives were in the balance and we were in a position to help. On an ordinary afternoon, Helen, Pat, Miriam, Juanita, and I sat in our sparsely furnished living room and weighed the consequences: this would be very risky; were there other options? Were they just using us as "*tontas útiles*" (useful fools)? As someone said, "Better to be a useful fool than a useless one." We understood the danger. Pat Downs was in the process of moving to Colegio Loretto where she taught math classes. She chose that moment to confirm her decision and abstained from voting. It was decided that we would take them in only if all of us were in agreement. It was unanimous, and we turned to Juanita. Fully grasping the seriousness of the moment, we said, "Tell them they can come tomorrow."

By the time we came home for lunch the next day, Juanita had already installed the guerillas in one of the small bedrooms. I had walked that hallway many times, but now the closed door took on an ominous aspect. No hint of sound or movement came from behind it. Luisa, our cook, was summarily dispatched to the corner store to buy sugar, and while she ran the errand we hurriedly scooped up large portions of food from the table and Juanita whisked them off to the "guests." The unknowing Luisa, her eyes as round and bright as was her figure in colorful Indian skirts, was astonished to see how our appetites had grown!

At night, when we were sure there would be no visitors calling, we decided to let our guests out to move about the house. Three non-Bolivian men stepped briefly into our lives. Well-educated, one a doctor, another economist, and a student, they were quiet-mannered, surely incapable of mindless killing. They were eager to let us know what they were all about. No, they didn't like the idea of violence. But "depriving a child of bread, an education, medical attention, these too are acts of violence, and against the most vulnerable," they explained. Did we really think that significant changes in the system could be brought about by peaceful dialogue? These idealistic young men were willing to risk everything - home, career, comfort, their lives: to make the world a better place, and they justified taking up arms and violent revolution as a last resort. The vision they shared struck a sympathetic chord in us. The conversation lasted well into the early morning hours, and that night we became part of an underground that harbored and aided members of the ELN.

Sister Mary Magdalen came to visit us from Racine just at this time, and, not wanting to put her in danger, we temporarily found another place for the ELN members. She was not at all timid about the arrangement, and in fact, chided us for putting the young men at risk by moving them. "How could you do that? Bring them back immediately. I want to meet them." The nightly debates continued with a stamp of approval we hadn't expected, but welcomed with great relief.

We had some things in common with the ELN: a vision for a better world, a commitment to the earth's most needy and, apparently, a common enemy. The capitalist system and its transnational companies, spearheaded by the USA, controlled and concentrated wealth, designed foreign policy for their own benefit, and regularly cheated and stole from poor countries. The USA was busy reinforcing and training the Bolivian military in methods to keep the people in line. Yes, our concerns were the same, but we did not necessarily share a common strategy. Especially as foreigners, especially as religious women, we couldn't accept violence. They understood our hesitation. They spoke a language of struggle and hope and urgency. Maybe they were right. We did not have any answers. Most remarkably, the spirit of Che Guevara's "*hombre nuevo*" filled that dimly lit little room and we knew we were with men who were generous and courageous.

The risk involved in this operation was very real, and we learned to live with fear. A raid or a shootout was a real possibility. I think we all became very serious during this time. This was no game. We were in deep and had to look behind us wherever we went. One morning in particular, the danger became alarmingly clear. I made the trip to the corner puffing in the freezing air to buy the newspaper, and when I spread it open on the dining room table, we all suddenly stopped. The names and photos of ELN members stared at us from the front page of <u>Presencia</u>. They were accused of setting off explosives the night before and a price was on their heads. We knew with total certainty that they could not have been involved. They hadn't left the house the night before, not even for a minute but had as usual, been busy weaving plans for revolution and social change. The story was an outright lie and a blatant example of how the government spread fear and terror among the population in order to justify a permanent state of siege and curfew. Phony stories of hidden caches of arms were often front-page news, prompting of course, a cycle of raids and arrests.

These ELN men were Che Guevara's recruits and he was their fallen *comandante* and comrade. They knew him and were inspired by him; they were his men. In this way, Che Guevara became very real to us. I began to understand why he fought and died, what he may have meant by the creation of a "new society," the birth of a "new man," a world where everyone's dignity is respected, where every voice is heard. We had already come to understand that it was not enough just to feel indignation and outrage for the bitter inequalities we saw all around us. It was necessary to work for change, to understand the underlying causes of the injustice, to understand the political and economic system festering with poverty, inequalities and repression.

After a few days, the young professionals moved to another hideout, and a second group came to stay with us. In the next weeks, a variety of young people, men and women from the ELN came through our house. I became adept at receiving messages about when and where contacts were to be made. At work I would find an anonymous handwritten note with coded instructions. Since Juanita spent most of her time in the barrio, she arranged to be on hand to open the door.

As the time passed, the ELN members who came for our help became younger and younger and not as articulate or well prepared, as were the first groups. There was no doubt that the leaders were mature, courageous and well educated, but we began to have reservations about these youngest members.

We felt that the government was watching us closely. Even though churches and convents were still respected as places of sanctuary at that time, we lived with the constant fear that something would happen and the only question seemed to be when.

The answer came all too soon. Now in command of the ELN guerrillas was Coco Peredo, who together with his two brothers, Inti and Chato, had been recruited by Che Guevara. (Inti, the eldest was second in command to

Che Guevara, and was killed in the Ñancahuasú guerrilla war waged in 1967.) Coco was holed up in a room in an old house above the Plaza San Francisco, and he heard about the American Dominican *madres*. He sent a note through a messenger saying he wanted to meet with us.

On the designated night, at the designated time we waited, and we waited and waited. He failed to come and we tried to tell ourselves there was nothing to worry about. But the next day we awoke to frightening news. Early that morning the army had discovered his hiding place and made their move. Official reports said there was an exchange of fire and that he attempted to hurl a grenade through a window at his assailants. His missile hit the wall of his room, bounced back and blew him to bits. According to other sources, he had ventured out to meet someone who would bring him to our house, but his contact was a no show. He was followed back to his room and that was when the raid took place. Possibly, someone had betrayed him. This was terrifying. If someone had set him up, that same person would most certainly know about us. Our house was no longer safe – not for us and not for the ELN. We dropped out of the network but certainly not out of the government's crosshairs. The fear of reprisal was constant. We did not know whom we could trust. We did not know who else had been collaborating as we had been or who might know what our role had been. We lived under a necessary and real cloud of paranoia.

By some quirk of bad planning, all of the sisters were scheduled to leave La Paz at the same time for studies or return visits to the U.S. That left me alone in La Paz for a couple of months. I slipped into an uneasy solitary routine, working at IBEAS until 6 p.m. and staying on for youth meetings or workshops for a couple of hours more. The late hours were no particular concern and, the #4 bus took me to our doorstep.

Then one evening, I returned home from a late meeting and noticed the reflection of candlelight behind a neighbor's half-open door. She was an elderly diabetic who had recently had a leg amputated and was in a sad way. As I often had done, I stopped in to see how she was doing. She lived in one room with a dirt floor and a burlap ceiling and not much of anything in between. We talked in the shadows barely distinguishable to each other. I planted a quick kiss on her leathery cheek, promised to bring flowers the next day and crossed over the narrow street to our blue door.

I flicked on the light and froze in fear when I saw the educational material and contents of the trunks and storage boxes strewn over the brick floor of the entrance. Clothing and personal belongings littered the hallway. Beds were undone; lamps, dishes, books, papers and more personal belongings were everywhere. The whole house had been ransacked. I slipped out to get a young neighbor, Nelly, who lived a couple of doors away.

Together we checked out each of the five little bedrooms, the kitchen, chapel and dining room. Nothing had been stolen. Typewriter, radio, anything that had any value was still there. Tossed to the floor, here and there was a broken item, but there was no evidence of theft.

Nelly saw that I was shaken and volunteered to keep me company that night. The next day she helped me clean up and put things back in order. I knew it would be useless to make a police report. There was no doubt in my mind that the Ministry of Interior had sent us a chilling warning.

In the following days, the tension made it difficult to concentrate on my work. I wondered constantly what would happen next.

Later in the week, I received word that the ELN recruitment officer wanted to meet me. It was arranged for a contact to take me to a secret location in a comfortable middle class neighborhood. We entered a small, sparsely furnished house. For security reasons, I was asked to choose a *nom de guerre* and an assistant recorded it. Then I was escorted to the dining room. Seated at the head of the table was a nice-looking motherly woman in her forties with light hair and a fair complexion. With a welcoming smile, she explained that she was in charge of recruitment for the ELN and that she had been the secretary of Camilo Torres, the legendary priest who had died as an ELN guerrilla in Colombia a few years earlier. She had heard much of the American Dominican *Madres* and the work they were doing. Then after the introductions and the friendly conversation, came the reason for the interview.

"I understand that you and the other *madres* have noticed that some of our young recruits do not have much preparation and seem to be floundering. You are right. We do have a lot of new recruits, young people who need formation in revolutionary thought. We think you would be just the person to do that for us. I'd like you to join us. We would like you to be our ideologue."

She said I would be part of a team that would further develop their revolutionary vision. There would be no violence involved. I would help with the ideological formation of their members and participate in top-level leadership discussions and strategy.

I stiffened at the thought but was also deeply moved by the confidence being placed in me. Revolutionary thought? I was only a beginner myself in that area. I had so much to learn. It was outright frightening to have my ideas taken seriously, especially since I'd never taken them very seriously myself. For a moment I said nothing but I thought, "My God, am I the best they can get? They must be out of resources or out of their minds."

Finally, I said that I fully sympathized with their cause. Would I harbor young people who were being hunted by a repressive *de facto* government because they rejected the social status quo? Of course. I understood that the

United States and their local lackeys represented a system that was running roughshod over the rights of the Bolivians, that they were lying, cheating, stealing and killing their way through history. I agreed that changes had to be drastic. I could even understand why they felt violence was the only way to turn things around. Maybe dialogue between oppressor and oppressed was not a realistic option and the use of violence was necessary. But personally, I did not come to Bolivia to harm anyone. So with a very fuzzy fine line between yes and no, between heart and head, I declined. We talked a while longer. She did not pressure me. I never saw her again and often wondered how the course of my life might have changed had I accepted.

CHAPTER 22

SIGLO XX

The weeks of tension and soul-searching solitude were finally broken by the welcome arrival of the sisters from their vacations. We took advantage of the Easter holidays and set out together to visit the Llallagua-Siglo XX tin mines. Most of the day was spent on the road traveling by bus on narrow dirt roads carved out along the barren mountainsides. Along the way, we passed through several bleak mining camps hugging the Andean slopes, and by late afternoon descended into a small oasis-like valley with vegetation, neat buildings and comfortable homes. We inquired, "Who lives and works here?" We were told, "The engineers and their families."

In just a few minutes we climbed abruptly to Llallagua-Siglo XX, once the world's biggest silver mine and in recent decades still a major supplier of tin to modern nations – until it was largely replaced by plastic. The mining camp consisted of dismal row houses quickly slapped together with no concern for taste, comfort or privacy and without running water. There may have been an electric light bulb, but certainly not enough space to house a family. With a glance back and well within view was the valley below, the homes of the bosses and the engineers standing in stark contrast to the barracks-like buildings where the miners lived. The engineers even had a swimming pool.

The next day one of the Oblate missionary priests made arrangements for us to go down into the mine. We were outfitted with helmets, big boots and bright yellow raincoats. An elevator took us several levels deep into the earth. It was another world, an underground city, with a myriad of tunnels and shafts each with its own name and lore. There were offices and, small trains transporting raw mineral. We sloshed through sticky, slippery and wet muck, with water dripping from above. It was pitch dark, except for the lamps on our helmets. Some areas were sweltering and others bone chilling.

Supposedly, the miners considered it bad luck to have a woman in the mine, but all the same we were warmly welcomed wherever we shuffled along. Our guide told us of new technology and safety equipment and demonstrated a blast of dynamite. But the miners spoke of another reality: of miserable and unsafe working conditions and slave wages. They explained their belief in the "*Tío*, the devil image they pay homage to with alcohol, coca and cigarettes; the spirit who protects them from accidents and helps them find mineral deposits. Mining anywhere in the world is a dismal and dangerous occupation, but here it was even far more depressing than we had expected.

We emerged into daylight with a sense of relief, at least momentarily. The heavily armed uniformed soldiers occupying this mining camp made us uneasy. I could see why the ELN had given up on non-violence. It hardly seemed likely that peaceful negotiations could be possible under these circumstances.

We spoke with *palliris*, women sitting on the ground pounding rocky waste discarded from the mines and sifting through the pieces for bits of mineral. Young and old scavenged on the hard earth, some with infants at their side. They took time from their labor to feed tea or watered down milk to the babies and to rest briefly. Many worked in the mines for pennies a day in this desperate fashion after the death of their husbands.

A major lifeline and voice for the miners was Radio Pio XII, owned and operated by the Canadian Province of Oblate priests. Originally, Cardinal Cushing of Boston funded it as part of the Catholic Church's anti-Communist thrust. Its mission was to offset the growing leftist influence of the network of radio stations transmitting throughout the mining centers. These radios ran programs in Quechua and kept the miners' resolve alive and strong. They regularly criticized Pio XII and accused the Oblates of deliberately undermining their struggle for better labor and living conditions. But after the brutal June 24, 1967, massacre of the miners and the destruction of the miners' radios, Pio XII emerged as the sole voice of the miners and its mission made a sudden turnaround. Taking their cue from the grim reality, the Oblates became defenders of the miners' rights and unrelenting critics of the government and the military occupation. Although always under threat, Pio XII valiantly kept the country informed about what was happening in the mines.

If the hours spent in exchange with members of the ELN had been formative, the trip to the mines was a sobering taste of reality that sent the wheels of my mind whirling. I returned to La Paz convinced that there would have to be a new kind of commitment on my part, and began to question my work at IBEAS.

CHAPTER 23

CRISIS AT IBEAS

For some time my dissatisfaction with my work at IBEAS had been growing. I was increasingly uneasy because much of their funding came from the United States, and by then I knew that we were probably a source of data (useful or not) for American intelligence. The final test came when we were asked to review and approve a proposed project to study occupations in Bolivia. Professors from San Jose State University in California were to direct it and the budget was roughly a million dollars, an enormous sum at that time for a research project in Bolivia. The total amount would be in the form of a loan to the Bolivian government, but 90% of the money would be paid in wages to the visiting San Jose State researchers. Why should Bolivia pay gringos for something they could do themselves? Who would profit from this study? I balked at this and wanted nothing to do with it. I knew that the U.S used research results for its own unsavory interests.

My position was clear, "If you accept this contract, I quit!" I don't know if my stance had any influence, but the project was rejected and I agreed to stay on . . . for a while.

When the time came shortly after to give the Dominicans notice of my resignation, there was an unexpected turn of events. It was when Alberto Bailey, the Minister of Information, authorized a radical leftist weekly, "*La Prensa*," to go to press. The editors zeroed in on IBEAS with a vengeance and began a smear campaign, using half-truths and lies to link it with the CIA. Out of a certain loyalty to the Dominicans, who had been so kind to us during our first years in Bolivia, I decided to remain through the crisis. The articles in "*La Prensa*" had a devastating effect on the center. Our regular work stopped completely and the days were spent in frantic meetings in the priests' residence behind the office building writing responses to the accusations. But the weekly barrage from *La Prensa* was so intense that it was impossible to arm an effective defense. I felt the center's work should go on, that the stoppage was only playing into the hands of the people behind *La Prensa*, but the Bolivians on the staff were concerned about the damage to their careers and to their futures within the country, fearing reprisals or even exile. The attacks were personal with almost every employee targeted, in some way or another, by name.

La Prensa accused a Dominican brother of getting into a brawl with a priest and breaking his arm. Actually, the broken arm in question was the result of an accident. Notes from board meetings were quoted out of context. Zip codes from mailing lists were touted as secret CIA codes. Had the circumstances been different, these accusations might have been laughable but in 1971 Bolivia, they were deadly serious.

We later learned that a disgruntled former employee had revealed "information" to the paper. Although I may have been one of the few people not attacked by name, a friend told me later that an article had been in the works accusing me of, "cultural imperialism," and that an anonymous ally on the inside prevented its being printed.

La Prensa's tirades about IBEAS being an instrument of U.S. imperialism stirred up deep suspicion and strong opposition to IBEAS, so much so that on April 13, when we arrived to work at IBEAS, police were at the door to greet us. Earlier that morning a group of armed university students had roused the Dominicans at gunpoint and occupied the buildings. By the time we got there, the students had been expelled and uniformed officers were searching the buildings and grounds.

Understandably, everyone was nervous. We stood by while bombs were located, one in the toilet tank in the bathroom just outside my office. Now, besides fearing reprisals from the right for having collaborated with the ELN, we were fair play from the left as well.

A student, who had been part of the youth groups we worked with, confided to us months after that he was at the university meeting when the decision was made to occupy IBEAS by force. He maintained that the instigators of the takeover were outsiders unknown to him and that after checking with others, it turned out that no one really knew exactly who they were. They were the ones who provided the arms and the impetus. He suspected that they were provocateurs sent there to cause more chaos. Given the strong anti-American sentiment at the time, it certainly would not have taken much provocation to pull this off. He, along with other students who had been helped by the

Dominican priests over the years, slipped away from the meeting and did not participate in the assault.

Oscar Uzin, a Dominican priest who was there that morning, gives the following account of this attempted takeover of IBEAS in his book Luz de Otoño:

> The university students kept us incommunicado in a classroom for several hours of great confusion. We saw that the Institute was filled with people coming and going in and out of offices. They opened desks and read files looking for some incriminating evidence. Finally, the door opened and we saw the Interior Minister standing there . . . .
>
> He told us that the Archbishop had advised him of what happened and that he had brought troops to remove the students and return the building to the Community.

He added, "The seeds of IBEAS' destruction had been planted and the rest was only a question of time."

We continued our work, but everyone's attention was on the assault and press attacks. Helen's work in the library came to a standstill. There was no point in renewing her contract with the Institute, so in June we said our good-byes and she returned to Racine. It had been just one year since her arrival in La Paz, a year she would never forget!

CHAPTER 24

SAN FRANCISCO

Shortly after, it was my turn to make a trip back to the States for a meeting in Racine. I went first to San Francisco to spend a month with my Father and my brother John. I helped him finish building his art studio at the back of the cottage he had just bought. Evenings, I put together a family photo album, calling on my Dad's help to identify long gone relatives and friends. His memories were fading and I wanted to get them on paper before they were completely gone. I felt very much at home in San Francisco. It was wonderfully relaxing, and although I was six years younger than my brother John, we were close. We had spent a lot of time together when we were younger, possibly because our Mom had died when I was five and he eleven. Now art was his life, with painting and photography filling his days. Good books, music and the works of the masters surrounded me. San Francisco brought a welcome respite to soothe my very ragged nerves.

Although my Dad had become very mellow after his stroke, he was definitely showing signs of senility. Moreover, his smoking drove John crazy. He would light up a cigarette and blithely toss the smoldering match into the air. John could see his 1907 wooden cottage going up in flames and decided to hide the matches and light Pop's cigarette for him. It was a solution of sorts except that Pop would want a cigarette at any time of day - - - or night. At least this was better than having his house turned into a pile of ashes. To keep me from getting bored, John took me to old silent movies at the San Bruno Theater, to an art exhibit or two, a theatrical production, and always, on Saturdays, to garage sales. I spent time shopping for things I couldn't buy in Bolivia, shoes my size, for one.

During that month I also visited my brother Ed and his wife, Ruth in gorgeous Washington State. Ed was a reading specialist in the Bellevue public school system. Good food, warm company and fabulous scenery made for all the therapy I needed,

I then went to Detroit to see my brother, Chuck and his family. As president of the Communications Workers of America for the state of Michigan, he understood social and political struggles from the inside and he was no stranger to dedicating his life to a cause.

Finally, it was back to Racine and the Community meeting. By now it was evident that I had changed and that the Community had as well. Many of the Sisters had requested dispensations from their vows, reflecting the general exodus that characterized religious life at that time. Those who remained were struggling with new ideas and challenges. The spirit of Vatican II brought with it a long and unsettling process of soul-searching in religious communities and Racine was no exception.

I had very little patience with the long discussions and especially the excruciating self-scrutiny. It was impossible to put Bolivia on the back burner for recent events there had compelled us to look outward, to respond to immediate needs. Compared to what we were facing in Bolivia, the problems in Racine were of "another world." "Today's needs are too urgent, we have little thought of tomorrow," I had written. I understood, of course, that someone had to work out the details and plan for the future of the Community, but I wasn't that someone, certainly not at that juncture.

I felt I didn't make any contribution to the discussions. I couldn't find the right words to share our insights, nor did I feel at liberty to talk about our experiences. Even if I had found the adequate vocabulary, the most important part of the story couldn't be told. It was a frustrating time, but I knew I could rely on Sister Mary Magdalen for support and an acceptance of my person and my judgment. I was satisfied that she trusted me and approved, and that was enough.

At the end of two months, I was more than ready to return to Bolivia but sad to leave loved ones and apprehensive about what might lie ahead.

CHAPTER 25

TEOPONTE, THE HUNGER STRIKE
AND THE FALL OF IBEAS

While I was in the United States, I breathed easily without having to watch my back at every turn but in Bolivia, tensions, indeed, had been mounting. We learned just how deeply we were involved in events there when a former classmate of mine, Vivian (Madre Viviana), arrived to replace Helen. She held the dubious distinction of having a close relative employed by the CIA. When he learned she was going to Bolivia; he contacted her and urged her not to go because, "the sisters there are being watched very closely." She did not take the warning seriously and brushed it off as a relative's unwarranted concern. However, we knew there was reason to worry and that our greatest fear was from U.S. and Bolivian CIA operatives who followed, spied on and often arrested anyone who worked with the poor and had their welfare at heart.

Even the Ovando regime could not ignore the pressure from reactionary forces within the Bolivian military and Washington and he was forced to dismiss his liberal cabinet and appoint members more to the satisfaction of the right. The liberal General Juan Jose Torres, who had written Ovando's "manifesto" at the time of the takeover, was also targeted and relieved of his post as Commander in Chief of the Armed Forces.

Repression intensified and armed civilians led by the Marquese brothers occupied the University of San Andres. Basically, they were nothing more than a gang of thugs employed by the government to brutalize students. Unfortunately, they were never brought to justice, even though the students were unwavering in their demands that judicial action be taken against them.

Then, the Bolivian government proudly announced a new program. The Ministry of Education sent out a call for students to participate in a national literacy campaign in the campo. The response was immediate and enthusiastic, but the young men who answered the call had an agenda of their own. The episode that followed caused embarrassment to the government and, though ending in tragedy for the young people, set off a series of remarkable events.

I wrote home at that time,

> . . . the guerrilla movement in Bolivia, silent since the execution of Che Guevara, burst into the open once again. A group of university students, clothed as volunteer teachers, boarded trucks provided by the Ministry of Education to begin their "work" in Teoponte, a gold mining center in the interior of the country. The government hailed them as heroes and with great pride and much publicity gave them a rousing sendoff. The open-air trucks had hardly begun the trip into the interior when the robust sound of protest songs rang out from the young revolutionaries crammed atop. Unwittingly, the government had trained, supplied and transported a band of young rebel guerrillas. The Ovando government was mortified and furious and swung into action. But the students' daring captivated young imaginations.

> It was, of course, more than a mere embarrassment. A new guerrilla campaign had begun and bitter fighting ensued. In August, the government reported eight casualties among the guerrillas, whose identity they refused to make public. Later accounts of the event, reveal that the young men could not withstand the demands of guerrilla life, and that, whether frightened, sick or disillusioned, or all of the above, they abandoned the fight and were ready to return home. At that time all we knew was that they had been killed. Their families requested that their bodies be returned for burial and the government answered with a firm denial. The government's response immediately aroused questions about the circumstances of their death and suspicions that the students had been executed.

In face of the government's adamant refusal to return the bodies and growing reports of executions, support grew for the families of the guerrillas. On September 3, a hunger strike was declared. The strikers camped out in the cafeteria of University of San Andrés in La Paz. On Sunday evening, Miriam and I joined the group, as did hundreds of students and workers in universities all through Bolivia. On Monday, more hunger strikers arrived, and by Tuesday the university dining-hall was wall-to-wall with sleeping bags and blankets. The newspaper *El Diario* reported that among the hunger strikers were "ten priests and five women religious (two of them North Americans)". And it published a photo of Miriam and me.

We spent much time in conversation and joking to hide our real concern about the possible consequences. Someone kept us supplied with Chiclets for three days. Even now, years later, my stomach churns at the thought of chewing gum. The Red Cross checked our blood pressure each morning and served us a kind of watered down porridge to help us keep up our strength.

The hunger strike must have gained some international notice, since Oriana Fallaci, the Italian reporter famous for interviewing Fidel Castro and other world figures, showed up one morning looking for a story. I had no idea who she was, and when she promised that the Bolivian crisis would receive international attention, I naively agreed to an interview. Some months later I saw the article she wrote and it was not at all sympathetic with the Bolivian cause. It was, in fact, a very cynical and sensational piece of yellow journalism including a photo of an Italian priest, posing with his hunting rifle. She irresponsibly labeled him a "guerrilla." The bishops threatened to have him exiled and it could have cost him his life.

By noon on Wednesday, through the mediation of Archbishops Gutierrez and Manrique, the government showed a change of heart and agreed to return the bodies of the fallen guerrillas to their families. They also promised to protect the hunger strikers. We had won and we were elated by the results! One of the students, Hugo Rocabado, invited us to his home where his mother had prepared a nourishing bowl of soup to ease our stomachs back to normal. We were happy to be sipping the broth, but at the same time, were, in reality, very uneasy with the victory.

The next day I woke up early for my first class at the university. It was one of those rare and delicious balmy mornings in September. I hopped off the bus with new energy, crossed the street and headed for the main entrance of San Andres. I felt a hand on my arm, "What are you doing on the street? Haven't you heard?" A student whisked me aside. "The government is rounding up the hunger strikers and it isn't safe."

Although not fully aware of the details and relying on rumors passed by word of mouth, I wrote home.

On Tuesday, . . . at midday: Jose Prats, Spanish Jesuit and nationalized Bolivian citizen, was arrested by Bolivian police

---

in the city of Sucre and flown to La Paz, where he was held in custody. At 1 o'clock in the morning, Pedro Negre and Luis Espinal, also Jesuits were roused from sleep by ten armed men and dragged off to spend a night of terror and interrogation. At 3 o'clock, Anibal Guzman, a Methodist minister was taken from his home in the same way, without any warrant. Another Jesuit, Federico Aguilo, was arrested as he left his monastery at 8 o'clock that morning and Mauricio Lefebvre, a Canadian Oblate, disappeared on his way to a meeting at the La Paz Chancery Office. By one-thirty p.m., all five men were secretly flown to Salta, Argentina and held in the local jail until the present moment.

All had participated in the hunger strike in La Paz. Reaction nationwide was immediate. Days of violence followed - the gloves were off. For the first time in Bolivia, the Church was openly under attack. In response, the Jesuits and Oblates threatened to withdraw all of their members from Bolivia and the Oblates refused to hold religious services on Sunday. There were riots and casualties in all of the major cities. Funerals for those killed by the government turned into protest marches that brought on more violence, and the cycle was repeated more than once.

Within the government, military and political leaders became locked in bitter conflict. Labor leaders met with Generals Miranda and Torres and chose sides. Miners, workers and professionals lined up to mediate between the government and the Church. The upheaval at the highest levels of government was so intense that it almost overshadowed the issue of the exiled churchmen. The deepest division was within the military. The right wing accused the Ovando regime of being in bed with the left, and the left accused him of leaning to the right.

Then, on October 6, General Miranda, a reactionary nationalist, ousted Ovando, but within hours, the military edged him out of power and replaced him with a triumvirate made up of the commanders of the army, navy and air force. We kept glued to the radio, astounded by the political uncertainty. From 2 o'clock in the afternoon until 7 o'clock in the evening Torres threatened to bomb the government palace and planes menacingly circled the main Plaza. That night we climbed into our bunk beds expecting a blood bath. However, while we slept, General Torres came forward again and consolidated his leadership among the progressive military. All that night, troops marched quietly through the city and occupied all of the official buildings, the factories, streets and plazas, without firing a single shot. On Monday, dawn broke on a new day and another new government. There had been a coup followed by a counter-coup, followed by a counter counter-coup. In one weekend Bolivia had had six presidents.

Along with the political sweep, several U.S. installations were occupied, including (for the second time) IBEAS, the residence and research institute that belonged to the Chicago Dominicans. This time the takeover was definitive. The priests and brothers had been awakened from sleep, mistreated, threatened and herded into the dining room. They were ordered to leave and allowed to take only personal belongings. When all was over, the priests had lost their buildings, and the work they had begun with such enthusiasm and dedication came to an end. Some days later, the Department of Sociology of the University of San Andres hung its sign over the front door of the building.

Oscar Uzin phoned us that morning extremely torn by the events. Understandably shaken, and with a tremble in his voice, he said he felt relieved that it was finally over. The Dominicans moved in with the Franciscan Friars temporarily. Later, they moved to a residence in Miraflores and continued working quietly there for some years. Eventually, they would leave the seminary in Obrajes as well and turn it over to the Jesuits and the Catholic University. Later Uzin wrote of the incident, " . . . we had to accept the harsh reality: the work had been destroyed . . . . The buildings, the convent, the institution had been expropriated but the community never received a cent of indemnity."

We pretty much lost contact with the Chicago Dominican priests after that and what little communication we did have was very strained. They planned a yearly meeting to discuss and re-evaluate their mission in Bolivia, and we were not invited; we knew that we were not really welcome. A decade and a half later I received a surprising phone call from one of the priests. He called to apologize and to set the record straight. In the confusion and turmoil after the fall of IBEAS, they erroneously thought that because of my connection with the Sociology Department, I had had something to do with the takeover. Years later, they discovered that I had not. I thanked him, but in truth, had never even suspected the depth of or the reason for their resentment.

In the end I did not have to resign from IBEAS but now I was unemployed.

CHAPTER 26

LEFTIST INTERLUDE

Although the Torres coup had destroyed the work of the Dominican priests, it gave new life to movements on the left, instilling hope and reaffirming a sense of freedom. Torres was a man of humble origins with a simple manner of speaking. His populist rhetoric fueled long frustrated radical aspirations and soon the newly organized workers and students began to make their demands. The government lost no time in answering.

The Peace Corps was expelled for its perceived complicity with the CIA, Regis Debray was released from prison, labor unions and political parties were quickly legalized and the miners' radio stations were rebuilt. After investigation, suspicions were confirmed that the Papal Nuncio (the Pope's representative) had been complicit in the expulsion of the five churchmen who had participated in the hunger strike. Finally, by year's end the government had repealed all of the repressive decrees passed by Presidents Barrientos and Ovando.

One of the most controversial acts of the Torres regime was the approval of the *Asamblea Popular* (Popular Assembly) composed of representatives from labor unions, middle class organizations, leftist parties and *campesinos*, although no *campesino* actually was ever a member. After only ten days, mostly spent in bitter division and debate over specifics, it was agreed that the *Asamblea* would be at the center of the anti-imperialist movement. Its goal was to install socialism in Bolivia, and to make illegal all forms of repression against any organization or person involved in this revolutionary struggle. The whole country's attention was riveted on the sessions whose deliberations were reported each noon and evening on the news.

During the Torres regime, anyone in Bolivia who had any leftist inclination stood up and was counted. There was an explosion of artistic energy in film, songs and poetry. The music of Victor Jara and Benjo Cruz rang out at meetings and rallies. Students openly attacked the "*gorilas*" (military) and Yankee Imperialism and its lackeys. Intelligence sources were surely working overtime documenting and recording information on all of us. Needless to add, behind the scenes, the CIA and the Pentagon were paying close attention and making their own "plans." After all, leftist thinking or activities could not be tolerated.

Finally, with the stroke of a pen, the Torres government signed a truce with the ELN, bringing the whole guerrilla episode to an end. Unfortunately, this came too late for most of the idealistic young students who had formed the Teoponte band. To be sure, the guerrillas had suffered a bitter defeat at the hands of the Bolivian army, but no one can deny that they had triggered a chain of events that opened the way for Torres and all of these progressive reforms.

Many groups that had been oppressed for years were now filled with optimism, and formerly clandestine organizations now operated openly. Among them was ISAL, *Iglesia y Sociedad en America Latina,* a progressive international organization, a Latin American branch of the World Council of Churches, whose members were students, workers, professors and clergy of differing faiths. In Bolivia, ISAL took on a decidedly leftist political character and became the prototype of the Third World Church. Its members were often called *"Tercermundistas"* (progressive church people who work in the third world) and, rightly or not, labeled "marxist." Members of ISAL organized a national conference to explore the role of the church in the process of liberation and I helped prepare the document on the role of women.

Hugo Assmann, a visiting Brazilian clergyman, attended one of the ISAL meetings and enthusiastically told us about a new theology he was developing along with Gustavo Gutierrez in Peru. It was called a "theology of liberation." I was skeptical and impatient. "Theology is for theologians," I countered. "The people need work and bread and dignity, not a new theology." I could not know then that Liberation Theology would turn Central America upside down one day soon, or that it would be a source of a major division within the Catholic Church.

In the first days after the coup, I was still without a job and I spent much of the time at home writing letters and following up on several invitations to work. Plans were being made for a Workers' University and I was invited to be on the planning commission. The teachers union was re-organized and I was invited to give them a workshop, and I attended the National Congress of Juan Lechin's PRIN (National Leftists Revolutionary Party).

On one of those sleepy sunny afternoons when I was working on my manual of creative experiences for children, the roar of a motorcycle interrupted my concentration. I looked over the balcony, and there, coming up the hill in a cloud of dust, was Pedro Negre! He and the five churchmen had returned from exile.

He grew pale when he explained how he and the others were treated, of the cold cement floor in the frigid Altiplano night and the terror that tore through them during the flight over the Paraguayan jungle. He said that their captors had thrown open the doors of the plane and threatened to throw the churchmen into the black abyss below. History of the "Dirty War" in Latin America has since revealed that others were not lucky enough to survive those horrors.

As the country was enjoying a welcome respite from the repressive regimes, we too were able to relax a bit. Juanita, Miriam and I took in a couple of movies, enjoyed a roast duck dinner in Achachicala prepared by Pierre in his rustic adobe room attached to Our Lady of the Snows chapel. The meal was shared, incidentally, with son of forties' film idol Hedy Lamarr who was backpacking through Latin America. Also, our close-knit relationship with the members of ISAL was growing.

There was never a shortage of fiestas in Bolivia and this was a time when there was much to celebrate with weddings and holidays. Any gathering of students, political leaders and church members could turn into a festive occasion. Whether we knew how to dance or not, we would soon be linking arms and getting swept along to the strong beat of Bolivian folk music. This truly was Bolivia's heart: its music and dance. This was its carefree way of savoring the moment in all its intensity with no past, no future, no yesterday, and no tomorrow. We celebrated the return of the exiled churchmen with music, singani (Bolivian whiskey) and dancing.

Miriam, Juanita and I had finally found a meaningful niche in Bolivia and were confident that it would last indefinitely. Bolivians were no longer "they," but gradually becoming "we."

Amazingly, while all of this was happening, we were able to take time to make some major decisions. We sold our house to the barrio Junta in Achachicala on the condition it would be used for a small hospital. We got rid of most of our furniture and rented three rooms farther up the hill in the same barrio. We called this our "birdhouse," because the rooms were so small and perched high on the second and third floors.

We had a veranda from where we could view the whole barrio below and the stand of eucalyptus trees on the mountainside directly across from us. Vivian used her ingenuity to turn a nightstand and a bucket into a commode and a very large tin funnel and a piece of garden hose into a sink. Male visitors regularly mistook it for a urinal. We were lucky to have a spigot of water right outside the house, having only to carry the buckets up one flight of stairs. After helping us get installed with electrical outlets and a bathroom, Vivian moved to El Alto to work with the Sisters of St. Joseph.

Some of our American friends thought that we were becoming too culturally adapted for their taste and commented that soon they would find us in sleeping bags in a tent. The missionaries at the southern and wealthy end of the city found it especially hard to understand this radical move and, half-jokingly, they vulgarly taunted us for living in a barrio that was nothing more than an open latrine. But whenever there was a heavy rain we took the opportunity to alert them that the contents of the "latrine" was washing down the hill and that they should be prepared.

In the second patio behind us lived the owners of the house, a *campesino* couple who regularly had violent arguments. At first we sat through these confrontations tense and fearful, but later we knew to wait for the sound of the frying pan landing on the husband's head. That would end it and the next day he would inevitably appear calm but hung over with a bandage on his forehead.

An even more amazing achievement in middle of this political whirlwind was the transformation of our old house into a hospital by Juanita and a group of volunteer doctors, nurses and friends. We took time with the barrio to celebrate opening day. There was to be a doctor in residence 24 hours, 7 days a week. We trudged home after the dedication ceremony feeling great satisfaction. With the experience of IBEAS fresh in our minds, we realized that our decision to sell was a preventive measure, for we had decided to "nationalize" our property before the government got to us!

A group of well-intentioned wealthy women, who were the wives of factory owners and businessmen, opened a center for children in Achachicala in a small abandoned storefront located on the ground floor of our birdhouse. We called them "Damas Voluntarias." To their credit, they scrubbed and painted the walls and tended to the children with sincere concern. Daily, they brought them vitamins and milk served from whisky bottles donated by Bellows Distillery. But they did not hide their motivation nor did they suspect that I found it crassly self-serving. In their own words, it was to make friends with these children so that they would no longer despise the rich and so make the lives of their own children safer.

The children of Bolivia were my constant concern. They were the most innocent victims of the economic policies and the transnational monopolies. They lacked basic nutrition and sanitation, and in their innocence did not yet know how poor they were and much less, why. In my opinion, it is the purpose of education to sharpen children's wits and prepare them with the tools to identify needs and create solutions in freedom and confidence. The children I worked with were happy and innovative youngsters in spite of their poverty.

To this point, everything we sisters were doing in Bolivia was wholeheartedly supported by the Racine community, especially the leadership. Now the sisters in Racine chose Sister Suzanne as the new major superior. She was given the title of "President", not a particularly friendly term for us. One of her first acts was to visit Bolivia. Though quiet, we found her to be a good sport during her stay.

When news of her visit reached the Italian priest Oriana Fallaci had maligned in her feature article in _La Scala_, he invited us to visit Bolsa Negra, a privately owned wolfram mine right in the middle of his enormous parish. He picked us up in his jeep and in less than an hour, we arrived at the mining camp just south of La Paz. It was located on a dreary, gray slope facing, and seemingly within arms reach of, the snowy heights of Mt. Illimani. We gasped in amazement, as we stood face to face with this gigantic mountain, the backdrop for the million souls who lived at its feet.

We spent the day visiting the area and company officials proudly showed us the facilities they had provided for the miners: a cheerful dining room, a pleasant school and a clean, well-stocked clinic. That evening the padre explained that Bolsa Negra was one of the better mines, but that the following morning he would take us to one where the miners were not so lucky.

Early the next day, we started out to another mine carved into the side of the flat-topped Mt. Mururata. Legend has it that this poor mountain lost its peak in a love triangle struggle with a neighboring mountain that summarily cut off its "head" and left it flat for the rest of time. The jeep labored higher and higher into the mountain to a small private mine owned by Grace and Company of New York.

We were driving through snow and clouds when suddenly; we saw an Indian woman, dressed in _pollera_, shawl and derby seemingly suspended in the thick mist, splitting small rocks with a larger one, working the mineral with only the tools provided by nature. As we rounded the steep curve, her figure came more clearly into focus. She was sitting by the side of the road in the snow, working in the cold drizzle on this steel gray Sunday morning. The unspeakable misery of this god-forsaken place was part of the financial empire of Peter Grace, who, astoundingly, had recently been awarded by the Vatican the proud distinction of "Catholic Businessman of the Year."

By the time we wound our way down the mountain late that afternoon to head back to La Paz, it was raining and the road had turned into a river. The jeep slid through as far as it could and then with profuse apologies the padre left us and we had to go the rest of the way on foot. We plunged into water, which at one point was up to my neck. I would not have made it without the help of a couple of tall men, also on their way to the city, who pulled me through the current. Then the clouds parted and we continued on our way under a starlit sky. When we reached barrio of Calacoto, we boarded a bus. As we were jostled back and forth on the way up to Achachicala, the other passengers were oblivious to our clothes completely caked with mud.

There was something more than the dirt on our faces that went unnoticed that evening: a deep and ominous rumbling from the belly of Bolivia. A little General from Santa Cruz, Hugo Banzer Suarez, who had unsuccessfully attempted to overthrow Torres twice, had returned clandestinely from exile.

CHAPTER 27

MOVING OUT AND MOVING ON

February 1971 was a decisive time for Miriam, Juanita and me. The superiors in Racine asked all of us to re-examine our understanding of religious life. We were given a list of questions to guide a group discussion. Why had we entered the order; had our motivation changed in any way; if given the choice today; would we enter religious life; and why would we continue – or not. We came to the only logical conclusions: our motivation had changed radically; no, we probably would not enter if we had the choice; and after much reflection, we decided that we would not continue, each with her own reason.

After the group discussion we wrote to Racine to request formal dispensations from our vows:

> Our asking for dispensations is the most honest thing for us to do, not because we consider ourselves unfaithful to anything, but because we simply no longer fall within the church's definition of those who bear the name "religious". . . . We trust you to understand that they (reasons) spring from deep convictions and a dedication to the Bolivian people. We intend to continue a life of prayer and sharing in common, opening ourselves to a whole new development within ourselves."

We concluded with a gentle reminder, "You have set us on the road that has led us here."

We sealed the envelope, took it to the post office turned our attention to another decision, namely, to look for another place to stay.

While we waited we decided to move again, after just nine months in the "birdhouse" because the distance from our places of work proved to be a major inconvenience, and we needed be closer to the city. In May, we packed up our belongings and furniture and moved into two rooms, still at the north end of the city and located around the corner from the Canadian Oblates' parish house. There we had the luxury of running water right in the patio and were actually blessed with a flush toilet – across the patio and shared with another tenant– but genuine. No more buckets!

Juanita still was weak with hepatitis, and her work in Achachicala became more and more limited until finally, the doctor advised her to leave the high altitude indefinitely. She moved to Santa Cruz, which is at lower altitude, and so we were two.

One day we woke up and found that our electricity had been cut off. The Canadian owned Bolivian Power Company, had disconnected it because we had not paid our bill. I went down to "La Power" to explain that we weren't due for a bill yet, because our meter had just been installed. That didn't matter, and I had to pay the bill. What should I do if I didn't have a bill?

"Go home and get it and pay it," I was told.

I repeated that I had not received a bill. Then they insisted that I was Jose Rodriguez. I had no way of proving that I was not. I had I.D. that proved who I was but didn't have anything to show who I wasn't. Two days and eight candles later, Madre Viviana, who was a licensed electrician, hooked up the meter all by herself.

We plunged into the new freer political environment with enthusiasm. We marched with ISAL in Bolivia's biggest May Day celebration ever. We chanted "Que *Vivas*" and "*Que Mueras*" the length of the Prado. The rally stopped in front of the COB Headquarters for speeches railing against Yankee Imperialism, the School of the Americas, the war in Vietnam, the International Monetary Fund the World Bank and a host of foreign companies which had long exploited Bolivia's workers and resources. The *campesinos* carried banners that were beautiful works of art, mounted on exquisitely hand-carved poles. I wrote home that some day Bolivia might have an indigenous government, and that this would bring a new dimension to politics. We noticed that we were frequently photographed when we participated in these events, as we had been during the hunger strike. The pictures are undoubtedly tucked away in our CIA files. However, regardless of the exuberance, the triumph and the hope, there was an undeniable underlying sense of fear and mistrust.

I accepted a contract with the Catholic Bishops Commission to direct an analysis of textbooks and teaching methods. This became a benchmark study focused on cultural alienation in Bolivian education. I recommended a long time friend to be my assistant. I was also invited to teach a full schedule of classes at the Normal School, giving me a total of 74 hours per week. Although it sounded like an impossible task, especially considering time needed for class preparation and checking papers, I suspected that with the predictable delays, strikes and cancellations, I would never have to actually put in that many hours. Besides, I couldn't refuse the offers because some very good people had worked very hard to get them for me.

Just about that time a representative of UNESCO invited me to participate in a panel of seven or eight educators to review and evaluate a brand new innovative television program for children, *Plaza Sesamo* (Spanish for Sesame Street). I had never heard of it, but UNESCO gave it an impressive buildup and I eagerly took part in the panel. I anticipated an amazing production.

We were ushered into a small auditorium with comfortable theater seats and as I looked around, I saw that I was the only one on the panel who had direct contact with children in poor barrios and the campo. I knew well how serene the children were, how easy it was to motivate them and hold their interest, and I knew they had an exceptional capacity for concentration and reflection. The film rolled.

The Sesame Street programs (we saw three) were a rapid bombardment of images and sounds that left me as wired as if I had swallowed several of cups of strong coffee. It was a veritable assault on my senses. I took out the evaluation form and wrote. The films were neither appropriate for nor needed by the children I worked with, who were representative of the great majority of the school age population in the country. Motivating them was effortless; they were not easily distracted and certainly did not need a blast of images to stimulate their minds. Not to mention that most of the children did not have access to TV.

Mine was the only negative evaluation. I was the only panel member to reject the program. The government TV channel began transmitting the series shortly after that. So much for my opinion! Significantly, at this writing, a recent critique of Sesame Street claims that the program moves too slowly and that it should be speeded up.

Then came the reaction from Racine! There was disappointment and some anger. By that time as was true in many other religious orders, a good number of members of the Racine community had already left, and I think there was a fear that this would trigger an even greater exodus. Some fear may have been justified. In fact, the entire formation group had been sent home to "re-think" their vocation, and the sisters there were trying hard to deal with so many changes. It was a challenging time and more difficult for some than others. However, most responded with typical generosity, and wished us well, saying the door would always be open if we should change our minds, and warmly offering us a continued bond of friendship.

About that time, and in stark contrast to our experience, a group of seventy Colombian religious women received a serious blow. They had been making a sincere effort to draw closer to the needs of the Bolivian people, to set aside some of the practices and customs they felt were irrelevant to their work and to take the Church's renewal message to heart. Their superiors did not welcome their efforts at innovation and experimentation and the reforms they had initiated. Suddenly, without warning, they were all expelled from their order, in a foreign country and without support.

Without any fanfare or second thoughts, on May 16, 1971, we signed the dispensation forms that had been sent to us from Rome. Antonio Antezana, a factory worker, Pedro Negre and Sister Vivian were witnesses to the act.

We placed the documents in the mail and continued our lives exactly as before. We had broken legal ties to our community, but we still felt a strong bond with our Racine roots and deep gratitude for the moral support we received. We had walked away from privilege and all financial support. We were on our own but confident that new ties to Bolivian friends would help us define a new community, a new vision.

CHAPTER 28

THE BANZER NIGHTMARE

In addition to classes at the Normal school, the research study and other projects, I began the long drawn-out process of applying for a teaching position at the University of San Andres. I had the academic qualifications, but I was blacklisted because of my connection with the now ill famed IBEAS. I was informed that the "Revolutionary Committee" that reviewed and gave final approval of all teaching positions had considered my application and had identified me as an agent of American imperialism.

Several students and professors who had been present at the meeting knew me well and they appealed the decision in an effort to clear my name. Finally, by late July, my revolutionary credibility was publicly established and proved beyond a doubt to all. Thanks to the determination of my friends and their convincing arguments, I was indisputably on record as a bona fide leftist and, at last, I was awarded a professorship at the university! I would be co-teaching a rural sociology workshop with a friend from ISAL, Jaime Paz Zamora, a dashing young student from Tarija and brother to Nestor, the guerrilla who had lost his life in Teoponte.

In mid-August, and just before the start of classes, I met with Mauricio Lefebvre, a Canadian Oblate and Dean of the Department of Sociology (located in the IBEAS buildings.) We discussed plans for the workshop. Padre Mauricio, a tall priest in his early fifties with gray hair, a ready smile and lively blue eyes had two hobbies: tight rope walking and carpentry, hardly the signature of a rebel. He welcomed me warmly to Sociology, a department with a reputation for being Marxist, something he viewed with some reservations and an amused chuckle. We chatted at length and set another meeting to make final arrangements for scheduling and classrooms. We were to meet again on Saturday, August 21, at 3 pm, an appointment that would not be kept.

August had begun, as usual, with the barrio fiesta in Achachicala. There were processions, masked dancers, firecrackers, brass bands, and a lot of drinking. I stayed with the children in the center until evening. After sunset the temperature must have dropped below freezing but five little ones didn't want to go home and they clung to my side. I bought a sumptuous supper from one of the street vendors to share with them. We sat on a huge rock and shared a meal of potatoes, meat and rice smothered in onions and served on a piece of paper. With no utensils, we ate with grubby hands and laughed and shivered until the last bite. I found a few pesos in my pocket, about four cents, just enough to buy some peanuts for dessert. The city lights sparkled on one side of us and the dark hill of trees formed a jagged silhouette on the other. The last of the revelers stumbled down the dirt road, masks in hand and covered with confetti. After the last peanut was devoured, the children left and I hopped the next No. 4 that came along.

The crowd on the bus ride home was happy and bleary-eyed, completely insensitive to the blasts of wintry night air. A radio played *música bailable*, lively dance music, and passengers mixed political slogans with other more incoherent phrases. The driver and I were probably the only ones aboard who weren't sloshed. It was the end of a typical Bolivian holiday and I was tired and cold. Although I was sober, I was just as oblivious as the rest as to what was about to happen.

Less than two weeks later, on Saturday, August 21, we woke up to a confusion of unconfirmed rumors that some of the cities in the "Oriente" had fallen into the hands of the ultra right. Their residents were under the impression that La Paz had fallen, too. Bill Lange, a Chicago Dominican, arrived at the house after a ten-hour bus ride from Cochabamba with news that that city had been taken over by the military from the *Tarapacá* Regiment. It was still quiet in La Paz, but the coup had already begun! We turned on the radio and listened in disbelief while our world spun full circle round.

By mid-morning, the *paceños*, people of La Paz, were being called to arms by the official radio station and directed to go to the Stadium Plaza where rifles and munitions would be distributed. They were asked to take to the streets and defend President Torres. Shooting broke out all over the city. The rifles handed out at the stadium were rusty old relics from World War II. That and a shortage of ammunition left hundreds without defense in spite of being just a few blocks from the major military barracks in the city. As the day progressed and fighting intensified, the radio appealed for volunteers to pick up the victims. The streets were littered with wounded and dead. The instructions were to take a white flag and go to the Red Cross Center on the Avenida Camacho.

Pierre stopped by briefly to say that Mauricio Lefebvre had painted a large red cross on a sheet, draped it over the roof of his big blue van, which was known by everyone in the city, and left to help with the rescue effort. We listened, as the frantic radio announcer called for help at specific locations. There was a call to go the intersection of Capitan Ravelo Street and Montevideo where a doctor had been shot while going to get his little daughter from a neighbor's house. Mauricio and a young medical student were dispatched to the location. As they pulled to a stop at the intersection, the military entrenched in the hill of Laicacota spotted the vehicle and opened fire, blasting the windshield. Mauricio managed to jump out, and using the door as a shield, he yelled to his companion to run. Then, as he turned, he was shot from behind. We listened in horror as the Red Cross made an appeal to pick up another victim, driver of a blue van at the corner of Capitan Ravelo and Montevideo. It was Mauricio!

Pierre left in his little yellow Citron with hopes of helping. He found Mauricio in the middle of the intersection. Each time he tried to go to his side, there was a spray of gunfire over his head and he had to retreat. The shots came from the hill of Laicacota. Obviously, they did not want Mauricio to be rescued.

Later, under the cover of night, with bullets still flying, Pierre returned. Inching his way on his stomach, he hooked Mauricio's belt with a cane and dragged his lifeless body to his vehicle. There was no doubt that he had been deliberately targeted.

The shooting continued into the night and the next day. Juan Jose Torres was ousted and General Hugo Banzer Suarez, a small, bantam rooster in uniform, declared that as President he would restore "order, peace and work" to Bolivia. He spoke to the nation and invoked the help of God and the United States.

Mauricio's funeral was held two days later. Students and factory workers came out of hiding momentarily, some in disguise, to join the long, sad funeral march. Although no one knew who or what would be next, the final brave speeches and "*que vivas*" rang out proudly and tears were choked back. We bade each other "*chau*" followed by a hug and "be careful" and each withdrew to his own corner of tension and fear. As always, the cameras were aimed at selected individuals throughout the ceremony.

On August 26, we received a phone call asking if we would hide out a well-known leader of one of the leftist political parties. We quickly accepted. We were told it would only be for one night. Evening came and we waited. Around eleven o'clock we decided that there had been a change in plans and went to bed. At 11:30 the doorbell rang and I jumped to answer. Without a thought I darted out to the patio and through the dark passageway that led to the street. I unlatched the door and watched in terror while five armed civilians barged in, shouting, "Is this where the Sociology teacher lives?" My first concern was that we would be arrested and would disappear without any trace. I knew that we needed to let someone know what was happening. After they filed past me, I attempted to slip through the door to the street. And then a sixth paramilitary, who was standing guard outside, pushed a machine gun into my chest and forced me back into the courtyard. I returned to the rooms, where Miriam was calmly asking the men to identify themselves and by whose authority they had come. They said they had orders to arrest us. They showed us I.D. cards of which I remembered nothing. We were still in pajamas and I asked if we could get dressed. Once inside the bedroom, Miriam, muffling the phone under a blanket, called the Oblates to let them know we were being arrested. Juanita and I covered the call with coughs and loud talking. All of the Oblates from the parish, except Brother Miguel, had gone into hiding. Our call only succeeded in further frightening the already terrified *Hermano*, who spent the night thinking he'd be next.

Possibly because things were still in a state of confusion, the paramilitary sent to pick us up were not clear about what they were supposed to do with us. The usual procedure would have been to take us to the Ministry of Interior, and that would have meant prison and exile or worse. But learning that we were foreigners, they packed us into an oversized white jeep and drove us over the cobblestone streets to the offices of INTERPOL just off the Plaza Murillo. Two of our paramilitary escorts went inside with our passports and we stayed in the jeep under the control of the others.

We waited in silence in the jeep. Literally, shaking with terror I opened, at random, a small New Testament that I had put in my pocket. There was nothing particularly consoling in the words of St. Paul that I read by the light of a lamppost, "I know, friends, that the voyage will begin to be very dangerous and filled with prejudice, not only for the ship and the cargo, but also for our lives." However, it got a little better as I continued, ". . . the centurion gave more credit to the pilot and to the owner of the ship than to what Paul had said." (Acts: 27:10). But, of course, I knew that in the end Paul was shipwrecked.

The paramilitary returned with our passports and reported, "There isn't any record there. Take them to the house." The "security house," where the tortures were conducted? To our surprise, the jeep turned back up towards Achachicala and we were finally left at our doorstep with apologies. "There must have been some mistake."

Indeed there had been a mistake. The paramilitary sent to arrest us hadn't understood. They didn't know they were supposed to be carrying out the "Banzer Plan," drafted in Washington and by which, with the help of CIA informants and reports, the current Bolivian government eliminated anyone or any institution with the slightest left leaning, especially members of the Catholic clergy. The plan was to deepen the division within the Church, to smear and harass its leaders, and to arrest and/or expel foreign priests and nuns. We had been lucky.

In the following days, constitutional rights were suspended, as well as freedom of the press. We were denied the right to assembly and freedom of movement within the country. General Banzer announced that the members of ISAL were to be "liquidated."

The attack on the Church began in earnest and was unprecedented. Even temples and monasteries were not beyond the reach of the new regime. By then, almost everyone we knew had scattered and gone into hiding. The number of dead was never fully revealed. A new word was coined as the number of citizens who were "*disappeared*" mounted.

At first we were unaware of the many arrests, disappearances and exiles. It was only after two or three weeks when those of us who remained gradually and cautiously began to surface that we began to meet in secret and exchange information. Luis Espinal, Miriam, a couple of Oblate priests, a few students, and factory workers met clandestinely in a chapel under the pretext of celebrating Mass. We learned that most of the ISAL members were in exile or in prison. Many fled to Chile where they were safe under the Allende regime. Others could not be accounted for. We could not organize, we could not speak out. We could do nothing publicly. ISAL was finished. Except for an occasional letter from exile over the next months, we had no more contact with Pedro.

We learned to watch our backsides very carefully. Whenever we left the house we let someone know when and where we were going. And when we arrived at our destination, we called to let someone know that we were safe. As an extra security, we tried not to go anywhere alone. Paramilitary circulated in taxis looking for leftists or even sympathizers with the left. Friends disappeared from the street.

For the first time in Bolivia a regime was targeting ordinary citizens. Before the Banzer government, the violence and repression resulting from political unrest had always been limited to labor or political party leaders. Now anyone was fair game.

The new dictatorship closed the universities and that meant the students, who depended on the university cafeteria for their meals, hadn't eaten for several days. One Saturday evening, they assembled for a meeting in the auditorium to see what could be done to get food service renewed. Tanks immediately surrounded the building and planes circled overhead. The students huddled inside all day Sunday and into the night, too terrified to leave the building. On

Monday, the military mounted a loudspeaker on a truck and boomed out orders to evacuate the building. When there was no reaction from the students, the military offered that they would be allowed to leave peacefully.

An Italian priest, who had joined the group and had been meeting with them in their efforts to reopen the cafeteria, advised them to put white shirts on sticks and to hold them high as they left. When they filed out of the building, the military opened fire, killing a number of students. The students scrambled back into the auditorium. Then, thinking they had shot the priest, a voice on the loudspeaker blared, "Mission accomplished. We killed Padre Carlos!"

The soldiers had realized there were 300 students in the auditorium and decided against a mass slaughter. Again they shouted out, "Leave at once," and again promised that their safety would be guaranteed. Once again the students began filing out cautiously, hands behind their heads. Indeed, they were "safely" marched down to the Ministry of Interior at gunpoint. They were beaten and robbed of their possessions, even clothing. Some were never heard from again.

Churches and monasteries of known or suspected progressive religious and priests were broken into, paintings burned and destroyed, priests and nuns arrested and exiled. We know now that we were part of an experiment called the Banzer Plan, so successful that it would soon be proudly presented at international congresses as a model for stamping out communism and then adopted by other countries in the Southern Cone. For us at the moment, it meant the arrest of some priest or religious each week.

We waited anxiously for the Church hierarchy to speak out against this new self-declared "Christian" government. Finally, an official statement was released, affirming that it was not the place of the Church to judge the regime and that its relationship with the state was "very cordial."

The new President, General Hugo Banzer Suarez, spoke to the nation and invoked the help of God and the United States. There is no official record that the former granted any special blessings, but the latter responded most generously. Private capital flowed into the country almost immediately and continued in the following years. Skyscrapers went up, blocking the sun, and depriving *paceños* of much needed warmth in this crisp Altiplano climate. U.S. banks opened branches in La Paz and a new airport was completed. Military aid poured in and the heel clicking parades on national holidays became a proud and menacing display of newly acquired tanks and heavy artillery.

Whenever the government changed in Bolivia, as it did so often in those years, the whole atmosphere of the city changed. But never was it more evident than with the Banzer coup. The streets of La Paz were suddenly filled with strangers. Only days before, the Plaza Murillo was filled with *campesinos* and workers warming themselves in the noonday sun, some engaged in earnest debates during their mid-day recess from the sessions of the Popular Assembly. Others were downing *salteñas* and soda. Now, suddenly, in their place were businessmen in expensive suits and ties. Military officials saluted at attention at the gilded door of the government palace. The well-known figure of Juan Lechin, standing and chatting with his "*compañeros*" by a lamppost outside the headquarters of COB on the Prado, was also absent. Where long-time friends and students used to gather to eat, laugh and exchange stories, there were now upper middle class types in neat dresses and high heels. Before, I would meet a friend on every block, and there were frequent invitations to a cup of coffee. Now hundreds of students were in exile - the schools were closed, the university was empty, and the halls of Parliament were abandoned. All the familiar faces were gone. Central casting had brought in a new set of characters.

One of the very few who survived the purge was Luis Espinal, a Catalan Jesuit and a well-known film critic. Whenever we met, there was a knowing twinkle in his eye that said, "We're still here!" He continued his weekly film critiques in Presencia with razor-sharp social commentaries obviously aimed at the Banzer regime. He even managed to produce a TV documentary on violence in which he included clandestine interviews with hooded members of the ELN. Not surprisingly, after the program was televised, he was dismissed from the Television network. Although ousted from TV, Luis continued to walk a tightrope with his radio broadcast and column. It may have been his international reputation in the world of film that explained his uncanny ability to survive the Banzer days. He would not always be so lucky.

This was not the first time we had lived under a state of siege, but the Banzer restrictions were the most frightening and dangerous we had experienced. With other regimes, government clearance was frequently needed to travel within the country; but now busses and trains were subject to search at any time. Homes were broken into. There were no constitutional protections. Living under the Banzer dictatorship was like learning to live with a serious chronic illness: we became familiar with the danger signs and swallowed many bitter pills. But we never gave up hope for a cure.

I wrote home, "I think we may have come to the end of an era in our work here in Bolivia. The present situation looks like it will last a long time." And it did – for seven interminable years.

CHAPTER 29

THE JUNTA AND THE DAMAS

Sister Suzanne, the new President of the Racine Dominicans, paid us a visit again in October, to talk with Vivian, the only member to remain in the Community. She accompanied us on an official visit with Archbishop Manrique, with the purpose of giving him formal notice of our dispensations from the order.

The Archbishop was Bolivian and came from a humble background. A very dear and likable man he genuinely put the well being of his people first. He had a short and solid build, wore thick glasses and a kind smile for everyone. However, his peers among the clergy did not always see him in a kindly light. Often he stood alone defending the rights of the workers and *campesinos* and when he challenged the government, he was quiet but fearless. For that, he also became a target of the "Plan Banzer." His only comment to us about our leaving religious life was, *"Mal, mal. Muy mal."* (Bad, bad very bad.) The deed was done, but we knew we would still be friends.

Against the backdrop of the new political tensions, the next months were a kaleidoscopic blur of comings and goings. Vivian was in El Alto; Juanita was still fighting hepatitis in Santa Cruz; Miriam made several trips, including a prolonged one to Milwaukee to visit her family. Most of the time, I was on my own, but with plenty to keep me busy.

The non-functioning hospital in Achachicala was yet another victim of the Banzer coup, because the student volunteers and medical staff had gone into hiding, and Juanita, who had been spearheading the project, was in Santa Cruz. I tried to jumpstart the project several times but, besides not having anyone to work there, I was in a catch-22 situation. The agreement Pierre drew up with the *barrio* required the people to make monthly payments on the property we had sold them. On one bright Sunday morning, Pierre had explained that they were getting a health center for very little and, placing three bottles of beer on the table during an outdoor assembly on the hillside, and he said: "This will cost each of you less than three *cervezas*. Who of you cannot afford three beers a month?" It seemed easy enough, but the problem was that Pierre did not leave any instructions as to how this amount would be collected or who would do it, and after the Banzer coup, he did not return to Achachicala.

I wasn't concerned about the money and I was pretty certain that the nuns in Racine wouldn't care either. The problem was Bolivian law. If I were to donate the property outright, I, as previous owner, would have to pay a hefty 25% tax. I had no way of doing that. The other problem was that, even though we had required from the start that the barrio write statutes and apply for a "*personería juridica*", or legal status, the people could not get together to get this done. Without this, they were unable to get funding or financial help to keep the doors open and of course, there was no legal entity to give the hospital to.

In the midst of frustration, the president of the Achachicala neighborhood junta would regularly get drunk and pay me a visit, during which he would pressure me to turn over the building. He and his cronies would blame me for all of the ills that were befalling the hospital, such as thefts and irregular activities. I suspected then, and it was later shown to be true, that a relative of his had actually been responsible for thefts of equipment and the general mismanagement of the place. These visits began to wear on me and all I could do was keep trying to arrange for meetings to explain the situation. Unfortunately, no one attended the meetings and the hospital languished.

The *Damas Voluntarias*, feeling more at ease now that the government was protecting *their* class interests, decided to build a library for children in Achachicala. They invited me to attend their meetings (teas) and help plan the project. These were always held in the home of one of the volunteers. It was hard for me to find anything in common with them, and I soon discovered that they knew very little about the reality of their own country. They were more in tune with the interests of women of their class in Europe or the United States and had little in common with the poor in Bolivia, or anywhere else for that matter. When it came to furnishing the library, I suggested buying "*payasas*," Bolivian straw mattresses, for the children to sit on. They had no idea what I was talking about, had never heard of a *payasa*. Of course, I knew they had never gone to the Indian Market or seen a house in the campo.

Although the afternoon teas, usually on Thursdays, were mostly torture for me, they also provided a surprisingly pleasant respite from the harsh political realities. These were moments spent on the simple bus rides down to *Calacoto*, the wealthy barrio where the *"Damas"* lived. Since very few people who lived in that area used public transportation, I usually had the luxury of a seat on a half-empty bus, a real pleasure considering that passengers were usually bulging out the doors. As the bus descended the winding, paved avenue going lower and lower; the homes became more and more comfortable and elegant. Finally the road opened to a flat paved tree-lined boulevard where the air was warm and soothing. The scent of eucalyptus trees and *retama* bushes with their little yellow jasmine-like flower, filled the air with a sweet exotic perfume. I imagined lush gardens and other marvels hidden behind the walled-in mansions. For almost an hour I could ride in warmth and comfort and listen to music or the current *radionovela* (soap opera) of the day, depending on the bus driver's fancy. For a short time, I almost forgot the cruel political reality.

CHAPTER 30

SIMON BOLIVAR

Whenever the government changed, and, obviously, it did often, classes at all levels, were suspended until further notice. This was meant to discourage student protests and keep the powerful and rowdy teachers union at bay until things calmed down. Shortened school years were the norm. In all the years I lived in Bolivia, not once did the children complete the required number of school days. When Banzer seized the government in July 1971, the students had just returned from winter vacation, and barely 70 days of classes had been completed. The government, as expected, shut down all educational facilities and then in as expected, promoted all students to the next grade by "*decreto supremo*," or executive order.

Along with elementary and high schools, the *Escuela Normal Superior Simon Bolivar*, the main teacher preparation institution in the city also came to a standstill. But, unexpectedly, just one month later, it was singled out by the Ministry of Education to be reopened. It was at that point that I became the new psychology "*profe*" at the "Normal."

It just happened that one of the teachers in the Philosophy Department became seriously ill and would be on sick leave indefinitely. Through a friend of a friend, I was recommended as a replacement, and I was hired to substitute for her temporarily. I had the job of preparing students who were to teach psychology in high school. Since these students were not included in the government's "*decreto supremo*," they had to take a written test in order to pass to the next level. So, on my very first day, I gave final exams to students I had never laid eyes on before. There was, in fact, one subject in which the students had not even attended a single class with any teacher. I had no syllabus or textbook to guide me but did manage to come up with an innovative test they could not possibly fail. The authorities (and the students) were delighted. I even made arrangements for several students who were in hiding. I also had to arrange to test another who was hospitalized after being tortured. Everyone passed and I became the new Psychology *"Profe."*.

Soon, I was introduced to one of the most unpleasant tasks I had during my years at Simon Bolivar that of sitting on a panel of judges for final exams for the graduation class. During several mind-numbing days from 8:00 a.m. until 6:00 p.m. wrapped in scarves and coats, we crunched into small desks with very hard seats, and listened to six students teach six short philosophy and psychology classes each. (These subjects are taught as part of the high school curriculum in Bolivia.) In the first round, three students were very good. The others ranged from fair to hopeless. The other judges gave them all passing marks, possibly just to avoid a grueling second *desquite* or set of makeup exams. They would graduate, unfortunately, for their future students who would be subject to the tyranny of the inadequate teacher. I thought to myself, "I hope I never have to go through this again." But I did go through it - many times more in the following years. I stayed at the Normal School of Simon Bolivar (temporarily) for five years, teaching five psychology classes daily to future high school teachers.

CHAPTER 31

ON MY OWN

It was a time of many good-byes to friends who were leaving Bolivia and for many weddings, one of which was the French Oblate from Achachicala, who married his long-time secretary. I suspect that I finally made him decide to marry one day when he began to complain of her little deficiencies. I unwittingly agreed with him about her, and he armed an impressive defense, ending up convincing himself that he should take the plunge. Miriam sewed her wedding dress. The reception was replete with French Embassy personnel. After the wedding, the newlyweds moved to the safe haven of Chile, safe at least for a while.

Sadly, the three of us in La Paz also would go our own ways. Juanita's illness kept her in Santa Cruz, and it was uncertain whether she would ever be able to work in the high altitude again. Vivian decided to move Santa Cruz to work with the Sinsinawa Dominicans and then Miriam lost her job in La Paz and accepted a position in Cochabamba. I was alone in La Paz. We divided up the few things we still had - each taking what she needed. I got the bookcases, a couple of beds, a broken stereo and some used records I had brought all the way from garage sales in San Francisco. Our plan to remain together had lasted less than a year. We were still in Bolivia, but each in a different city.

I had no adequate cooking facilities and was in the process of looking for a *pension* where I could pay monthly for lunch. In a chance meeting on the street with one of the Canadian Oblates, I was invited to have lunch regularly at the parish. That was how I became a *"pensionada"* at Espiritu Santo. I hesitated at first, but soon discovered that the food was good, the cost was low and the company was first rate. The parish provided a safe place for progressive thought and a chance to form new friendships. Now I was to begin a new set of experiences.

I was not the only layperson at the table; besides the resident priests, there were a number of regulars and always many visitors. The group included a young widow, her one-year-old baby and two married couples. We celebrated holidays together, had a picnic or two and occasionally took in a movie. Brother Miguel forgave us for scaring him out of his wits the night we were arrested and, for the most part, and, in spite of the pall of the military dictatorship, life went on.

With time, I grew close to the group at the Oblates, eventually staying for supper as well as lunch and often remaining to play scrabble with others in the house. With teaching, research, writing, Achachicala, the Damas Voluntarias, and an assortment of meetings, this was one of the most productive times of my life.

That first Christmas, everyone at Espiritu Santo had plans or invitations to spend the Holiday somewhere else. I spent my Christmas Eve with a family that used to live next door to our "birdhouse" in Achachicala. They had moved to an even colder barrio, though it is hard to imagine a place colder than Achachicala, called Villa Fatima. It was located in a niche on another side of the canyon. On that chilly, windy Christmas Eve, and after a long bus ride and a considerable climb on foot up a dusty hill, I finally found their one-room dwelling. It had a dirt floor and walls blackened from the smoke of the *anafre*, a small, single-burner kerosene stove used before gas stoves became common. There were two creaky beds with sagging mattresses pushed together where the whole family slept. The father had been a shoemaker and had developed an allergy to the dyes he was using. His hands were crusted with scabs and he could no longer work. There were eight children in the family, the youngest a newborn. I brought them some food and a few toys and we spent the evening chatting. I wondered how they were able to survive at all.

One of the little girls had been adopted by one of the plans advertised on TV, and she received a small stipend each month from her benefactor in the United States. They showed me the letters she had received and asked me to translate them. They were pleased that she had been "adopted," but could not understand why only one child in the family could participate. That is a detail the commercials do not mention. It made a slight difference in her life, but it didn't get to the heart of the problem. They understood that they were the forgotten poor upon whose tired shoulders the rich built their fortunes. Some sincere and well-meaning soul in a faraway place would toss them a few crumbs of concern and they were received with heartfelt appreciation, but it was not nearly enough.

They thanked me for the gifts, but more than anything, they were pleased by my visit. They asked about the other *madres* and I told them that I was now living alone. They looked at me with great sorrow and came up with a solution. Each Sunday they would send me two of their children to keep me company for the day, and, to my delight, they kept their promise. Every Sunday for more than a year, two of the children rotated taking the long bus ride to my place to spend the day and cheer me up. I enjoyed their company. We took long walks, ate ice cream and looked at books. At days' end I hugged them and put them on the bus home. They were well behaved and never asked me for anything. They were there to be my companions and they took their job very seriously.

I spent Christmas day with the children in Achachicala who had been given a brand new playground as a present. In other barrios, the government had held toy giveaways and the people they sent to distribute them had no experience with small children who have never had a toy. The exuberance overflowed and the children couldn't be controlled. There was a rush for the toys, a stampede ensued and several were crushed to death. It was a tragic lesson. Fortunately, in Achachicala we made a better choice and the children were delighted with the playground equipment. We prepared hot chocolate and found some leftover cookies to share. I stayed until the sun disappeared behind the mountains.

In the quiet of my room that evening I knew I was exactly where I should be.

CHAPTER 32

DANGEROUS IDEAS

Emma Violand, my assistant from my days at IBEAS, helped me re-edit the Occupational Guide and the result was an impressive little paperback. Since we had begun the project during the fervor of the Torres regime, we had dedicated this new edition to the downtrodden and oppressed miners. But by the time it came off the press, the introduction could only have been interpreted as an inflammatory affront to the military government. Even so, Emma and I loaded the boxes of books into her car and bravely decided to pay a visit to the Minister of Education. We placed the *Guía* on his desk and hoped he wouldn't read the introduction. He did and he was not pleased.

He scolded us and insulted us saying that we hadn't read the newspapers and that we were unaware of his plan to change the educational system with a new reform (the eighth in just seven years) and that the universities were closed, anyway, so why would anyone be interested. Then he said we should have gotten his permission. He finished the tirade and we imagined ourselves being hauled off in handcuffs to witness a modern-day book burning. Instead, he bought fifty copies! The eighth educational reform was rejected in January and once again the Occupational Guide was current and up to date. Thus, Emma and I outlasted the Minister of Education and Bolivia was spared the circus of another educational reform!

In fact, education was a very sensitive subject. Words like "liberation" and "alienation" were too risky to be used in the press or in speeches. The consciousness-raising methods used by Pablo Freire, the Brazilian educator, were considered subversive and his books were banned, along with other "dangerous" writings.

It was right at this time that Maritza Balderrama and I finished the final draft of "Education and Liberation", a study of alienation in Bolivian education. Like the "Occupational Guide," it had been designed and researched in another political climate. Now, seeing the title, the Bishops who had commissioned the project, panicked and insisted we change the title and edit out certain anti-capitalist language. Halfheartedly, we plucked out a few phrases and left others in place, making no major changes. Although somewhat softer in expression, it pointed the finger at Bolivian education as a process of cultural alienation that impoverished the minds and spirits of the young. We were not particularly pleased with the final product and knew it was weaker than we had intended. We agreed to change the title to "An Analysis of Textbooks and Methods in Bolivian Education."

My job was to "market" the report to the city's bookstores. That meant walking the steep cobblestone streets with several of the heavy reports and showing it at every *librería* (bookstore) in La Paz. Even with the required changes in the title and text, no one was interested. Fear of government reprisals was on the face of every bookseller I talked to that day. In time, however, it would be hailed as a benchmark study of Bolivian Education and become the inspiration for a textbook reform.

CHAPTER 33

A DUBIOUS ALLY

From time to time, following the publication of the textbook study, I was invited to give talks to groups of educators. On one such occasion, I participated in a workshop in the town of Sorata. I made the trip in a jeep with a co-worker. We spiraled down out of the harsh altiplano terrain into a land of tropical vegetation and colorful wild birds. We swung around the curves in the road in time with music scratching out of a small tape recorder on the seat. We played "Samba de Mi Esperanza" over and over until the batteries went dead and the melody was recorded in my mind for days. For just a few hours I could pretend that there was no Banzer regime, no risks, except for the winding mountain road and remember what it felt like to travel safely in the campo.

The beauty of Sorata is legend. Bolivians claim that it is the scene of the Garden of Eden. Who knows? Its lush vegetation is pressed against the skirts of the immense snowcapped mount Huayna Potosí and the Rio skips and dances over the rocks on its way to the Amazon and then to the sea. It is one of the loveliest places on the earth, without a doubt. The week was filled with not very memorable conferences, good food and evening get-togethers that involved good stories and music.

One of the speakers at the workshop was a Bolivian physical anthropologist. He was an older man with a bushy mustache, five ex-wives and a declared interest in making me number six. He also had close and trusted contacts in the military establishment. In spite of this, he was oddly neutral politically and was more interested in performing autopsies on indigenous peoples.

When we returned to La Paz, he came to visit me two or three times, once with his sweet seven-year old daughter. He always had rare tidbits to share, such as the "Aymara Indian's liver has an extra lobe and his intestine is a meter longer than the western intestine." Once he brought a tape recording of indigenous music that he claimed no one had ever heard before.

He claimed to have earned his revolutionary stripes at the age of ten, when he carried a message tucked in his knee socks to a military installation, a message that set off a palace coup. He also saw firsthand how another coup was nipped in its planning stages when the non-commissioned officers tied the rebel commander to a toilet seat and prevented him from carrying out his plan. But now at this stage in his life, he was tired of politics. He wanted to return to the U.S. to pursue a third doctorate and, since I wasn't interested, a new wife.

He turned very serious when he explained that he had gone to the trouble of checking on my file with the government and had discovered that I was on a Banzer hit list. Of course, he did the only thing a gentleman would do. He did me the unsolicited favor of telling the Minister of Interior not to bother me, because I was his lover. Although there was not a grain of truth in this, I did appreciate the gesture.

For a time, I was safe from the military, but not from the anthropologist's unwelcome advances.

Although he was an interesting person, he was a nuisance and to my great relief, he was soon on his way to the U.S. He phoned me the day before his departure to tell me I would be on my own and that anything could happen. I should be careful and try not to go out unaccompanied.

I thanked him for the advice, wished him well and immersed myself in the work at hand.

At the end of July that year, I wrote home,

> Soon we will be celebrating last year's revolution. The first anniversary. The U.S. has given us so many gifts of tanks and planes and other armament that we ought to have a very impressive parade. The Bishop has blessed the gifts and so they are now consecrated to the service of God and the destruction of man . . . .

On August 20, the government staged a "liberty march," that workers were required to participate in or risk losing their jobs. Not much liberty there! Instead of going to the parade, I attended the Oblates' very touching and inspiring memorial service for Mauricio Lefebvre.

The following month, I received a letter from Suzanne, reporting that the Racine work in Bolivia was formally ended. Vivian had returned to Racine to recruit another sister to accompany her back to Santa Cruz but without success. Barely seven years after the first sisters received their mission crosses, the Racine community closed the chapter on Bolivia. At Siena Center, someone quietly removed the Andean weavings and woodcarvings that adorned the visitors' parlor that had been so enthusiastically dedicated to the mission.

For the three of us who remained, however, the mission was not over, Not yet.

CHAPTER 34

JUANITA'S RETURN

Halfway through 1972, Banzer seemed to get a second wind. With real or trumped up fears of a coup, he launched another wave of attacks on the Catholic Church and arrested 13 nuns and priests as well as a bishop. The response from the Catholic hierarchy was barely a faint whimper. There was no organized protest. No one dared. It was estimated that there were at least 2,000 known political prisoners at that time, an alarming number in a country of 5 million. We learned that the U.S. was paying the Bolivian government five dollars a day for the maintenance of each prisoner, most of which was most certainly not spent for that purpose.

Other "reforms" included a new Security Law, mandating a five-year sentence for any workers threatening to go on strike and allowing the government to open letters. After that, mail disappeared even more frequently than usual. A close friend said that while he was being arrested in the central police office on a bogus subversion charge, he saw a large sack marked "outgoing mail" being hauled into the station. Outgoing all right! Out of the Post Office and into the hands of the Ministry of Interior! The screws continued to tighten.

Then, the IMF monetary changes went into effect, devaluating the Bolivian peso by 60% and causing prices to rise by 75%. It had taken me three years to save enough money to make a trip home to visit my dad and brothers. With the devaluation, my meager savings dwindled and it would take more than a year to make up the loss. The government quickly and brutally repressed the brave little outburst of popular outrage and the protest marches that ensued. The voice of the people was easily silenced in the repressive climate.

Most people in the United States know very little about Bolivia, but

Bolivians know a great deal about the United States and they are very aware of U.S. problems. They are shrewd political analysts and don't need to be taught anything in that area. I saw a good example of their political savvy during the U.S. presidential election in 1972. A group of Bolivians were asked which candidate they'd choose and not surprisingly, McGovern beat Nixon with 60% of the votes.

Juanita returned to La Paz from Portugal early in 1973 and decided to give the altitude another try. It was good to have her back, and we jokingly took time out for a two-person "education convention," and spent days thinking up ideas for the manual, Creative Experiences for Children. With every sentence, Juanita found encouraging words to prod me along; in fact, if it hadn't been for her support, I might not have finished the publication. Besides the manual, another work was getting some unexpected attention at that time.

The textbook research I had done with Maritza Balderrama, though rejected by the fearful bookstores at first, was now getting considerable attention. The Bishops' office of education sponsored a series of seminars based on the study in La Paz and a Bolivian author and newspaper owner/editor, Mariano Baptista took up its cause. A textbook contest was launched and workshops were held throughout the country. I was asked to join the team of presenters, but suggested Juanita be hired for the job. She accepted and spent the better part of that year traveling to the remotest corners of Bolivia under every imaginable condition. Each time she returned to La Paz, there was reason for celebration and amazement as she told of her latest adventures.

That also gave us a chance, in between downpours, to check out new little boutiques that had sprung up along the Prado or to take in a Friday night movie with dinner out and a cab ride home – all for less than a dollar. And there was always the good company of the Oblates and the host of friends at their house. As enjoyable as those months were, they were always against a backdrop of fear and great tension, for we were not free to speak our minds or meet in groups of more than three. Beneath the surface, the repression was very real.

In February, we had two visitors from Wisconsin. They were two former Peace Corps volunteers who had been expelled from Bolivia by the Ovando regime. I couldn't help but wince at the idea of having two Peace Corps volunteers right there in our rooms after all of the vitriol we had spewed against them. It was one of those nights when the rain pounded on the pavement, and our soaked clothes took forever to be dried by the kerosene heater. We visited with the young Americans until the storm lifted. Oddly, they weren't resentful about our participation in their expulsion, and, in fact, confirmed that they and all of the volunteers they knew had been encouraged by the U.S. government to spy on each other as well as on Bolivians, to detect and report any communist leanings.

Looking back, what I remember most about that summer (Southern Hemisphere summer) was the exceptional rain. Our rooms were always dank and cold. Nothing ever seemed to really dry out: shoes, clothes, even the walls in the house were damp to the touch.

After that grueling year of traveling around Bolivia, Juanita accepted an even more challenging job, one that would keep her firmly anchored in La Paz. An Italian priest working in the southern city of Tarija asked her to manage a new co-ed residence hall for students located in the middle class barrio of Miraflores just a few blocks from the normal school where I taught. He was to finance the program in order to house the young people from his city who were studying in La Paz. Juanita packed her belongings and began to get the residence in order.

In April, the house was ready and President Banzer was invited to the opening ceremony. He showed up in full dress uniform, stiff as a stick and cocky as a bantam rooster. It was the first time I saw him up close. I was surprised at his size. I measure less than 5 feet in height and we looked at each other eye-to-eye.

During his brief speech, he promised all of the students at Juanita's residence hall a trip to Tarija for winter vacation. Taking the offer very seriously, a few days later, Juanita made a 30-hr. bus ride to the city of Tarija to make preparations for the arrival of the residents. She had scarcely embarked on the long trip, when she was informed that Banzer had changed his mind and had withdrawn his promise of a trip. Juanita came home mad as a hatter and sore in more ways than one. We speculated that he might have been too busy naming his next cabinet members, because just one week later, he dismissed them all and appointed an all-military cabinet. Juanita settled in to what quickly became a 24-hour, 7-day a week position as housemother, counselor, activities director, and policewoman.

As for Miriam, in 1972 she had married in Cochabamba, shortly after returning from her trip to Milwaukee and now, a year later, she and Bill were blessed with a baby girl. We were *tias (*aunts*)*

CHAPTER 35

THEY MAKE US DANGEROUS

I was invited to stay at the normal school for another year and became more and more absorbed by the needs and lives of my students.

With the rainy season in full force, there were few places where the cold and dampness were more penetrating than at Simon Bolivar. Because of the open hallways and courtyard, the only shelter from the weather was in a classroom. However, in my room all the windows were broken and we shivered through our sessions making class time absolutely miserable. I dipped into my meager funds and showed up one day with a complete set of windowpanes. The students were so appreciative that they pitched in to make the repairs. They bought paint and spent the whole weekend not only fixing the windows, but patching and painting the walls.

That was class that had wanted to get rid of me a year earlier because I taught them how to apply the experimental method in, of all things, experimental psychology. They had been accustomed to copying dictation word-for-word in a notebook (*cuaderno* method) and had no intention of actually performing experiments. No "learning by doing" nonsense for them! Surprisingly, one of the older and much revered professors, Federico Blanco, came to my defense and told them in no uncertain terms that they were lucky to have me for a teacher. Although he himself adhered strictly to the *cuaderno* method, he was gallant enough to come to my aid.

The collection of books in the library at the normal school was meager, actually pitiful. I found it necessary to start buying more books for my psychology classes. I made a sizeable collection and the students started using my place as a study hall. Together we prepared their practice teaching lessons as a team, drank tea and munched on fresh bread - fine ingredients for friendship.

The student enrollment at Simon Bolivar was about 5,000 - our department, philosophy and psychology had 180 students with a well-known reputation for being the most radical group in the school. The department anniversary party that year was not a festive event. We mourned the loss of two classmates and speculated that our next party might have to be in Paraguay, the favorite destination for normal school students who were arrested and exiled under cover of the now famous "Plan Condor." In fact, the Normal was having so many problems with the government that the administration felt it was necessary to name an intermediary with the Ministry of Interior. I was selected for the job, more than likely, I speculated, because they felt that as a foreigner I was "disposable." It was not a prospect I relished and it added another layer of tension to my life. Going to the Ministry of Interior could easily mean never returning home again. I wore the title reluctantly and fortunately, was never called upon to act in this capacity.

As a deliberate strategy, the Banzer government made many arrests of innocent people who were released promptly as a ploy, to make Banzer appear benign. One of my students from the Normal School, however, was not so lucky. He was detained and after going missing for several days, his body was found. He had been tortured and executed. The authorities, of course, said they knew nothing about it.

Always, always we were haunted by the political reality. The following excerpt from a letter I wrote to a friend at that time captures well the tone of life under Banzer,

> "One of my students was beaten to death, another shot. Yesterday I made my usual trip up to Achachicala in wind and snow (unusual for mid-afternoon). The medical student who is volunteering in our small hospital wasn't there; he had been arrested. I went further up the hill to the library and found it cold and empty. I only found a note telling me where I could find things and who would carry on with the work there "if something happened" . . and adding . . . "if for reasons that you know, we will not be able to work."

> "I walked home with the most desolate feeling."

> "Later I went to a party that some of my students gave in honor of Teachers' Day. For most of the evening, I was the

only teacher there. I told my kids that the rest were probably afraid "because you're dangerous."

One of my boys answered wisely, "No, señorita, we're not dangerous. THEY MAKE us dangerous."

Tonight the weather continues gray and cold and the surrounding hills are covered with snow. Every knock at the door or the sound of voices under my window makes me a little more than nervous. I think I will spend the night elsewhere – again."

He was right. Anyone who challenged or questioned the system was dangerous.

CHAPTER 36

AN IMF POLICY WITH TRAGIC RESULTS

By now, it was painfully obvious just how U.S. economic policies were reaching into the fabric of everyone's life from the tragic to the mundane. The new set of conditions tied to loans from the International Monetary Fund required, among other measures, the withdrawal of subsidies for a number of products, including flour.

When the parish household wanted to celebrate Lorenzo's birthday, I was elected to bake a cake. Using a tried and true recipe for high altitude, I prepared the batter but as I was about to put it in the oven, the electricity went off in the whole city. My only alternative was to scour the neighborhood for an oven heated by kerosene. Finally, after a balancing act with an 18" x 18" cake pan, I discovered a tiny door right across the street from the parish house. I knocked timidly. Speakeasy style with whispers and signs I was whisked into a garage with an enormous, clandestine industrial oven where the owner was baking without a permit. Once she knew I was baking a birthday cake for the padre, she generously allowed me to slip my pan in between her batches of bread. As we sat chatting beside the warmth of the oven, I looked at the garage door and was amused to see rags stuffed into every hole and opening where the aroma of fresh bread might escape and be detected by the authorities.

Not so amusing, however, was the scarcity of bread brought on by the IMF policies. For many Bolivians a small bread roll or *pancito* was often the only thing they had for breakfast and supper. Now, since flour was no longer subsidized, prices soared out of control and bakers who had flour were not about to sell until prices became stabilized. That, of course, meant that many Bolivian children went to bed with empty stomachs.

Then, on January 20 Banzer announced that prices of food staples - rice, sugar, flour, etc. would increase by at least 100% and other basic food products, by 219%. To offset the higher prices, workers' monthly wages were to be increased by 400 pesos, about twenty US dollars. It was hardly enough to make a difference. Even the repressive Banzer machine couldn't hold back the ensuing wave of strikes, marches and protests that swept across the country in the aftermath.

Things took the most tragic turn in the Cochabamba valley where *campesinos* and rural communities near Cliza, Tolata and Quillacollo, were outraged by the economic measures. They recognized the unbearable hardship this new policy placed on their families and because they had the leadership and a history of defending their rights, they reacted firmly. In a country where roads are sparse, a few rocks can effectively halt transportation and cut off cities from receiving food and goods. In desperation, the campesinos set up roadblocks. However, the Banzer government lost no time in sending in the army to clear the roads. There was no negotiating when it came to military force. In several communities the soldiers sprayed the protesters with machine gun fire.

At least 80 and perhaps as many as 200 campesinos had been massacred and disappeared. Once again, the voice of the oppressed had been silenced and the IMF prevailed.

CHAPTER 37

BANZER'S BOLIVIA

Shortly after classes started for a new school year at the Normal, Banzer also allowed the University of San Andres to open and I began teaching my favorite class - Design and Analysis of Social Research. With no computers to crunch numbers in seconds, my students and I had to code and tabulate data quickly using only a pencil and paper. That, however, was the least of my concerns.

My class was programmed for 6 p.m. the same time that the student rallies or emergency assemblies and protests were scheduled to begin. My class met only by luck and by chance. Because of this, I learned to do most of my teaching in the first days of the semester by inundating students with bibliography, basic instructions and a long-term assignment that could be completed independently. In the best of scenarios, we might be able to meet again at least for a final exam or maybe not.

It also was because of this that I adopted the habit of always approaching the university from the opposite side of the street. From a distance I could see if the students were milling around and if there were banners and shouts. I always had to be on the lookout so as not to walk blindly into a riot or police roundup.

That particular semester, we didn't have to wait long for the disruption. Right after the start of classes, Banzer tripled the salaries of the university authorities who were his appointees and close friends and supporters. Their monthly wages went from 8,000 to 24,000 pesos. Professors' salaries increased as well, but only to 8,000 pesos. This direct intervention by government in the affairs of the autonomous university caused outrage among both professors and students. Then Banzer further infuriated them by appointing an army colonel to head San Andres. From May 27 to June 27 there were daily demonstrations in the streets, and each time the police lashed back with teargas, severe beatings and dozens of arrests.

In order to distract public attention from the growing list of political prisoners, and specifically, from a prominent lawyer forced into exile, Banzer staged an auto-coup in June. This, in turn, justified another wave of repression at the Normal School and the disappearance of another student who was arrested before our eyes. We were helpless to prevent his detention. Before long, almost everyone including me had to go into hiding for a few days.

On the crest of this wave of repression and turmoil, Juanita made a major decision. After another arduous year, this time spent at the students' residence hall, she was ready to pursue a long-postponed dream to study medicine. She was accepted for a two-year study program in missionary medicine, and on September 2, 1974, she left for Spain. I accompanied her to the airport with a heavy heart, hugged her good-bye and wished her good luck. Just one week later, the scene was repeated at the airport with Bill and Miriam who pulled up roots and left for Milwaukee with no plans to return. Now I was truly on my own.

It was almost ten years to the day since I had set out for St. Louis to study and prepare for a new Bolivian mission for the Racine Dominicans. I had, in fact, studied and even became somewhat of an authority on Bolivian education. While some friends may have felt that this ten-year mission was a failure, I knew in my heart that the lessons we all learned echoed back to the community leadership in Racine and impacted decisions in ways that most of the sisters did not know. I felt that our influence in ten short years had been far-reaching and I knew that my own transformation was profound and lasting. Now I was alone and I intended to stay because I still had much work to do.

There was little time to think about being alone. My days and evenings were filled with teaching and research and in Juanita's absence, I was trying again to open the hospital in Achachicala. *Experiencias Creativas* was in print and eight children's centers were using the method. The training and supervision of the young people, who worked there, fell on my shoulders.

The center in Achachicala was especially promising with more and more children flooding into the program daily. Adrian and Maria Luisa, two dedicated *normalistas*, grouped them into "clubs" and were able to handle the large numbers by putting the older children in charge of the younger ones. The center in Achachicala could not have succeeded without the two young students who dedicated weekends and long hours to the work for more than five years. They miraculously kept everything going there, helped open new centers, and became expert teachers long before graduation.

Mornings I taught at the Normal School, and afternoons and evenings at the university. Former students of mine, who had graduated, were now doing research for private or public organizations, and occasionally invited me to assist them with the design and planning of their projects. I was still working with the *Damas Voluntarias* who had received a grant from Bread for the World to build and run a new center, which they called the *Biblioteca Infantil*, the Children's Library.

It was a very busy time, but not busy enough to distract me from the ever-present dangers under the Banzer regime. And now very soon the curtain would open on a new player in this political drama. Cocaine.

The first hint came when in October a scandal broke wide open. Banzer's brother-in-law was caught smuggling drugs into the Miami airport. Thanks to Banzer and his friends in Santa Cruz, cocaine production in Bolivia had been ratcheted up quite a few notches. This was the beginning of the kind of drug running that would mushroom in the 1980's completely changing the rules of the game and almost destroying the country.

Not surprisingly, the U.S. government turned a blind eye to the dirty dealings of the Banzer regime, and was more concerned about the flow of leftist ideas into Bolivia than about the flow of drugs into the streets of Los Angeles or New York. In spite of the growth of cocaine production during this time, U.S. Economic aid to Bolivia was not affected, certainly not until the DEA launched its anti-drug campaign in the 1980's.

In fact, the money continued to pour in through banks and loans to the rich, but I discovered, projects that would make a difference in the lives of the people often were only offers, and nothing more. Projects were touted in the press, as done deals yet often did not materialize. I remember one such project to amplify rail transportation. By some odd chance, I was asked to translate into Spanish a proposal for the Ministry of Transportation. As I poured over the proposal, I got an inside view of the reality. The requirements set by the U.S. were so unreal, that it was evident from the first paragraph that they would never be met. It was only a piece of paper and a total exercise in futility. Yet the next day, there it was, front page news in <u>Presencia,</u> "The U.S. has given Bolivia millions to expand rail transportation." It was pure feel-good fantasy.

Meanwhile, there were attempts, real or trumped up, to overthrow Banzer, each one leading to another brutal crackdown and a series of strict regulations. All types of leadership were outlawed; even private businessmen were not allowed to organize. In the name of "Paz, Orden y Trabajo" (peace, order and work), Bolivians were subjected to new disciplinary regulations.

The number of national holidays was reduced. Buses had to install doors and the drivers were ordered to wear a coat and tie. It struck me as peculiar that nothing was said about replacing their broken windows. Was it a realization that air had to circulate? No, it was more likely that the people making the laws had never ridden a bus and didn't know that the windows were broken. Passengers were not allowed to stand in the buses. This rule was actually enforced for a short time until the drivers lost too many fares. While it lasted, it was a pleasure riding on the new little microbuses. Clearly, these reform measures had U.S. Embassy fingerprints smeared all over them.

The year ended with a letter reminding me that I would have to move out of my rooms at the Yanez's house in May, or come up with another chunk of cash for my "*anticretico.*" If I were to move out, I would no longer have the safety net the Oblates had tossed me three years earlier, when I first found myself alone. Their kindness and generosity had been a great support, but it was time to move on.

CHAPTER 38

THE DESTRUCTION OF RADIO PIO XII

Ibegan 1975 with serious doubts about staying in Bolivia. I was forty years old, and although I had made many friends, I had also lost a good many of them. Did I really want to spend the rest of my life in La Paz? Could I? But I knew that I was not in a frame of mind to make a big decision. I would wait maybe a year or two. It was something that I definitely had to consider "some day." But for now there were too many things I could not leave behind. There was the colonial style *Calle* Jaen with its antique lamplights reflecting on wet cobblestones after an evening shower, and Plaza Riosinho, with a strange turn-of the-century flavor. I imagined echoes of tangos pulsing in its shadows at night with ghosts from a time of romance and high starched collars. The city was so much a part of my life, filled with many memories of happier times like walking home after a good movie or with students after an evening class, and always the many parties! The view of the city from the arch in the Alto still thrilled me beyond expression, and Illimani at twilight took my breath away. One of the Oblates told me that it would be a terrible mistake to go back to the United States. "What would you do there? No, Bolivia is where you belong." Although I was beginning to have misgivings, I suspected that was there still more for me to do.

I was on this mental crossroad when I met Enrique Bachinelo. It was January 3, a Saturday morning, and I was cleaning my room. I hung my hand-woven blankets on the clothesline to air. The rope stretched across the sidewalk blocking the entrance to the patio. A hand timidly pulled aside one of the blankets and a thin man in his forties with curly hair, seventies-styled sideburns and dark-rimmed glasses asked, "Señorita, would you mind if I slide your blankets aside? I need to move my furniture into my room." He was very serious and formal. Startled and embarrassed for having blocked the entrance, I quickly whisked the blankets off the line and retreated to my room. The *caballero* moved into the one vacant space in the courtyard. I wondered who this new tenant was, but the events of the next weeks would overshadow my curiosity.

On January 25, 1975, at 4:00 a.m. government agents broke into Radio Pio XII owned and operated by the Oblates priests in the mining center of Llallagua/Siglo XX. The radio station was destroyed, their houses ransacked and stripped. Two of the priests were arrested and taken to La Paz. Another, Roberto was beaten severely and left for dead in the road. If it hadn't been for a young girl who found him and helped him, he would have bled to death. Two others were lucky enough to find refuge in homes of miners. Three more hid out in the church. That same morning troops destroyed radio stations in three other mining camps. The Oblates were accused of subversion and of "agitating" the miners.

By mid-morning the people of Siglo XX surrounded the Church to protect the priests who were inside. The two who had been arrested could not be located. All communication with the mining centers was cut off. As it happened, there was no electricity in La Paz on Tuesday, and so even short-wave contact with the other Oblate houses in the country was not possible. The priests in La Paz were especially eager to contact the parish in Oruro (halfway to the mines) and make sure that they would send someone to check out the situation in Siglo XX. Without radio communication, the only alternative was for someone from La Paz to hand-deliver a message. I was still on summer vacation from classes and so agreed to make the three-hour bus ride with a letter for the Oblates there instructing them to go to the mines with a camera and document the damage. By the time I reached Oruro, however, the priests had already left and were on their way to get pictures and record eyewitness accounts of the assault. I returned to La Paz that night to a tense and outraged community of Oblates. Lorenzo, as acting superior for the Oblates, took the lead and immediately began negotiating the release of the two who had been detained.

In Bolivia at that time Catholicism was the official religion and there was an official concordat between Church and State. The photos of the sacred areas of the church in ruins with altar breads, wine, chalices and other holy vessels strewn on the floor were printed in *Presencia* and the entire nation was outraged. Everyone knew that these were acts of desecration that should have warranted immediate excommunication from the Catholic Church for those involved, and the people took to the streets while the Catholic hierarchy did nothing. As with the Massacre of *Campesinos* in the Cochabamba Valley, even Banzer's repressive apparatus couldn't hold back the tide of outrage, spontaneous strikes and protests that followed. The government was peculiarly up against the wall; because having successfully decapitated labor and student organizations, there were no leaders to negotiate with.

The Oblates circulated a report complete with more photos exposing what the army had done. They waited again for the Bishops to follow up with an appropriate supporting statement. They waited; we all waited. The only valiant voice heard among the hierarchy was that of Archbishop Manrique who protested vehemently; the other church leaders remained silent as stones.

The Catholic Church's Peace and Justice Commission, though suppressed, met clandestinely to determine a plan of action. They asked me to direct a campaign to circulate a petition and get 100,000 signatures in support of the Oblate Community. Then, before the campaign even began, Cardinal Maurer derailed the whole effort by publicly declaring the Peace and Justice Commission "temporarily defunct" because "he wanted to restructure it." He said he would reveal the details of his new plan "after returning from Rome." The Cardinal saw no need to rush to judgment.

Instead of denouncing what was an unprecedented attack on the Church, and coming to the defense of the Oblates, as would have been expected, Cardinal Maurer, the highest-ranking prelate and spokesperson for the Bolivian Church made peace with the government and offered only to mediate. It was a crushing disappointment for the Oblate community and in the end they lost their fight with the government.

The day Maurer denied support for the Oblates, I met a glum looking Archbishop Manrique walking through the Plaza Murillo almost oblivious to the light rain falling on his tired shoulders. We shook our heads in sorrow and disbelief and continued together to his office in silence - significantly, under my red umbrella.

Finally, the government signed an agreement promising not to arrest or deport priests or religious "without giving prior notice to the church authorities." Not surprisingly, the government was up to its tricks again before the ink dried on the paper.

In spite of having been suspended by the Cardinal, the Justice and Peace Commission continued to work clandestinely. It investigated the January killing of campesinos in the Cochabamba Valley and published a report, condemning the Banzer government. Two Belgian priests, who were distributing copies of the study, *La Masacre del Valle (The Massacre of the Valley)* were kidnapped in broad daylight. They were pushed into taxicabs three blocks from the Oblate house on the Avenida Peru and taken to the Peruvian border. One was an Oblate from Espiritu Santo Parish and the other a Belgian Dominican.

This time the bishops reacted quickly, and denounced the arrests, but their outrage was not caused by the deportations; instead, they were upset simply because they hadn't been advised of the arrests beforehand. Obviously, they were accustomed to being "in the loop." The government responded to the criticism by publicly calling the bishops liars. This happened the week before the sacred high feast of Easter, and tensions were extreme.

It was Holy Week, the time of year when government dignitaries as dutiful and faithful Catholics, expected an official invitation to attend the solemn services in the Cathedral. Archbishop Manrique publicly announced that he would not issue the traditional invitation. Nor would he reserve places of "honor" usually designated for the political leaders in the Cathedral on Holy Thursday. Instead, he opened the door wide and filled the church with poor people and children who occupied all of the pews. Then suddenly, as the Mass was about to begin, five hundred officers and soldiers burst through the rear doors of the temple and ordered the people out at gunpoint. They then stood guard at the door and prevented anyone from reentering. From the altar, Manrique shouted his condemnation of the invasion and refused to celebrate Mass unless the people would be allowed to come back in. After a bitter, hour-long standoff, the cathedral doors were again opened and the faithful poured back in. This was church leadership that could be trusted, in the person of a little man squinting through thick glasses and wearing a pacemaker who had the courage to face up to an armed battalion.

My Easter Sunday was spent up in the barrio at the Center with the children. They were used to working in small groups, playing, reading and generally enjoying themselves. I served them milk and cookies in the afternoon and at dusk I sent them home and closed up. The last rays of sunlight were hovering over the crest of the mountains. The street below was quiet and empty already in the shadow of darkness. I sat for a while on a flat rock overlooking the houses below and the stand of eucalyptus trees rising up on the other side of the *Choqueapu* River. The chill that always comes just before nightfall cut through the heavy poncho I was wearing. I shivered a little, but didn't move. It was good to be there. I was exactly where I should be. I felt an easy familiarity with everything: the hills, the sound of the train across the ravine, the smell of eucalyptus, and the dirt road under my feet. I was grateful for so many things, especially for a courageous archbishop who stood up for what was right.

CHAPTER 39

MORE OF BANZER'S BOLIVIA

One of the many projects the Banzer government signed on to that year was a $65 million loan from the U.S. to restructure the educational system. The loan would be payable in 50 years, but all conditions laid down would hold for five years beyond the final payment. Chief among the conditions was that everything in the plan needed Washington's stamp of approval, from the formulation of the objectives of the reform to the hiring of personnel. This was a classic case of the Washington stranglehold on the internal affairs of Latin American countries. Education was an extremely hot political issue, and the USAID office in La Paz was particularly interested in reforming early education (pre-school and kindergarten classes.) If the U.S. government wanted to make sure there would forever be a source of cheap and willing labor and devoted consumers of North American products, it would be necessary to nip indigenous Bolivian culture in the bud. Where best to start than with its youngest and most impressionable citizens.

I had the good fortune to work with many projects that went contrary to those objectives. One of these was in the barrio of El Carmen, where together with a Maryknoll priest, Roy Bourgeois, we opened a storefront center for children. Later Roy became one among other church members who were arrested and deported from Bolivia. He went on to found the School of the Americas Watch, hell bent on closing the center at Fort Benning, Georgia where the Latin American militaries are taught how to repress their people.

I visited El Carmen weekly and trained the young students who worked with the children.

It was located on an unpaved dead-end street where there was no traffic.

The children used the street to play outdoors from time to time and it gave them a safe place where they could come and go. One day, the owner of the bus that drove through the barrio, decided to use that particular space for and end-of-the-line parking area. The bus drivers bullied the children and began parking their buses right outside the center's door. In danger and deprived of their play area, the children swung into action and held a meeting. In true Bolivian style, the little ones (ages 2 - 10) set up a barricade with their tiny tables and chairs, toys and their little bodies. They stood their ground until the bus drivers were shamed into retreat and backed the buses out. It was a perfect lesson in popular education and community action. It was an especially sweet victory because the bus and taxi drivers were great allies of Banzer and they sorely deserved the upset.

At about the same time, repressive tactics used by the police and military were beginning to take a new turn, as I experienced first hand when I was on my way to meet with the new head of the Sociology Department at the university. The street erupted with exploding teargas canisters and gunshots, not an unusual occurrence, but there was something different this time. The soldiers were now in full riot gear and marching in formation, wearing helmets, sporting big protective shields and, for the first time, holding dogs on leashes. I tried to outrun the melee and ducked into the restroom at the theater, 16 de Julio, a block up the street. I no sooner got in when there was a crashing knock on the door and a soldier shouting, *"Sal de allí o vamos a romper la puerta!"* (Get out or we'll break down the door!) The point he was making was that no one was allowed in the area. I exited quickly and after a couple more blocks ducked into a little restaurant along with about fifteen teary-eyed students. The soldiers followed us, stopped short of storming the restaurant, looked around, and then left us alone. Being routed from the university by soldiers was nothing new, but the use of dogs was a brand new tactic with "made in the USA" stamped all over it.

A story circulated later that when university students in Peru were faced with attack dogs, they took appropriate precautions for the next march. They came prepared with cats hidden under their shirts. When the soldiers appeared with the barking dogs, the students tossed out the cats behind them. A good part of the security forces was dragged away by their four-footed accomplices.

Later on in June, I was invited by a group of young teachers (ex students of mine) to give some talks in the mining centers of Llallagua/Siglo XX, which were still under military occupation. The head of the department thought it was a great idea and got the director of the Normal School to approve. After following a maze of paperwork and visiting several offices at COMIBOL, the national mining company, to get the required permits, we were on our way.

This was, of course, Banzer's Bolivia and the trip would not be peaceful. An hour or so out of La Paz at one of the newly created checkpoints, government agents boarded the bus. They walked up and down the looking over the passengers menacingly. Suddenly, they singled me out and ordered me to turn over my bags. Then as the other two professors looked on in disbelief, the uniformed agents angrily and rudely emptied my belongings in the middle of the aisle. At first I was frightened but when they told me I could pack my things up, I was mostly embarrassed. As was my custom, I had stuffed everything into a couple of old threadbare shopping bags. There was no point in ruining a decent piece of luggage on one of those dusty trips.

Once at the mines, we were shown the damage that had been done to the Oblates' radio station. I realized how effectively the government had silenced the miners. The next day we began the workshop and spoke at length with students, parents and teachers. The state owned National Mining Company (COMIBOL) was known for taking an interest in the education of children. And the teachers received better salaries than those in public schools. In fact, it was COMIBOL that had paid for our trip to the mines.

The arrival of our team from La Paz was well publicized and the miners opened their hearts and homes to us. They had had so much grief and suffering that a little positive attention was welcome relief. During those meetings it became obvious that there was little need to convince them of the importance of an education. It was for them the one ticket out of that god-forsaken place.

Evenings after supper I ventured out alone to walk along the slag hills and chat with the women who were just finishing their work. It was the middle of June - this meant it was winter in the Southern Hemisphere and it was very cold. This visit was very different from the one three years earlier when we had reason to be optimistic. The mines, again occupied by the army, were more dismal than ever. The streets were filled the stoic faces of the military ready snap into action. The young, uniformed men were on every street corner with orders to maintain the peace. An icy, bitter calm it was. A metallic dust from the tin mines hung in the air and settled at the back of my throat. It was so cold I had to wrap my scarf twice around my neck.

Adding to the somberness of the evening was my visit to Lorenzo, who had recently transferred to the mines to replace the priests who had been arrested months earlier. I delivered some letters and personal belongings to him. Then, alone in the night, I returned to the school where we were being housed, recalling how thin and tired Lorenzo looked.

Each morning, I peered out the window on a landscape of varying shades of gray against a cobalt sky. The only sounds were those of the small carts on rails moving the minerals, the grunts of the men working behind them and the sharp echo and steady pounding of hammers splitting rocks left by the side, the beating heart of Bolivia's economy. The wealth from these mines filled the nation's treasury but gutted the lives of the miners as surely as it dug into the hills.

Incredibly, this dismal life was a step upward for *campesinos* whose land no longer yielded crops, or whose parcels were too small to feed their families or produce crops to sell. As miners, they lived in row houses, lucky to have a bare bulb hanging from the ceiling. Water had to be brought from a spigot in the street. Poverty was in the air they breathed.

This was Siglo XX, the mine once owned by the infamous tin baron, Simon Patiño, which was the scene of massacres and indentured slavery. It was home to some of the most volatile and fearless miners in the world, men who could make governments tremble when they announced their arrival in the cities with dynamite explosions. I felt strangely relaxed on this trip and was put at ease by the pleasant smiles from the passers by. Here, I was just another teacher from the normal in La Paz, nothing more. I was told on the last day that they were pleased that I walked around the town like everyone else, that the only people who drove vehicles there were "the bosses and the missionaries," but of course, they were missionaries to be respected.

The first months of the year had been difficult for me personally. My two closest friends as well as several others had left Bolivia, and the Oblate community had been brutally attacked and scattered. Also there was always the nagging problem of the hospital in Achachicala, which caused me no end of grief. Moreover, the constant fear instilled by the Banzer regime was nerve wracking. Unexpectedly, though, the trip to Siglo XX was a turning point for me, and I returned to La Paz exhilarated, feeling strong and optimistic and ready to go back to work.

CHAPTER 40

COINCIDENCE

O ccasionally, while I was in Bolivia, a visiting stranger from the U.S. would knock on my door with a note of introduction from someone I knew back home. This particular time, it turned out to be a tall, husky blond woman who was an astrologist by training. She insisted on interpreting my astrological chart and told me I had a special affinity for men born under the sign of Gemini. After giving it some thought, I wrote home in June that it might be true, since my dad and two of my brothers were Gemini's and I got along very well with them. I said to myself, "I don't know any other Gemini men, but I'll keep an eye out."

I wouldn't have to look for long. My work on the Creativity Manual was in its third revision and a student, Hugo Rocabado, volunteered to help me with Spanish on weekends.

On one of these Saturdays, a balmy afternoon with the sun pouring in through my wide open doors, I was preparing a pot of tea and waiting for Hugo. My new neighbor of seven months now, who had asked me to slide my blankets aside and whose name I hadn't even bothered to ask, approached me in the patio. I became a bit unnerved because in a completely justifiable state of paranoia, I suspected he was a government agent planted there to control the house. It was strange to see a businessman living alone, and once he had even called me by my name, stiffening my resolution not to have anything to do with him. I was careful never to say more than a *"Buenos días"* or *"Buenas tardes."* I was wary.

He saw the open door and stopped on the ledge politely. He smiled and asked if I had a phone. "My daughter took my keys and I can't get into my room. She is a student at the Normal." The request seemed harmless enough. Cautiously, I showed him the phone and he made his call. "Lourdes, it's Papito. You have my keys. . . .!"

By the time he finished his conversation with Lourdes, the water was boiling and I invited him for a cup of tea. His name was Enrique Bachinelo. He told me that he had been watching me. But his reasons weren't political. He knew my name because my students had been knocking on his door for seven months asking for me, and he would patiently show them where the *profe* lived.

In short order, I learned that he had been a political prisoner and had been ordered not to return to his home in Potosí. He was living in a kind of exile within his own country. He was employed as Public Relations Representative with the National Federation of Mining Cooperatives that ran the old depleted mines, which were sold to the workers by outgoing companies after the riches were sucked out. He was a lawyer and also a journalist.

He was surprised to learn that I was an American. He thought I was a teacher, maybe from Santa Cruz, where the people have hair that is a little lighter than that of the dark Indian population in the Altiplano. Almost always with Bolivians, one of the first topics that come up in conversation is your birthday. So it didn't surprise me when Enrique asked me when mine was, and I in return asked about his. That was when I discovered he was a Gemini!

When Hugo arrived, the two struck up a friendly conversation as if they had known each other for a long time. When Enrique left, Hugo remarked that he was an "interesting fellow."

Enrique turned out to be interesting, indeed and a very kind person, as well. When he received a prized ticket to the national folklore show, he insisted that I use it, saying he would watch it on TV at a friend's house. Then one Sunday morning, while taking a walk with him up to Achachicala and hiking up the mountain overlooking the barrio, I told him about the problems with the hospital. He volunteered to help by writing the by-laws and getting the legal papers in order. This was the best thing to happen in a long time.

He frequently stopped in to chat and, little by little, he told me his life story. His father, an Italian from Venice had been a sailor during World War I. When the Italian naval ship docked at Buenos Aires, the lads were told that the war had ended and that they could return home or stay in the New World. Enrico decided to seek his fortune in South America. Gradually, he made his way to Potosí, Bolivia. His first night in town, the locals discovered he had experience in construction work, and on the spot he was given a contract to build a new social club. He stayed on in Potosí doing more and more construction work, eventually putting in the railroad from Potosí to Sucre. During that project, he met a Quechua Indian girl who brought food to the workers. That was Enrique's mother.

Soon after, Enrique told me he had been the head of the FUL, the student organization at the University of Santo Tomas in Potosí. I interrupted his story, " So it was you! It was your name that I had tucked into my pocket in 1965; I needed to contact you for information for my thesis."

Washed out roads had prevented me from reaching Potosí to meet him then but now, ten years later, circumstances had brought us together.

CHAPTER 41

CLASS TRIP

One of the most hated institutions created by the Banzer government was CNES, the National Council on Higher Education. It was a supra-administrative body that replaced the Confederation of Bolivian Universities (CUB), co-government and autonomy. So despised was this organism that one evening, the students risked their safety and lives by making a fifteen-foot papier-mâché pig with the letters "CNES" painted on its side and parading it up and down in front of the university. After everyone had had a good look at it, they doused it with kerosene and set it on fire. The fire department, which rarely responded to fires, reacted quickly, first turning the hose on the students, and then on the flames. Then the military took charge tossing teargas canisters into the crowd. I was in the process of giving a final exam in a classroom on the fifth floor with windows overlooking the spectacle. We stared out the windows during most of the exam until the glass was shattered and the teargas forced us out of the room. It was almost a routine procedure. Always take the stairs; never take an elevator when there is teargas in the air. If it has been on the ground level, it will fill with teargas. Getting trapped inside for several floors can have serious results. Run out the back door and check the news that evening to see if classes will be suspended. That time they were – indefinitely. With the closing of the university, I had time to accept an offer made to me by my students at the Normal School.

In September, the students I had been with for four years were ready to graduate. They planned a trip and asked me to be their chaperone. I accepted and the class made all of the arrangements. Along with a score or more of students, I boarded a bus one evening to begin another small adventure, Bolivian style.

It began with an all night ride to the accompaniment of guitar and flute music until we fell asleep. Early in the morning we arrived in Potosí, the frigid hometown to several members of the group at 14,000 ft above sea level. We toured the city and were treated to Potosi's finest cuisine. We spent the next night in the home of one of the students and then headed out for a visit to the mines in complete mining gear: boots, helmets and raincoats. Potosí was Enrique's home, too, and he had been careful to take advantage of our trip to send *"encomiendas,"* or packages, to his family there. Besides the daughter studying in La Paz, he had three younger girls still in school in Potosí who were living with wife and sister. I did not go to meet them, for which he roundly chided me when I returned.

When in Potosi, we visited the *Casa de la Moneda*, where coins had been stamped for all of South America and Spain during colonial times. Potosí and its *"Cerro Rico"* were filled with history. I remembered doing research on the *"mita"* system of labor when I was studying at Saint Louis University, and was entranced with the tradition of this old and decaying city, at one time the most populous and wealthiest in the world. Long before Madrid, London or Paris, Potosí was world famous. It was also infamous for the cruel exploitation of the Indian population who were served as slaves in the mines and to carry the mineral on foot over the Andes to the mercury mines in Huancavelica, Peru. Now I was seeing for the first time, what had happened to this beautiful old city with its colonial churches and buildings. It was a city that I had studied and read about with such awe. The Potosínos were pleased to have visitors and graciously showed us everything we had time to see. I was impressed with their friendliness and hospitality. They had so little, but they did not think twice about sharing with strangers.

From Potosí, we headed south to Sucre. On the way, I had a front seat in the bus, alongside the driver, with my nose almost pressing against the windshield. About halfway through the trip, on a nearly deserted road with nothing in sight, a truck piled high with *campesinos* and bundles rounded a curve and headed straight for us, advancing, seemingly, in slow motion. Neither of the drivers put on the brakes. Both could easily have stopped, but stubbornly advancing, the two vehicles crashed. An Indian woman, who was sitting cross-legged at the front of the truck, sailed through the air, unbelievably, still cross-legged and landed on the side of the road, shaken, but unharmed, probably well cushioned by the thick layer of skirts she was wearing. Much yelling and swearing ensued. The driver of the bus was a social notch above the driver of the truck. The poor truck driver said he had just had his vehicle repaired for 700 pesos the day before and now it was completely wrecked.

We got off the bus, glad that no one was seriously hurt and began the long wait. The passengers, including a couple of French tourists, stood around and grumbled in three different languages, maybe four. Nothing could be done until the "highway patrol" officers would show up and do the proper paperwork. We had already descended a distance into the valley from the highlands and the weather was pleasantly warm, but there was nothing to do. The passengers looked around as if expecting something more to happen. Then, as if by some mysterious signal, it did. Several *campesinos* appeared carrying bundles and sticks on their backs. In no time, a roadside cafeteria was set up with soft drinks, boiled corn and fruit. Word had spread that there were travelers stranded on the road and the enterprising locals came to the rescue.

A group of us bought something to eat and crossed over to a hill and had a picnic. Four hours passed before the officers came on the scene. To my horror, when the poor truck driver tried to explain what happened, one of the officers whacked him across the face and told him to be quiet. In a short time, we, of course, were on our way, but the truck driver sat sadly by the roadside contemplating his wrecked vehicle.

We arrived in the proud city of Sucre that evening and were housed at the local normal school. The students there were fine hosts to their colleagues from La Paz. In return, my students put on a show. They had written an original anti-government play, complete with background Andean flute music. They even managed to get military uniforms from someone. It was a "closed door" performance because it could have gotten us all in serious trouble with the Banzer government. The "accommodations" were similar to the night before and I resigned myself to another night on a hard floor.

The next stop on our trip was Cochabamba. We feared that news of our clandestine anti-Banzer performance had reached the authorities there, and we were extra careful at the checkpoints. Besides, the Ministry of Interior had already blacklisted two of the students and the others had to periodically think up ruses along the way to throw the police off track. When asked for ID's, they pretended to be sick or sleeping. Those students, who were not in danger, would pass their ID's to the ones in trouble, and then brush past the soldiers to pee behind the bus or make some joke with the guards about why they forgot theirs. That portion of the trip was touch and go, but, luckily, we reached Cochabamba without incident, and the students again put on the political drama. Tired but still in good spirits, we headed back to La Paz.

On the first day back at classes, the director called me to her office and told me that in our absence, the Ministry of Interior had sent an official to the school with threats to expel the students, and an order for me to report to the Ministry for special interrogation. Mysteriously, though, someone intervened and the problems went away. At times I suspected that the director manufactured these alleged crises and that they were then suddenly resolved by the same hand just to keep us in line.

One morning, I arrived a few minutes late for an assembly in the philosophy department and the students were loudly proclaiming that there was a traitor present, possibly the informant who reported the show put on during the graduation trip. They demanded that he leave the meeting. Red-faced, a student standing in the back of the room stomped out. Then they said there was another one, who was also on the CIA payroll. However, they let him stay because, "He just needs the money and besides, he only turns in the names of the students who support Banzer. He's on our side."

The students at Simon Bolivar were not only courageous but also informed and astute. I was amazed when they introduced me to Noam Chomsky's writings in 1972.

The normal school was not for students with money. The really wealthy sent their children to Europe or the United States to study or to prepare for the more expensive careers like medicine or engineering at the University of San Andres. Others went to the newly opened Catholic University, which was run by the Jesuits, in the former Dominican seminary. The normal school was left for students with meager resources. Many of them came from the campo or the mining camps and saw this as a way up the social ladder.

Most of the teachers at the normal were strict and very formal, in fact, somewhat pompous. They demanded unquestioning militaristic respect from the students, who oftentimes graduated and went on to perpetuate the same authoritarian pattern in their own classrooms.

The school year neared an end with more arrests, and I again was named as intermediary between the school and the Ministry of Interior, a role I feared I would not play very well. Strangely, someone volunteered to take my place again. By the time classes were over, well over a hundred university and normal school students were jailed, a raw reminder that all was not well.

CHAPTER 42

BECOMING FRIENDS

With the school year over, I had time to turn my attention to a notice I had received earlier from my landlord. My contract had expired and I could either increase the *anticretico* amount or find another place to stay. Enrique found out that he, too, would have to leave his room at the Yanez house on Chacaltaya, and when he learned that I needed to move he suggested that we house-hunt together. I welcomed the help of a Bolivian. We began scouring the newspapers and visiting the *Comerciales*, as Felice and I had done in 1967. I knew the routine and he had the lingo. We searched all of the month of November but without luck.

That year Enrique was doing some looking for funds for a school and a small clinic in a rural community named Sankayuri where there was a mining cooperative that produced salt. Because I had some experience with writing grants, I was invited to go along and see what I thought could be done.

The Sankayuri *campesinos* treated us like royalty. After meeting the leaders, we toured the salt deposits and talked about the needs of the community: a school, a clinic, jobs for the young, and the commercialization of salt. The number of members was dwindling each year and there were no resources for any of the projects they proposed. Afterwards we were ushered into an 8' x 8' mud hut with a thatched roof. Enrique and I sat on a bed raised on a low platform of adobes and our hosts covered us with animal skins to keep us warm. It was time to eat. We were each served the head of a lamb, with its eyes still staring accusingly at us. I had a little trouble with this, but I found that the cheeks were actually quite delicious. The Sankayurians crowded around a rustic table right next to the bed and told us stories for several hours until the candles burned low and we all were ready to sleep. Then, realizing that I was a "señorita" and not Enrique's wife, they whisked me off into the night.

By candlelight, I could see it was an even tinier hut. It had no windows, but a door barely a yard high, a typical campesino dwelling well sealed to keep out the cold. Inside, was a cot with animal skins for covers. I climbed in between them and our hosts bade me "*buenas noches, señorita.*" When they left with the candle, I was in total darkness. I was just beginning to doze when I sensed I was not alone. I heard a thump at the door and something or someone stumbled in. There was another thump and some grunting and heavy breathing right over my head; he didn't smell of liquor. Then there were voices and much excitement outside the door.

A lantern lit up the doorway and I saw the shadows of agitated community members wrapped in ponchos and flap-eared caps milling around. There, hovering over me and breathing in my face, was a curious mule that had come to check me out. The campesinos apologized to me, pulled the friendly animal out, whacked him soundly on the rump and sent him running off into the night. I wondered if I was occupying his bed.

The next day we considered the feasibility of a clinic and a school. The problem with this was bigger than just a new school. The young people were leaving for the city and the old folks had no one to care for them. The only possible solution would be to mechanize the salt production. That might give the young people work and then they might not leave for the city. We returned to La Paz with a project to work on, and the following week, the grateful *campesinos* from Sankayuri came to my door at the *Casa* Yanez with a bushel of potatoes and a whole slaughtered lamb.

Certainly, I admired Enrique. He was a lawyer and a journalist yet he was as comfortable with campesinos as he was with jai alai. He was unpretentious and had a good sense of humor. I began to wonder about his charms, though, when once in the middle of the night, he knocked on my door, totally drunk. He explained, as best he could, that his friends were drinking in his room and they fell asleep. When he went out to use the bathroom, the door closed behind him and locked and he couldn't get back in. His buddies were out cold and didn't answer his knocks. I had no other alternative than to let him in and point him to the interior room where there was a cot. He stumbled in and promptly fell asleep. Then, about an hour later, his friends, still very drunk, but now awake, started making a terrible racket in the patio. Eventually, they found their way to my door to howl and complain because they wanted to leave and didn't know how to get out of the courtyard. By that time all the lights were on in the patio and curious eyes were peering from the windows. I got up and showed them the door to the street. Enrique, of course, slept like a rock the whole night through.

The next morning, I sent him on his way with a "this won't happen again!" speech. How could I expect guarantees? This was Bolivia.

It had been a typical *Viernes de Soltero* or Friday-night-out-with-the-boys, a sacred ritual in Bolivia, and especially in La Paz. By Friday noon, every office in the city sends a representative to reserve tables at a local *boliche* (bar or canteen) everyone takes off work a few hours early and the drinking and carousing begin. In Bolivia "having a drink" loosely translated is, "Get very soused," and that is just what happens. The evening starts with a round of drinks and then a few hours of *cacho*, a game of dice. When the dice are eventually set aside, the conversation begins in earnest and the rounds of beer or Singani start hitting the table. No one worries about designated drivers because no one has cars. Besides, there was always a cheap form of transportation to be had. The canteens stayed open well into the early morning hours, and if not, the crowd headed to someone's house to finish the revelry. Only a government enforced curfew could put a damper on the occasion. Without doubt, it was an important time for male bonding, for making deals and promises that could not be broken, that is, if they were still remembered the morning after.

Saturday morning was dedicated to curing the headache, first with a very hot dish of stew or soup, and then washing that down with a couple more drinks. If a man was up to it, he might take in a *futbol* (soccer) match at the stadium and collapse exhausted at home that evening. The long-suffering women just shake their heads and hope that nothing serious happens. Although I had been in Bolivia eleven years, this was my first up-close and personal experience with *Viernes de Soltero*.

The Friday night incident cooled our relationship and I set out on my own to find an apartment. In short order I came across a place in Achachicala basking in glorious sunlight. It had two big second-floor rooms and the luxury of wood floors. I immediately paid my *anticretico*, which was considerably cheaper because of the barrio and with the help of students from the normal school, I packed up my books, records and furniture. On December 5, I moved back to Achachicala, on a hill across from the children's library. From my window I had a panoramic view of the streets below and the mountain across the way. A train labored its way through the stand of eucalyptus trees that covered the hillside. I was especially delighted to have sunlight because for five years I had been living in rooms where the sun never shone.

My new landlords were a *campesino* couple named Maria and Mario Coronel. They assured me that there was water in the house, but I quickly discovered that there was none, except for the bucketful that I hauled from the local spigot a block away. I didn't really mind because I was glad to be back in Achachicala!

Enrique, knowing I was still upset about the nocturnal visitors, had cautiously phoned me a few days before the move to ask how the house-search was going. I told him I had found a place and he wanted to know if there were any more rooms available there. I said I thought so, but that he would have to talk to the owner. "The house has two patios and maybe there's something in the other patio," I explained. "Just don't get any ideas," I added. A week later, Enrique followed me to Achachicala and moved into two rooms in the second patio. He and Mario became occasional drinking buddies.

Once settled in the new rooms, I made a trip to San Francisco where I spent the Christmas holidays with my father and brother John. First, I needed to get accustomed to sea level, which meant a very long night's sleep. Then, as I came out of this stupor, I realized that this was a world I could no longer relate to. The shopping malls and the supermarkets were monuments to consumerism. I panicked on freeways as the world whizzed by insanely with no time to appreciate it, and the violence on TV appalled me. It was a pre-packaged culture where everything was neatly wrapped and concealed, under glass, plastic or tin. What was this place where even foul odors weren't allowed to escape, without some artificial 'poof' to counteract them? Still, in spite of my difficulty in adjusting, I spent a restful and thoroughly enjoyable two months. John was a nonconformist, wise and knowledgeable, somewhat of a bohemian spirit, and after all, this was San Francisco. His was a painter's soul, but he drove a cab to put food on the table. He cared most tenderly for Pop, who was gradually declining in health. That didn't stop him from making three trips to Europe with our dear, loving and gentlemanly father (words that describe him perfectly). And we were all on the same page politically. So what was there not to appreciate?

Enrique wrote frequently and to my surprise, I received all of his letters from Bolivia opened and inspected by U.S. Customs! When I complained to the local post office in San Francisco, the clerk told me that they had legal authority to open foreign mail. I thought they did that only in Bolivia!

CHAPTER 43

MEDDLING FROM WASHINGTON

I returned to South America in March. First on my agenda was a visit to the normal school to check on my status. I had been there for five years and was still only a substitute with a temporary assignment, so I shouldn't have been surprised when the director told me that my position was cancelled. However, the explanation was chilling. "By orders of the Ministry of Interior," the Director said, "You will not be allowed to teach here any more." Was it the class trip? Did my past catch up with me? Was it serious? Once again I was reminded that this was Banzer's Bolivia and all was not well.

Actually, on a practical level, I welcomed the change, because I was now free to accept a research position I had been offered with a brand new institute, CEBIAE, *Centro Boliviano de Investigación y Acción Educativas*. I could now return to my first love – research. CEBIAE was designed from the outset to avoid the pitfalls of IBEAS, the Dominicans' research center taken over during the Torres coup. It was organized so as to maintain a balance of powers: the Board of Directors included members of the Lutheran, Catholic and Methodist churches, as well as government officials. The entire staff was Bolivian, except for a Spanish Jesuit and me. The organization was democratically run, had fair salaries for all, and policy decisions made by the entire staff, even the choice of research projects. Everyone had a voice and a vote. We started out temporarily in a large room located on the property of the Methodist School. As there weren't enough desks, I eagerly volunteered to share mine. That way I only had to show up part time and could do most of my work at home.

One of the first controversies in the group was whether or not to accept grant money from the World Bank. I held out firmly and stubbornly against it, along with Gonzalo Gantier, a likeable maverick intellectual, who had an endless supply of raunchy jokes and who frequently scrawled colorful epithets against "Yankee imperialism" on the office blackboard. We shared strong feelings about accepting money with capitalist strings attached, but the others used the most common argument for accepting tainted money, "If *we* don't use the grant money, someone else will – and for the wrong kind of project." The majority won and CEBIAE went ahead with the study. All of us were about to learn a hard lesson.

Gonzalo and I refused to budge and the team did not pressure us to participate in the study. But CEBIAE began in earnest to document the history of Warisata - the indigenous teacher-training school founded by the Aymara people for their own needs. The center assembled an indigenous team to direct the research, and after months of intense work, they produced a project steeped in the rich tradition of the school. They had surveyed the current needs of the area surrounding Warisata and designed a plan for a teacher-training center that would reflect and be in harmony with the indigenous culture and social structure of the Altiplano. The results were both professional and culturally sensitive.

Finally, the day came when the visitors from the World Bank descended on our office. By chance, I happened to be at my desk that afternoon. I was close enough to hear every word, yet far enough away not to be a part of the discussion. A team of three very tall, arrogant *gringos* had flown in from Washington and came directly to CEBIAE from the airport. They listened briefly to the presentation centered on the cultural and historical importance of Warisata and the objectives sought in the expansion project. Impatient to give their own opinion, the representatives of the World Bank abruptly cut into the presentation and "got down to basics." "You didn't calculate cubic meters correctly. You have too many light bulbs. You can't train that many teachers. It is too expensive," they complained in embarrassingly poor Spanish. Every time the Bolivians tried to explain something, they were countered with, "It's too costly." I hung my head in shame as they ranted. The final decision came, "You have to pretend that we will give you no money at all. How would you proceed without money?" The project was rejected and in less than two hours the gringos, having torn the project to shreds, were in a cab and on their way back to the airport.

Sadly, our fears had been justified, but Gonzalo and I said nothing. Eventually, the Warisata project did become a reality, no thanks to the World Bank.

Among other foreign aid projects, USAID offered $100 million for educational research, and this sent educational groups scrambling to design studies to compete for the funds. Even well intentioned progressive groups felt they could use the money to the advantage of the country. This almost seemed to be another ploy to flush out progressive thinking in the guise of planning the ninth educational reform. We also prepared a proposal at CEBIAE, knowing it would very likely be rejected. We gave it our best shot and devised a well thought out and professional plan firmly rooted in Bolivian culture and based on sound principles of popular education. We submitted the project to the U.S. Commission.

Just then it turned out that my good friend, Emma Violand, had an offer I couldn't refuse. She was a counselor at the American School and had contacts with American Embassy personnel who were parents of her students. She had planned an evening at her home with the embassy cultural attaché who was responsible for reviewing and selecting the educational reform proposals. He was new to the country, and Emma knew I'd love to corner him to get some inside information, so she invited me to dinner. Since my name did not appear on the CEBIAE proposal, I could ask him whatever I wanted to in perfect anonymity. The conversation eventually turned to the subject of the education proposals. I asked him how the selection process was going. He said, "We have received some excellent proposals. Without a doubt the best proposal," he said, "is from CEBIAE. Very professional, but it won't receive the funds because we have to fund the ones that are in line with our interests." He told me that it was far and away a great proposal, but too far to the left. Emma nearly choked on the fondue while I made careful mental notes.

CHAPTER 44

PROGRESS IN THE BARRIO

Meanwhile, back in Achachicala, we were being asked to pay 5 pesos a month for using the public water spigot, which we had installed ourselves. On a couple of Sundays, we had helped, along with the neighbors, to dig the well and put in the pipes. Now we had to turn it over to the city and could use it only for an hour in the morning and another in the afternoon. There were barrio meetings to see if we could extend the pipes closer to our houses and hook up to the source. No permits were allowed. Now that the rainy season was over, our barrel was empty and I learned to survive on four buckets a week.

About that time I started helping Enrique with grant writing for the mining cooperatives and learned more about minerals and mining than I ever intended. In turn, he helped me solve the problems in the hospital in Achachicala. It had fallen on hard times due to misunderstandings and thefts, and together, we started working on a proposal to remodel it in hopes of getting it off to a fresh start.

During the next months, Enrique and I plugged away at organizing the hospital. It was then that the Calvo brothers came there to help out. Freddy and Carlos, dedicated doctors who heard about the small clinic contacted me about volunteering there. They simply wanted to help out, knowing the value of getting as much medical practice as possible. Both were graduates from the University of San Andres in La Paz, and Carlos had done post-graduate work at the University of Michigan in Ann Arbor. They took the long bus ride up to the barrio several times a week to tend to the patients, receiving no payment in return.

Both doctors were just what I needed when I was suddenly flat on my back with a burst ovarian cyst. On short notice, late one Friday night they scheduled an operating room in a small clinic and got the equipment ready. They phoned an anesthetist friend who was in hiding from the government and needed a job. So, without wasting a minute, the three of them took me under their care. Enrique found a pharmacy and got the medicines I needed.

I was in their capable hands! The first diagnosis was a burst appendix. It wasn't but they figured that as long as they were inside, they would take it out. "It was the smallest appendix we ever encountered," they told me. It is still on display at the medical school in La Paz.

Friends were also there to help. Sonia Davila, a co-worker who had a jeep, picked me up when I was ready and drove me home. Enrique slept on the floor in the kitchen for a few nights, until I was able to move around by myself.

When the day came to have the stitches removed, I slowly eased myself down the stairs and then down the hill to wait for a bus. The No. 4 slowly lumbered to a stop on the dusty road. I gingerly climbed up and found a seat in the back. Then, as if possessed by a demon, the driver stepped on the gas and bounded down towards the city, jolting back and forth, bouncing up and down, over ruts and railroad tracks, around curves, and jerking to a stop wherever there were people waiting. I clutched my incision tightly fearing it would split open at any minute. Even under ordinary circumstances, it would have been a wild ride. I survived and, in due time, recuperated from the surgery and from my fear of the No. 4 bus.

Every year the university departments in La Paz celebrate their anniversaries with parties, days off and other celebrations. The students and faculty in the medical school always commemorated the anniversary of their founding day by playing a prank, and Carlos and Freddy were often behind the tricks. That year they gathered all of the babies in the maternity ward for a picture with a *cholita*, who agreed to climb into a hospital bed and pose with her "quintuplets." The spread was in all of the newspapers and on the radio until the gleeful students announced it was a fraud. These practical jokes always worked on the unsuspecting public.

However one such prank almost caused an international incident. Carlos, who as a oung student, was dating the U.S. Ambassador's daughter, convinced her brother to go along with a phony kidnapping plot. The medical students and the U.S. teenager thought it was great fun until the CIA, the FBI and INTERPOL got hot on their tails. The ambassador's children had some tall explaining to do.

Freddy Calvo was the younger of the brothers and had just finished his studies. He started bringing along fellow-students to help out as in the hospital, sometimes a dentist, and sometimes a nursing student. News of the doctors working in the clinic spread quickly and our little hospital was abuzz with activity again. They delivered babies and began prenatal classes. The waiting room was filled with expectant mothers, newborns and neighbors with an assortment of ailments, cuts and bruises. Excited by the newfound success of the center, Enrique, Carlos, Freddy and jumped into action and finished the grant proposal to expand the facility. Things were definitely looking up!

CHAPTER 45

PROGRESS A LA BANZER

The first week of June, the news ran the disturbing story of Juan Jose Torres' assassination in Buenos Aires. He was still very popular among Bolivians and this came as a terrible shock. There were protests and manifestations petitioning the return of his remains for burial in his home country, and his wife made a formal request to repatriate her husband's body. Having overthrown Torres, President Banzer refused. Then in a saccharine and totally hypocritical speech, hailed the fallen general as his "best friend."

Interestingly, at this same time, a "distinguished" North American statesman visited Bolivia. Henry Kissinger was given a warm welcome and even allowed to make a nationwide broadcast, giving a speech filled with arrogant clichés. The press noted that while a much-loved ex-president was not allowed, even in death, to return to his own country, the government rolled out the red carpet for a foreign official. The protests continued.

Because of the unrest, the government closed down the university that semester after the first day of classes, and the students joined the miners in their newly declared a strike. The government responded to the miners' request for dialogue by cutting off food, water and electricity to the mining centers. The third week of the strike, the factory workers joined in and then a state of siege was declared - again. This time the miners were completely isolated because the radio stations had been taken over by the military. There was a complete news blackout in the mines, and newspaper reports about the strike were conflicting.

In the wake of all this turmoil, repression was intensified with more arrests, more disappeared, more exiles. However, this did nothing to alter financial prospects for the Banzer government, and the Bank of America made a $50 million loan to Bolivia for development projects.

During the seventies, TV was starting to invade the homes of families with a little more money at their disposal and Enrique thought that I was woefully behind the times and that I should get a television set. It was a hard sell, but he finally convinced me to at least go shopping. We scoured the popular Indian Market several evenings after work, and I tried to remember what little I knew about TV sets back in the fifties before I left for the convent.

Television came to Bolivia in 1967, but I hadn't seen any programs or even cared to since arriving there. Enrique kept nudging me, and soon, a small white box invaded my home and my life. In La Paz there was only one black and white channel, and programs were televised from 4 p.m. until about 10 p.m. with a late movie on Saturday night. When the station celebrated its anniversary, there was no programming at all.

The sole channel was government run, and there were no commercials. Many programs came from the USA, and at the commercial breaks, only the word "Commercial" would flash on the screen in English for a split second and then the program would continue. Under the Banzer government, television became a useful tool to "educate" Bolivians in the ways and culture of the United States, regularly exposing us to reruns of I *Love Lucy*, *The Flintstones* and *Love Boat* translated into Spanish. Not only were we subjected to gringo entertainment, but significantly, one of the first programs I saw was a talk in English by Dr. Musgrave from Cornell University, who spoke about restructuring the Bolivian economic system and maintained repeatedly but unconvincingly that he had "no interest in ideology." Television sets were made available to families in mining communities at cut-rate prices with easy term credit plans. The newscasts were especially fascinating: friends and acquaintances were on every night. Occasionally, Enrique would phone me to let me know who was going to be on that particular evening. Often it would be Enrique himself, sitting at some meeting taking notes.

At this time, Enrique was making many trips to mining cooperatives and as a reporter, also covering many of the meetings and events in the city. He always took along a small tape recorder, fresh batteries and a tape. He would record everything and do his writing from the tape later on. One of the most disheartening aspects of Enrique's work was that he often brought back news of exploitation and misery. For example, from the gold mine in Tipuani, he wrote of how the children panned naked for gold, in the cold water, how sick they got from this work. It was one more example of the dirty underside of capitalism.

At other times he returned with stories that never made it to the newspapers or television reports. One of these was the November 10 celebration of the founding of the department of Potosi. It is the day when Potosinos commemorate the day Simon Bolivar climbed to the top of the richest silver mine in the world and declared their department officially liberated from the Spanish Crown. This year President Banzer planned to lead a march up Cerro Rico, the same hill that serves as backdrop to the city. Once at the pinnacle, overlooking the city and with great fanfare, he would hoist the Bolivian flag for everyone to see and honor.

Enrique was assigned to accompany the delegation and report back for Radio Cruz del Sur. He made the trip to his hometown to witness the spectacular event. As usual, the festivities were late in getting started. There was music, confetti and the townspeople wore their Sunday best.

Finally, Banzer arrived and proud as a rooster in dress parade uniform, he signaled the start of the march. The climb uphill was long and steep, a small sacrifice for the honor of having the president raise the flag on their notorious hill. It took longer than expected, and the immense crowd reached the top with their tongues hanging out. There were speeches and music and more speeches. The wind and cold were unbearable. But the band members played on with stiff fingers. Finally, the long-awaited moment arrived and Banzer would imitate Bolivar and hoist the flag. Everyone looked around. Flag? Where was the flag? The unthinkable had happened. They had forgotten to bring a flag! The crowd stood dumbfounded, somewhere between horror and laughter. Everyone blamed everyone else. Finally, Banzer angered and humiliated by the oversight, spotted a little boy who was waving a little 5" x 7" flag. He yanked it out of his hands, attached it to the rope and pulled it up until it whipped "gloriously" in the air!

During the Banzer dictatorship, traffic in La Paz turned into a nightmare. Before the Banzer days, the streets filled with cars only early in the morning, at lunchtime and then again at 6 p.m. when the offices closed. The old buses that transported three times their capacity, with people hanging from the doors and clinging to the sides were removed from the streets. The new ones carried only 22 passengers. Also, the narrow streets were clogged with *trufis* or *Taxis de Ruta Fija*, a new mode of transportation. Microbuses and taxis jammed the city streets. At the same time pedestrians insisted on recklessly owning the streets with seemingly little awareness of the dangers posed by the moving vehicles. More than once, I heard an irate driver, cupping his hands over his mouth yell out the window, "llama!" at a slow-moving *cholita*.

The traffic glut, however, was more than just an irritating part of economic development; it was politically driven as well. The *transportistas* were key players during the Banzer years. It was important to keep them calm, satisfied and on his side because they had the power to disrupt daily life, schools, business and government. A transportation strike would paralyze the country and that was a risk the government did not want to take. The Banzer regime took special care of the bus and taxi drivers: they could import vehicles and parts duty free, they were allowed to increase the fares slightly, and gasoline prices were deliberately kept low. They were among Banzer's favored allies and supporters and sometimes even collaborators in "disappearing" dissenters from the streets.

CHAPTER 46

PROGRESS AT CEBIAE

Just about then, CEBIAE moved to a new location, a cramped office in a storefront at the northern end of the city. Just as before, there was not enough space for everyone, so I volunteered to work without a desk. I began what I have always considered the most enjoyable job of my life. It was a project that was intended to last two or three weeks, a search for all of the bibliography on Bolivian Education. At that time I recalled amusingly the advice I had received when I first started out on this search in 1964: "Don't even bother looking for bibliography. You won't find any. There isn't anything worthwhile." Even my co-workers at CEBIAE thought I wouldn't find much material to document. We all had a lot to learn.

I began by making regular visits to the used bookstalls on the Avenida Montes and to all the bookstores in the city. The items I picked up from the street vendors were fascinating, old essays and articles, magazines out of print, each containing more bibliography. I set to work cataloguing and summarizing each book, study, article or critique on file cards. Bolivia had had several educational reforms, many teacher strikes and volumes of legislative acts, besides the books and published lectures and congresses. The documentation work kept mushrooming and I loved being out in the city all day, chatting with the vendors and fellow bookworms at the colorful bookstalls. Always, there were new contacts among the customers and another lead to track down. Three thousand titles and 33,000 index cards later, CEBIAE had an education documentation center. The "two-to-three weeks" had turned into three years.

In the meantime, at CEBIAE we were meeting every Tuesday to form and inform our own ideas about education. We analyzed *Education and Class Struggle* by Anibal Ponce, an Argentinean who had written a history of education from a Marxist point of view. He asserted that education was always the privilege of the dominant class and, when not explicitly denied to the masses, it was used as an instrument to control and oppress them. This was evident through the centuries, in royal palaces, monastery halls and in the factories and countryside. But the wisdom of the masses often broke through the wall of ignorance and created its own body of knowledge, i.e., a popular education, the intelligence of the common woman and man.

For us in CEBIAE this was not just an intellectual exercise. We began to develop our own theory of popular education, methods of working and organizing for action. We saw both research and education as participatory processes with less defined lines between learner and teacher. We thought both research and education should create basic "tools" to interpret and respond to reality. In this thoroughly indigenous country, something new was needed. I knew by now that the Indian population rejected Marxism as energetically as it did capitalism, for neither had focused on or understood adequately Latin America and its indigenous cultures and history. Marx did not know about or write about Aztec or Inca societies and modern economists focused only on their natural resources, not their welfare. There would have to be another body of theory, one that would take into consideration the indigenous peoples, their values and way of envisioning the world.

When the year ended I planned a fiesta for my co-workers at my place in Achachicala. Of course, there were inconveniences: no bathroom, no running water, and there was another problem, one I solved in an unusual way. The Coronels, owners of the house in Achachicala, had two dogs, a mild mannered cocker spaniel and a feisty big black and white mongrel. The spaniel was Mario's shadow and he would cower in the presence of strangers. He accompanied Señor Coronel wherever he went, stayed under his chair while his master drank himself stiff.

The mongrel dog received no such attention and was not so kindly. One day Maria and I tried giving him his very first bath. He became so upset that he sulked in a corner and refused to eat or even look at us for the next two days. Gradually, though, he attached himself to me. I began feeding him scraps and from then on, he assumed the role of my self-appointed protector and guardian.

This was where the real problem started, because he had the nasty habit of nipping at people's heels and could be quite threatening. On the evening after Christmas when the CEBIAE get-together was to happen, I didn't know what to do about the dog. As a last resort and just about half an hour before the guests arrived, I poured him a plate of eggnog laced with Chuchuhuasi, the local whiskey from the Bellows distillery. The innocent and trusting animal lapped it up and started down the flight of stairs with some difficulty on four wobbly legs. He curled up in a ball and slept soundly until noon the next day.

CHAPTER 47

CHRISTMAS CRISIS

Enrique often got interesting invitations, either through his press contacts or through the Federation of Mining Cooperatives. One of these was to spend an evening with a Spanish Theater company that was touring Latin America to put on a series of *zarzuelas* (operettas). After a satisfying meal and a glass of San Pedro wine, we settled back to listen to their very strange story. They recounted how they had flown to Arica, Chile from Lima, Peru and wanted to make arrangements to travel to La Paz overland. Not having a specific plan, they spent a few days in Chile and eventually found a bus driver who offered to take them to La Paz. From Arica to the Bolivian border, the roads were paved and in good condition, and all went well. Once over the border, however, the road disappeared and the Chilean driver did not know the way. They crossed over rocky terrain, mountain grass, mud and wilderness. Finally, at nightfall, the bus got stuck in the middle of a river. The panic-stricken driver, fearing for his life, abandoned the bus and took off on foot to the west. The actors were stranded. What to do! They were in a god-forsaken place and wandered for three days in the cold and desolate Andean mountains. The meager snacks they had packed were soon gone and they were very hungry. By sheer luck, on the third day they stumbled upon an indigenous tribe, whose members did not speak Spanish. With great difficulty, they tried buying meat and potatoes from them with dollars, but the locals had no use for green paper. Trying further with signs and gestures, they understood that the *campesinos* would gladly give them food but only in exchange for their clothes. The exchange was made and they then walked with the Spaniards for hours until they reached the main road where they were able to climb atop a truck going to La Paz. Two days later, they arrived in La Paz, shivering and wrapped only in blankets.

Now it was December and it was time to celebrate Christmas with the children in Achachicala. The *Damas Voluntarias* had made plans for a fiesta and the children rehearsed dances and poetry. When the day finally arrived, it was one of those unusually hot afternoons in La Paz when the blazing tropical sun beats fiercely on the dry ground. Adrian and Maria Luisa took care of last minute details for the performance, and then herded the children outside to wait for the *Damas* to arrive. I sensed some restlessness among the older children and moved closer to see what was up. They said they did not want to dance for the volunteers. "Last year only two of them came to see us. And they always make us wait." This year they had decided to perform only for the barrio.

As the children had predicted, the women were an hour-and-a-half late. By then the heat was almost unbearable. The scene was touching, even sad, as the line of waifs, some without shoes, wound around the yard waiting for a Christmas treat. Soon Adrian and Maria Luisa called me aside to tell me that the women had not brought enough ice cream to serve the 120 children who had stood so long and so patiently under the hot sun. I approached the women, expecting a quick and simple solution since a store close by sold ice cream. To my total surprise, they refused. They saw no problem in turning away forty little ones at the end of the line, children who may not have had anything else that holiday.

I couldn't believe they would be so cavalier about disappointing the children. But the *Damas* said the budget would not allow for any more ice cream. I knew they had just returned from Holiday shopping in New York and Europe and I spoke my mind. "Surely, you could dip your hand into your pocket and find enough loose change to buy a few more cups of ice cream." The disagreement escalated and the *Damas* became furious. They ended by stomping off and accusing me of being a "communist." My relations with them had always been strained, but now the differences had come to a head and I regretted ever having brought them to work in the barrio. Soon I would regret it even more.

Adrian, Maria Luisa and I put our own pesos together to cover the cost. The amount needed was truly insignificant. Adrian quickly ran down the road and bought more ice cream. No one was left out and the fiesta was a success, of course the *Damas Voluntarias* saw none of it.

After our exchange of words, the *Damas* remained indignant and maintained an icy silence. Weeks passed and there were no calls, no meetings, nothing. This is how and when my work with the children in Achachicala came to an abrupt end.

CHAPTER 48

UNEXPECTED CHANGES

As so often happens on the journey of life, 1977 began with delight and sadness, the former because of Juanita's return to Bolivia, the former at the sudden death of Enrique's wife. Enrique left for Potosí where he attended to the painful affairs that surround the death of a wife and mother. Life would change for him, for his daughters and eventually, for me.

By the time Enrique returned to Achachicala, Juanita was already in La Paz. The Coronels had an empty room and I fixed it up for her to stay in until she decided what she would do and where she would settle. After having studied for more than two years in Spain, she entertained me for hours with her tales of her adventures. First, she had been nursemaid to the elderly matron of the Marsh family (the Rockefellers of Spain), then after the matron's death, became governess to the family's three-year-old great grandson. She worked with lepers, sailed the Mediterranean on a yacht and met princesses, kings and other celebrities, all this while studying Missionary Medicine, the details of which are in her book, Journeying to Justice.

As delightful as her company was, one thing became clearer each day. The cold and the rain in the Altiplano were more than she could tolerate and that summer it was terribly cold and wet. For that reason she moved to Tarija shortly after arriving. We had little contact with each other in the following years.

Enrique and his daughters, in keeping with Bolivian tradition, wore black for an entire year while they bravely struggled with their loss.

In May, my Father was to celebrate his 80th birthday and I convinced Enrique to accompany me on a trip to San Francisco so he could be with us for the occasion. It was Enrique's first trip outside Bolivia, and we planned several stops along the way. In Lima we walked the beach and ate fish that went straight from the ocean to the skillet. In Quito we gathered around a TV set in the very small *alojamiento* lobby jam-packed with guests and neighbors and watched a Mohammed Ali boxing match – the first such event to be televised internationally via satellite, I believe. In Panama we experienced bitter anti-American vitriol. I was strip searched in the airport and Enrique was mugged in broad daylight. Cabdrivers, waitresses and store clerks all spewed hatred for Americans. We could understand the roots of the bitterness, but it still made our stay very uncomfortable. Our nerves were ragged by the time we left Panama, but there was an opportunity to calm them during our stopover in the Guatemala City airport where passengers are served free rum to make the wait less painful. After Mexico City, we headed for San Francisco; I quite relaxed, but Enrique very nervous about meeting my family.

Even with the language barrier, he passed review with flying colors. We spent two weeks seeing the sights, from Fisherman's Wharf to all the quaint corners that John had discovered during his cab driving days. The two weeks passed quickly and soon it was time to return to La Paz. Or at least that was my assumption.

Before leaving the United States, we had to make a trip to the Bolivian consulate on Market Street to get my passport stamped with an entry visa. We waited quietly, confidently. Then the Consul General called us into his office and looked at me coldly. He said, "I have orders to deny you entry into Bolivia." I could think of any number of reasons why, and when Enrique asked for an explanation, the Consul simply said, "Your name is on the list of persons not allowed to enter the country."

The following day we drove Enrique to the airport and he returned to Bolivia alone. I was frantic. There was no recourse. I knew nothing and had no way of finding out anything. Communication with Bolivia had to be made through a short wave connection in Chile or Peru and then by radio patch to La Paz. The only way to do that was by making arrangements well in advance. It was too complicated and even risky under the circumstances. I suspected the *Damas* of having done this - they were angry enough to denounce me and certainly had influence in high places. Or was it because of our earlier involvement with the ELN guerrillas?

I could only wait and nurse the lump in my throat. For more than a decade I hadn't considered living anywhere but Bolivia. La Paz was my home. My family, however, felt relieved. In short spurts of interest, I would think about looking for a teaching job or renting an apartment, but mostly I could only fidget and worry and politely pretend that I enjoyed staying in the U.S.

Then suddenly in July, and without any explanation, I received a telegram saying that I could return and that I should check with the Bolivian consulate. The Consul General stamped my passport as if nothing had happened and I was on my way back to Bolivia. I struggled with doubts and fears until the last moment when the flight attendants closed the cabin door. I loved Bolivia and was growing close to Enrique, but how much more was I willing to risk?

I suspected that Enrique had pulled some strings for my reentry, but when I asked him, he said no and that he was as puzzled as I was about the incident. It wasn't until I returned to classes at the university that I discovered what had really happened. Several university professors had been imprisoned at that time and the students went on a rampage and negotiated with the government for their release. Someone had the kindness to include my name on the list and it was thanks to the students that I was approved for a visa. What did remain a mystery was why I was denied the visa in the first place.

Shortly after that, Enrique received a scholarship to attend a three-month workshop in journalism at UTAL, the workers' university in Caracas, Venezuela. While he was away I spent the time delving more deeply into the documentation of Bolivian education, teaching classes and writing letters to Enrique.

CHAPTER 49

AN UNRAVELING DICTATORSHIP

Rumors of a return to democracy began with the historical signing of an agreement by the U.S. to turn over the Panama Canal Zone to Panama. Not only was this a signal event for Panama, but for all of Latin America. In addition, news spread that President Jimmy Carter had used this opportunity to meet behind closed doors one-on-one with each military dictator of South America to issue an ultimatum banning military dictatorships on the southern continent and to affirm that the military had no business running any country. We imagined that he said something like, 'Get your fanny out of the presidential palace or it will be blasted out.' Whatever the words he chose and whatever his motive, he made it clear that democracy must return to these countries, or there would be a price to pay.

We sat mesmerized, as much by the miracle of modern television, as by the wonder of the treaty signing ceremony. This was a monumental historical event no one in Bolivia wanted to miss. We were glued to the TV set waiting for the ceremony to begin. The image was crystal clear, but as soon as the speeches began, something seemed terribly wrong with the sound. After much static and sputtering, the voices rang through clear but undecipherable. We strained close to the set and turned up the volume. Someone at the controls had pushed the wrong button and all of Bolivia listened to the ceremony in impeccable Portuguese.

In the first week in November, the political course in Bolivia took a swift and sudden turn, with elections promised for 1978. A period of "institutionalization" was to begin as a preparation for "constitutionalization." Political leaders were summoned out of the mothballs to meet with the president. Political parties were to be allowed to organize first and then the labor unions, this being a deliberate strategy orchestrated to keep workers out of the political arena. It was important because, historically, the labor unions were the mainstay for the parties. The government's intention may have been to hold elections, but the first order of the day was to weaken the political clout wielded by labor.

Banzer's speech was telecast. He appeared with half a dozen military men in uniform surrounding him. The lighting on the set came from below, casting huge, sinister shadows on the wall behind. As Banzer solemnly read his pronouncement in slow, warning tones, the camera backed up and focused on an old colonial crucifix dripping with blood. Even though the president spoke of democracy and amnesty, the visual image was positively hair-raising, undermining all confidence in the promises. We turned off the TV and waited for the publication of the regulations that would govern the electoral process.

Banzer declared amnesty on December 23, 1977, but it was partial. More than 300 names were still listed as "delinquents," among them past presidents, two children, a gentleman who had died a year before and a number of people who had been in the country with all of their documents in order. It became obvious that without political parties, labor unions or student organizations, the planning for elections would be a big joke. With the majority of the opposition leaders still in exile, there was even less hope for a fair election. Soon, there was a general outcry for a complete amnesty without restrictions.

Among those calling for a complete amnesty was a group of four housewives from the Siglo XX mines, whose husbands were in exile. Banzer responded to their plea by throwing them out of work. On December 28, they brought their protest to La Paz. Along with 14 children, they began a hunger strike in the *Arzobispado* (the main offices of the Catholic Church). They made four demands: 1) amnesty without restrictions, 2) return of their jobs, 3) free functioning for labor unions (so far it had only been granted in theory) and 4) removal of the occupation army that had been in the mines for over a year.

Four days later, another group of eleven, representing various organizations, occupied the offices of the Catholic daily, _Presencia_. Then hundreds of groups throughout the country joined them in solidarity, in universities, in schools, in churches, and even in the offices of the World Health Organization.

Cardinal Maurer stepped in thinking he could mediate, but because of his record, the hunger strikers rejected the offer. He returned to Sucre with his agreement crumpled up in his back pocket, and feeling a bit less important than he did the day before.

From his office at FENCOMIN, half a block from the Arzobispado, Enrique prepared press releases denouncing the government and supporting the hunger strikers. He reported the events minute-to-minute for the radio.

Observers began to arrive from the National Conference of Male Religious in the U.S., the United Nations' Human Rights Commission, Justice and Peace and a host of international organizations and governments.

Soon the opposition to Banzer gained momentum and there were labor strikes. The government responded with a counter-strike. Ministers of government resigned, the mayor of La Paz walked out, and the military published a document demanding that the government be placed in the hands of civilians. Everything came to a standstill. Half of the stoppages were in support of Banzer and the other half, in opposition. Everything was in turmoil. Before it ended, more than 1500 people were participating in the strike and literally thousands more were protesting in various ways.

On the January 13, sixty armed civilians (government agents) entered the parish church of San Jose Obrero in Santa Cruz (run by the Boston Archdiocese), arrested 16 hunger strikers and took them to an unknown location. They broke through the roof, windows and doors, destroying everything in their way. When news of this reached the other cities, the strikers prepared themselves by resolving to remain calm and offer no resistance. Many were too weakened to do anything else.

The next day, all activities were suspended in the country as a show of support for the government, and the government-run TV channel programmed a day of cartoons and nonsense to distract those of us who had to stay at home because of what was going on. And to add insult to injury, commercials made their entry into Bolivian television for the first time.

The hunger strikers were hermetically closed up in their various centers of protest. At three-thirty a.m. January 17, every center in every city (with the exception of the chancery and one church in La Paz) was taken by assault and the strikers arrested. The scene in the offices of the newspaper _Presencia_ was one of the most touching and dramatic.

After seventeen days without food, the strikers were extremely weakened. Heavily armed and helmeted, the police forced their way in, in the middle of the night, and demanded that the strikers accompany them. A doctor who was attending them indicated that they were too weak to be moved. An ambulance was called. The director of the newspaper read the Beatitudes from the New Testament. The voices of the weakened strikers could barely be heard as they sang "Viva Mi Patria Bolivia," Long Live my Country, Bolivia.

The police carried the prisoners off on stretchers. The photos in the newspaper portrayed a heart-wrenching contrast of brute force with the strength of moral determination. These cowardly acts of aggression were carried out even as the representative of the Human Rights Commission was in dialogue with the government and close to a satisfactory agreement. Observers from all over the world were present, waiting for a resolution. They and the entire country were in a state of shock.

I seriously considered joining the strikers, but decided to remain on the margin and let Enrique take the risks. He covered the events and ran between strike locations, trying to keep up with what was happening. He reported the details to me by phone as a precaution in case he would not get through to his radio station.

The next morning, Archbishop Manrique threatened the perpetrators, the police and others responsible for the raids, with excommunication and interdiction, giving them 48 hours to resolve the crisis. Bishops in other cities followed suit. Even Cardinal Maurer had to abandon his position of neutrality and came out with a statement praising the courage of the hunger strikers.

The following day was extremely tense and Banzer made a few more weak attempts to continue the repression. Archbishop Manrique was severely criticized by the extreme right. Then another student was killed in the street riots in La Paz, and everyone pressured Banzer to concede. By this time even his closest supporters were demanding his resignation. That night, just two hours before the excommunication was to take effect, Banzer signed an agreement. All political prisoners were released immediately.

However, the victory sparked no celebration, no jubilation. We were all too exhausted from those three weeks of tension and very wary about the future. In spite of the concessions by Banzer, we knew that the U.S. state department was calling the shots and we were not convinced that things were really going to change.

Nevertheless, in the following days, everyone came out of hiding like hungry mice. Was this to be truly the beginning of a new era? The government did let up on pressure by leaps and bounds. Leftist leaders returned to the country, and in no time, the number of political parties mushroomed to 51.

Six months was not much time to organize a presidential campaign, given that the political parties had been underground for six and a half years. The mimeograph machines were old and rusty, and the ink had gone dry. Some members had gone on to pursue other interests or had changed political stripes. The only candidate with an organization and money behind him was General Juan Pereda Asbun, who had been handpicked by Banzer. Suddenly, inexplicably, campesinos, workers and an assortment of unaligned leaders proclaimed him "our choice."

Meanwhile there were changes on the home front and at work. The city cut the water service to Achachicala to only one hour every morning. All afternoon service was cancelled. That meant we had to get out of bed in the dark and bitter cold to stand in line with everyone else to fill our buckets between five and six a.m.

Then, Honoria, my long-time helper, gave me a fluffy white puppy with brown spots. We named him Bobo, Spanish for "dopey." On Saturdays, he would follow Enrique to the FENCOMIN office on the main plaza to catch up on the week's work. After that they went to the local market for lunch. One evening Bobo fell off the porch and spent the night under the wings of Maria's hen. He disappeared mysteriously one day and then just as strangely, reappeared seven months later – fully grown, muddied and hungry. The dog and I looked at each other momentarily and I asked, "Bobo?" His tail began to wag and we both knew he was home.

At work CEBIAE moved to a two-story house on the Avenida 6 de Agosto. I shared an office with Juan Martinez, Toribio Tarqui, and Isabel Siles, who had just returned from Spain after graduating in anthropology. Isabel was the youngest daughter of ex President Hernan Siles Zuazo. She had been born during her father's term in office and was brought up in a very politically charged atmosphere. Her political insights were hard to match. Although she was almost twenty years younger than I, we became close friends. I had already worked with her older sister, Marcela, in the startup of children's centers and we needed no introduction. Isabel, tiny and almost bird-like, is on my list of all time favorite people. We shared many jokes and laughs and enjoyed working together with Juan and Toribio.

We were a team with no one in charge. We worked on a project to study education as it occurs in a proletariat family and researched how family members interact and what outside pressures influence them. When I wasn't training interviewers, I continued chasing down obscure historical documents and chewed over ideas and plans with this very compatible team of researchers. Also at about that time, my work was beginning to show some results. People from UNESCO visited me at CEBIAE and showed interest in financing the education documentation center I had been putting together.

It wasn't long before Isabel's father started to organize his presidential campaign in earnest; he turned to Isabel, the apple of his eye. She became his "right hand," and helped scout for possible candidates on his ticket as well as for activists to work with him. She approached me to see if Enrique would be interested in helping out. Enrique, instead, recommended his boss, the head of the Federation of Mining cooperatives, who was a miner, a native Quechua speaker and a dynamic leader in the North of Potosí. Siles recognized his merits and asked him to run as Senator for that department. Since there had been no democratically elected government since the coup of 1969, all offices needed to be filled and the slate of candidates under the name of the presidential pretender was long.

CHAPTER 50

THE CAMPAIGN TRAIL AND A DOUBLE COUP

At last, we were on our way to Democracy. In fact, a Washington Post article written by the Washington Office on Latin America (WOLA) claimed prematurely and euphorically that Bolivia was "the only free country in Latin America." We definitely were taking an enormous leap forward, however shaky it may have been. The Carter initiative opened the door to democracy, but we had serious doubts about where it would lead us.

The United States typically talking out of both sides of its mouth, was on the one hand pressuring Bolivia to end the march of the dictators and on the other, turning again to arm twisting tactics. In order to make sure that Bolivia would not deviate from policies in line with its interests, the U.S. threatened to take 45,000 tons of tin ore from its buffer stock and dump it onto the world market. Since Bolivia's economy depended for survival almost solely on its tin sales, of about 23,000 tons yearly, the effect of that amount of tin reserves would be nothing less than disastrous. The world market price would drop drastically and there would be no way for Bolivia to compete with countries where the cost of production was lower. Headlines about this in the La Paz papers brought the university students back into the streets in a frenzy of protest against Yankee Imperialism.

The way this came about is a story in itself. At the start of World War II, President Roosevelt invited Bolivia's President Peñaranda to the White House for a visit. He convinced him that it was his patriotic duty to sell 180,000 tons of tin ore to the United States at a bargain basement price. This would be Bolivia's contribution to the war effort. Tin was a strategic metal and the U.S. made it known that a large reserve would be necessary. Roosevelt placed a cowboy hat on Peñaranda's head and had a photo taken with him at his side. After this show of camaraderie and celebrity status treatment, Bolivia's leader was delighted to make the sale. The reserve was never used in the war, but has been dangled as a hangman's noose over the head of the Bolivian economy ever since. Unfortunately, the Bolivians had just bought the most expensive ten-gallon hat in history.

It wasn't long before all democratic institutions in Bolivia were back on track. Union leaders were elected and the university swung back into co-government, electing commissions, committees and councils. However, for the political exiles from 1971 who were swarming back into the country and to the university, things were going too slowly. These newly returned exiles, not understanding the degree of repression and control the country had been under, were impatient to forge ahead with change. They wanted immediate results. But those who had suffered the Banzer years were mistrustful of the democratic opening and wanted to proceed with more caution. This friction came to a head when, after only one day of classes the students misjudged the government's words as conciliatory and occupied the buildings. They boarded up classroom doors to protest the government's bypassing the university's autonomy by appointing new administrators. Sadly, their trust in the dictatorship was misplaced and that night the government took possession of the campus by force. Our suspicions were confirmed. It was obvious that prisoners could still be taken, that dissidents could still be exiled and that the transformation to democratic rule would not be easy. An editorial in Presencia, the daily newspaper run by the catholic church, sarcastically commented: "it was too bad they closed the university because there was still so much space left on the walls for graffiti."

The U.S. outwardly wanted a return to democratic rule in Bolivia but it was not ready to give up control of Bolivian education. A new director was named to head the United States Information Service (USIS), and I came face to face with him when collecting and documenting material written about Bolivian Education. I had located a reference to a compilation of statistics published by USIS and wanted to include it in my bibliography. Although I didn't particularly like the idea of going to the U.S.embassy, I was curious to see what kind of information had been compiled. After all, these were studies paid for by American tax dollars, and since I was an American, I would surely get easy access to them. There was nothing confidential about education. Or was there?

The USIS (often referred to as "USELESS") offices had moved to a new location, so it took me a while to find their library. I confidently presented my credentials as a researcher with CEBIAE and expected that my own government would welcome my interest at least as much as Bolivian officials had. Surprisingly, the receptionist told me to fill out a form and return the following day. I could only assume they needed time for a background check.

I returned the following morning for the most bizarre encounter. I was ushered in to the office of an unpleasant "gentleman" with stringy hair and a gaping space between his two front teeth. He introduced himself as "Billy Bastard, U.S. citizen born in Puerto Rico," who had no idea who his father was "because his mother slept around so much." He hurled a few demeaning inferences in my direction to let me know I was not exactly welcome, and then told me he was directing the new Educational Reform in Bolivia and that he was, indeed, "proud to be a bastard." He asked an employee to bring me a couple of pamphlets about Bolivia, but not the study I had requested. Without any explanation, I was roundly denied access to the library or any further data produced by USIS. The U.S. Information Service had no information for me now that it was in the safekeeping of a disgusting piece of humanity. Was he typical of embassy personnel? I don't know. I didn't stay around long enough to find out. Eventually, I did manage to get hold of the study through another contact, not an American.

Isabel Siles kept asking me about Enrique - did I think he would want to work on the electoral campaign with her father. Quite unexpectedly, Enrique had caught the attention of Siles Zuazo and Isabel phoned to say that her father's campaign manager wanted to meet him. As a result of that meeting, Enrique arranged for Siles' tour of the department of Potosí. At first, Siles' alliance was called the Popular Democratic Front (FDP), and later the name was changed to the memorable Popular Democratic Unity (UDP), a coalition of centrist and left-of-center parties. I wrote home, "If the elections aren't stacked, he has a good chance of winning." Fat chance!

Enrique reflected, "by the end of the week, I will be a marked man and there will be no turning back." Potosí contributed more than half of the country's wealth and was the heart of the roughest and most militant rebels in the mining country. Even after the years of military occupation and repression, the candidate on the right did not dare go close to the mines.

During the campaign, the government monopolized TV, radio and newspapers for the official candidate, making it nearly impossible to get time or space for non-governmental publicity. However, since Siles was very popular and had what we would call "name recognition," he had other means of getting crowds out to the rallies.

In fact, when Enrique started out on the campaign trail with Siles, his job was to make contacts beforehand in every village and town to make sure that there was a good turnout for Siles' appearances. Enrique saw to it that the campesinos were given something for their trouble. Usually coca leaves were distributed in gratitude because tee shirts and campaign buttons were not appropriate. He and Siles left a trail of promises: jobs and better times. In Potosí, Enrique's hometown and a Siles Zuazo stronghold, the turnout was massive. Enrique enlisted a group of husky university students to stand guard around the crowd to keep an eye out for possible acts of violence. The *matones*, as he called them, hung around the edges of the rally and when they caught an occasional troublemaker, they summarily hauled him off, disarmed him and left him bruised, but not disabled, on some side street. Fortunately, there weren't many such dissidents. The crowd in Potosí stretched for fifteen blocks with onlookers hanging from lampposts and out of windows. In exchange for the risk of managing the campaign, Enrique returned to his native city in a blaze of glory, in sharp contrast to his having been dragged off in the night like a criminal seven years earlier.

Political alliances resembled the combinations in Alice in Wonderland. Pursued and pursuer were aligning together to make unlikely pacts with predictably tenuous results. Meanwhile, Banzer and his official "stepson" Pereda Asbun, were re-writing the book on dirty campaign tricks. They set up roadblocks to keep electoral material, including ballots, out of populous rural areas. They ordered police to stop electoral vehicles and destroy pamphlets and portable P.A. systems. In some cases, the notaries who were registering voters actually turned away anyone who might not vote for the Banzer ticket. In the Altiplano, just outside La Paz, hundreds of campesinos were assembled for a demonstration in support of Siles, and when they got there they realized they had been duped - the trucks appeared with enormous photos of Pereda Asbun. The campesinos threw rocks or anything they could find, and hurled insults in Aymara at the candidate. Soldiers marched in and hauled off three truckloads of campesinos. When they got to the jail, the fighting continued between soldiers and campesinos.

Among the planks in Pereda's party platform was a laughable one calling for the installation of parking meters. This was not really a pressing issue for most Bolivians, who usually rode on the back of old trucks or jammed into rickety buses. However, just for the record, some meters had already been installed and the boots were being used for violators. Up to that time, the only ones caught were the mayor, the Ministers of Finance and Education and Pereda Asbun, the presidential candidate himself, which may have explained his interest in the subject.

Just one month before the election, there was a sudden explosion of new candidates: with the final total being eleven presidential candidates and twelve vice-presidential candidates. One presidential candidate named two vice-presidential candidates, so that the people "would have a choice". This was the election where Domitila Chungara, a housewife from the mines, ran as vice-presidential candidate, a first for Bolivia and a tribute to the miners' wives who had been instrumental in achieving democracy. And even a student of mine, Isidoro Copa, was on the list of presidential candidates. At first Siles put Enrique on the slate as "deputy" or representative for Potosí, but two weeks later he was listed as substitute senator. Enrique was worried that if I wrote home about the switch, my family would get the idea that Bolivia was disorganized.

This was the first time television was used in an electoral campaign. The program, "National Debate" arranged a setting that looked more like a grilling than an interview. Four mean-faced journalists sat comfortably on a platform, while the candidate sat on a swivel chair below them. After a brief biographical sketch, the reporters hurled a battery of aggressive and insulting questions at the candidate. I wondered what would be in store for Pereda Asbun. Would they raise the level of the chair and would the journalists possibly smile? When the Casiano Amurrio, *campesino* candidate, was interviewed, they ridiculed him and asked if he was a terrorist. They didn't give him a chance to talk about issues or any intelligent subject. As Election Day neared, the TV turned into a little machine that churned out swill in industrial quantities.

Because of the high rate of illiteracy, the candidates had to be identified by colors on the ballots. Throughout the whole city, there were signs reading "*Verde es mi color.*" (green is my color.) Under the cover of night and with a few quick strokes, the letters were changed. We woke up the next morning and read, "*Verde es mi culo.*" (Green is my ass.) The Banzer supporters, in turn, painted pink tinted glasses on all of the Siles posters.

Each party had a separate slate or ballot for the election. The government paid for the printing of the ballots, but each party was responsible for getting its own ballots to the polls. This presented major difficulties. Some parts of the country could be reached only by air and only candidates with hefty financial backing could afford that. The distribution of ballots was almost impossible in isolated areas where there were no roads or transportation. Worse still, Enrique's jeep was stopped several times by thugs armed with machine guns. Only ballots for Pereda Asbun got past the government goons.

On Election Day, July 9, normal life screeched to a stop in the entire country. Everyone was expected to vote. Stores were closed; there was no commerce, no travel. I had signed up to be an observer for the UN but did not get my bid on time and stayed home to watch the "show" on TV.

Early in the day radio and television reported total chaos and confusion, but the press did a fantastic job of documenting the problems. By mid-day hundreds of complaints had been registered, some polling places had ballots only for Pereda Asbun and some had none at all. Some ballot boxes were being turned in from polls that didn't exist. Observers from the UN Human Rights Commission counted an astounding number of "phantom voters." Members of the military complained that they were being forced to vote for Pereda Asbun in their barracks. One observer understated the situation, "It is too early to say yet if there is a fraudulent plan, but there sure are plenty of irregular and strange things going on!" The Government did not hide its irritation with the international observers and complained continually that they should keep their noses out of Bolivia's business and that they were too partial in their judgments. Siles announced, "1952 will be repeated if fraud is proved."

Meanwhile, Enrique was observing in the mines where he uncovered more dirty play. He reported on radio Cruz del Sur that he had found ten ballot boxes pre-stuffed with official ballots and he named the colonel who was responsible. He told of other threats and pressures used in the mines. By evening, the fraud carried out in the north of Potosí was a done deal. The air force and the army had the whole area sealed off and operated a modern system of radio communications, to make sure no opposition ballots came in to the region. Jeeps loaded with stuffed ballot boxes circulated openly.

A flashback is appropriate here. While he was President of Bolivia in the 1950's, Siles was invited to observe the presidential electoral process in the United States. His American hosts proudly showed him the newly installed electoral machines and they told him that it was the "modern way to vote" adding that "with voting machines, we know the results of the elections as soon as the last voter casts his ballot." Siles grinned and answered, "Bolivia is more modern than that - we know the results of the elections the day before they start voting!"

In the days that followed the election, Banzer repeatedly insulted the international observers who had called the fraud "shameless." They were especially taken aback by his reaction because the Bolivian ambassadors abroad had assured them they would be received in their country with cordiality and enthusiasm. The final recommendation of the international visitors was that Pereda not be recognized as President, should he be declared the winner.

There were instances of campesinos walking miles with ballot boxes tied to their backs, of others getting beaten and having the boxes stolen from them. Some campesinos managed to get hold of the ballots they wanted ahead of time and did a little of their own stuffing. One such group arrived in La Paz beaten and bloodied to report that the ballots had been stolen by the army, but with big impish grins, they opened their ponchos and revealed crumpled tally sheets in plastic bags, complete with official thumbprints and X's.

One of the photos in the newspaper showed a voting booth located in a bathroom, ballots displayed on the toilet seat. The caption read, "One smiling voter came out and commented, 'If we have to vote in the bathroom, it's bound to be a dirty election.'"

The votes were counted between July 10 and 18. They were counted and recounted by the members of the National Electoral Court. Report of assaults and ambushes on ballot boxes grew, and hundreds of instances of falsification of ballots were discovered.

Siles Zuazo declared a hunger strike at four in the afternoon on July 18 and campesinos set up roadblocks all over the country. Then, in a "Through the Looking Glass" moment, Pereda Asbun, who had earlier declared himself a winner, now requested the annulment of the elections "in order to avoid violence." Banzer, still in power, announced he would abide by whatever the Electoral Court decided. He promised to hand over the reins of government to the winning candidate on August 6 and that in the absence of a clear winner, to turn it over to the armed forces. Half an hour after his announcement, the National Electoral Court officially annulled the elections "because of the many illegal practices and irregularities."

At midnight the Air Force and armed civilian groups occupied the city of Santa Cruz, and in Cochabamba the radio stations were forcibly taken by the military. Banzer declared a state of siege and imposed a ten o'clock curfew. By six-thirty in the evening, a teary-eyed Banzer gave a very long speech, stating that he would step down as president in order to avoid more bloodshed. Juan Pereda Asbun appeared on TV the next day and announced he was the new President.

Radios stations were assaulted and trashed and political leaders were arrested. Candidates and party leaders were again forced into hiding. The cities were under a cloak of deadly calm, and Bolivians were tense and completely disheartened. We dragged ourselves to bed that night with our hopes completely dashed. When I awoke the following morning, I pulled open the curtains and was shocked to see a soldier, turn toward me threateningly with a sub machine gun, apparently startled by the rustle of the curtains. During the night the armed forces had spread throughout La Paz and occupied government offices and the city streets.

We were back to square one. Had we on the left once again been duped into showing our hand? If so, this time there was no place to run to since Argentina, Chile, Brazil, Paraguay, Peru, and even Uruguay had all been recruited by the Cold War against their own people.

From the United States, Jimmy Carter flashed his electronic glance at the U.S. ambassador to La Paz, Paul Boeker, and he withheld official recognition of the new regime. Carter was reported to have said, "The elections in Bolivia were as crooked as a picket fence." Welcoming the pressure on the Pereda Asbun government, I wrote the ambassador a letter to show my support for this policy and urged him to continue it. On August 8 he answered,

> "For over 200 years the United States has stood for the same noble ideals which Jefferson wrote into our Declaration of Independence . . . . The United States are what we are because of this creed and we cannot but continue to represent it. I gather you feel this way and so do I."

Unfortunately, but not surprisingly, by the time I received his letter, the ambassador had turned about and had already given full recognition to the Pereda Asbun government.

It was not long, actually by November, before some elements within the military were grumbling that the inept Pereda Asbun was ruining even their inglorious reputation, and they decided to clean up their image. Pereda had been dragging his feet about elections, postponing them for another two years, with the excuse that 1979 would mark the 100th anniversary of Bolivia's loss of the seacoast and that the country would be too taken up with festivities "celebrating" this glorious defeat to hold elections. He further unnerved everyone, the military included, by stating that the armed forces would have to ratify popular decisions and that there really was no need for a congress. Such a blatant showing of dictatorial intent led to the ousting of Pereda four months after the coup by the friendly and kindly General Padilla. The general immediately promised that elections would be held in July. We braced ourselves for another campaign.

With a promise of new elections, the atmosphere became a bit more relaxed again, enough to allow the presentation of the political documentary, "Courage of the People," a tribute to the hunger strikers and a strong criticism of the military dictatorships. For the first time in almost a decade, we went to the screening of an anti-government film without the fear of reprisal.

CHAPTER 51

LIFE AS TWO

With the military machine in check, we were able to turn our attention to other concerns. The day was approaching when Enrique's and my *anticretico* contracts with the Coronels were about to expire and we would have to find another place to rent. But Enrique talked Mario Coronel into selling him the portion of his property where he had his rooms. By that time Enrique and I had become necessary and permanent fixtures in each other's lives and we decided to get married. Our time and interests had become so intertwined that we couldn't imagine living any other way. In a simple ceremony with Simon Yampara and Freddy Calvo as witnesses, we were married in the home of Oscar Bonifaz, ex- minister of mines and boyhood friend of Enrique.

We then decided to build a house. We drew up plans and discovered that our area of Achachicala had not yet been zoned, and for that reason, we could not get a building permit. We still were not on the city map. As was common practice, we went ahead with our plans. We made a drawing, hired an *albañil*, and bought bricks, cement and sand. As luck would have it, on the same day the truck delivered the building materials and as the workers began tearing down the old wall, an employee came from city hall to officially "urbanize" our section of the barrio. We were cited and fined for violating the urban code.

By Christmas, the house was well on its way to completion and I was expecting a baby. My flexible work schedule gave me ample time to pick out diapers (no disposable ones, thank you) clothes and everything we needed. At the same time we made many trips to hardware stores to pick out bathroom fixtures (hoping to have water some day) and to lumber yards for doors, beams and baseboards. We had to buy everything ourselves, from the nails and door hinges to the electric wiring, and deliver them to the workers. I added a whole new category of words to my Spanish vocabulary.

Hiring an *albañil*, or construction worker, was a major decision. Because so many houses in the barrio were badly built, sporting chipped and broken bricks or crooked windows, we proceeded very slowly. We kept noticing one new house that we passed every day on the bus. Then, unbelievably, a man showed up one day who told us he knew who built that house. We set out in search of the builder and hired him immediately.

In the first stages of construction things went fairly well. However, Enrique, whose father had been a construction worker, had some reservations about the albañil's ability. We thought we had estimated the quantity of building materials we needed, but several times we noticed that we fell short. A bag or two of cement here, a few bricks and two-by-fours there. I kept an eye on the work as much as I could in between classes and my work at CEBIAE. One day, when I happened to be working at home, I went over to the work site and climbed the ladder to the second floor. I sat on a beam and watched as the workers put in a raised platform where we wanted a fireplace. I questioned the size of the platform and got out the drawing to show him how it should have been done. The one he was putting in filled almost half the room. When I showed him the drawing, it was already too late, but he responded, "Oh no, I always make the ovens like this. In fact, the lady I made the last one for, still gives me free bread every day." He thought he was building an industrial oven. Enrique wouldn't tolerate another day and got rid of him immediately, even though the work was not finished. We made a thorough inspection and found he had made several other mistakes, like hanging the closet doors backwards, so that they swung inward, leaving no space inside for anything but the door. A further background check revealed that he was not an *albañil* at all, but a shoemaker and that while he had worked on the house we had so admired, he probably just carried water for the other laborers. Later we also learned that on his days off he was building himself a house using the materials he managed to spirit away from our place during the week.

We puzzled over what we could do to use or hide the big brick platform in the front room. I suggested that "Senator Bachinelo" could always use it for speeches." Enrique wouldn't have any jokes for the moment and the word "fireplace" suddenly became a dirty word not to be used in our house for a few months. Enrique brought in a carpenter and an electrician and things got off to a second start.

The workers on the house took a long vacation during the Christmas and New Year holidays. In their absence, we decided to cut and put the windows in ourselves. That was a mistake. Getting the huge sheets of glass up to the house on the steep dirt road filled with ruts was a feat in itself. It was hours before we found a truck driver willing to make the trip over the bumpy streets but finally and gingerly, we set the panes in the patio.

After considerable practice and a lot of broken glass, and nicks and gashes all over his hands and arms, Enrique mastered the trade of putting in windows. We had to mix our own putty, which also was a trial-and-mostly-error process: first it was too dry, then too runny, and finally we made one that seemed to work out, but not without disaster. I remember the look on Enrique's face one day. He worked all morning putting in four windows with dozens of small panes. Satisfied with a job well done, he took a break for lunch. The noonday sun made the putty run and then a good wind came down from Mount Chacaltaya. After lunch he returned to continue and all the glass was shattered on the floor. By the time we finished, we knew exactly how to and how not to do it.

We suspected that a goodly part of the construction materials were getting spirited away by the builders while we were away at work, so we both took some vacation time to observe things more closely and also to do more buying. We spent Christmas not quite in the new house and not completely out of the old one.

In January 1979, the house was ready! With the help of Honoria, we made the final move. It was very simple. We only had to slide the furniture and belongings over the porch railing of the Coronel house on to the rooftop of the new house and down to the second floor rooms. We would live on the second floor and Enrique's four daughters would use the rooms on the first floor whenever they would be there to visit.

The new house gave us a great sense of security and stability. No more landlords, no more *anticretico*. Even though it was just a basic structure, it was ours: a simple two-story house with a very small patio where the sun never shone. The second floor had two large rooms with huge windows and a very small room that didn't have any special purpose. And there was a rooftop where we could hang clothes to dry and sit in the sun and watch the neighbors. We had a bathroom complete with shower on both floors and two big barrels for water on the rooftop, and we were ready for water, if it should ever come our way. I loved decorating and doing all the domestic things that go with a home. We shoved furniture over the troublesome brick platform and forgot about ever having a fireplace.

Our dog, Pastor, was the only one who was not happy with the move. For a few days he stubbornly refused to come to the new place even for food. He stayed all by himself on the porch at the old house and I took him his meals. Finally, when he realized we were serious about not returning, he decided to make the move. He took all of his rags out of his box, dragged them out on the street and flopped down to sleep. He was a strange dog, a loyal gray mongrel that, with the exception of his reluctance to leave his old house, stuck to me like glue.

Once he became very sick with a dried and cracked nose. I tried taking him on the bus to the veterinarian. The bus driver got pretty upset, so I had to leave him home and go by myself. I sat in the waiting room with a parrot, two dogs and a monkey who sadly pondered his bandaged finger. His owner told me he had slammed a door on it. When my turn came, everyone wondered what kind of pet I had. Was it in my pocket? I marched in to the office and laid out the facts. The vet, somewhat amused, gave me a prescription, which I filled at the pharmacy for humans right across the street.

Poor Pastor was terrified of any kind vehicle. Once, when he was just a puppy, he got too close to a bus and the wheel ran over his paw. It did no damage, but it left him traumatized for almost a year. He was a homebody and it was a chore to get him out of the house for a little exercise. We'd throw him out a couple times a day and later, when we'd open the door, he'd just be standing there waiting to come back in. All that changed later, and the turning point came one day when Enrique went to a barrio meeting at the hospital. Who should he find sitting there with the members of the junta, but Pastor. He stayed for the whole meeting and seemed intensely interested in the proceedings. Afterwards, Enrique stayed behind to work on some papers, but the dog left with everyone else and went home.

Concerned about my pregnancy, Enrique accompanied me to natural birth classes. I was the only woman in the class of ten or so whose husband showed up. Embarrassed, he was afraid that the teacher would think he was responsible for all of the women there. Nevertheless, he valiantly persevered. Those months were very happy months. In spite of my age, forty—four, I had what the doctor called a "perfect pregnancy," no aches, no pains, no morning sickness. Just a big stomach - a very big stomach. At CEBIAE, five of us were expecting at the same time. That gave rise to more than a few jokes about what kind of work we did, but for us it was a great chance to share maternity clothes.

CHAPTER 52

HEARTBREAK

In mid December of 1978, key political leaders met to draw up rules for the next elections. Enrique was involved in the process and, after going to a dinner where the cabinet members were present, he remarked that they all seemed very young and fearful about what Banzer and the older military were secretly cooking up in Santa Cruz. It was clear by this time that the generational split in the military was and had been driving the political sideshow and that it would be some time before it would be resolved. An end-of-the-year news summary had commented sardonically, "Bolivia is back to normal now with two revolutions a year."

During the Banzer years, millions of dollars flowed into the country's coffers from international financial lending institutions, and because the beneficiaries of these loans had no intention of repaying them, foreign aid was being withdrawn piece by piece almost on a daily basis. To add to the economic gloom, the rainy season that year was especially severe or at least it seemed that way. A good portion of the country was flooded. With no resources, the only thing the authorities could do was fly over the devastated countryside and lament. The country was sinking in water and in debt.

By February, Padilla set the ground rules for the next election and plans got under way. This time around, Enrique was put in charge of publicity for the Siles campaign, but things were coming unglued in the coalition. Isabel confided in me one afternoon that her father felt that there was no one he could trust. People were after power and might just jump off the bandwagon if they felt they could get it somewhere else. There were also ideological differences and personality clashes. Siles had told her that she was the only one he could talk to and that he had doubts about running for office. Besides, his half brother, Luis Adolfo Siles Salinas, also threw his hat into the ring as candidate for president. By March there were 57 political parties lined up, a veritable Heinz's- variety.

Bolivia celebrated the 100th anniversary of its loss to Chile of its outlet to the Pacific Ocean. As promised, at noon the factory sirens sounded and the whole country was enveloped in five minutes of silence to commemorate the iniquitous deed. Enrique had hurried home in a flurry. He charged up to the rooftop to "listen to the silence." The sirens pierced the air with a deafening whine and then, silence! Or so it should have been. Pastor, whose canine ears had never heard anything so god awful, howled in pain for the full five minutes. Enrique threatened to expatriate him.

Padilla's investigation into the Banzer presidency revealed what we knew all along: that he and his cronies had ripped the country off handsomely. Natural gas, oil, minerals, valuable reserves of precious lumber, all these resources had been stolen and sold to the highest bidder while the government officials turned a blind eye. Never missing an opportunity for a peso, he had even sold the blood of the young military conscripts for a profit.

These revelations did not deter Banzer from participating as a candidate again. Unashamedly, he put his name on the ballot and tried campaigning. Fortunately, the people did not receive him well. In some small towns, the crowds even chased him out. It warmed our hearts to hear that he was begging the Padilla government for security protection for his campaign.

Although Democracy was struggling at the national level, it was up and running in the neighborhoods. One political observer notes that Bolivia is one of the most organized countries on earth. That is true. Local neighborhoods elect official representatives to a local governing body called a *junta vecinal*. These leadership groups, in turn, elect a central *junta* to work with the mayor. The *juntas* have real power and they know how to use it. They move the masses. The barrio of Achachicala lost no time in electing its leaders and they recruited Enrique as candidate for secretary. "Dr. Enrique," as they called him was a shoo-in. We were on our way!

Two weeks before the baby was due, I became very sick and the doctor decided to perform a cesarean section. Enrique was away campaigning, so, I tacked a note on the door and took a cab to the hospital with Carmen. The next morning, Saturday, May 5, as I was being wheeled to the operating room, Enrique appeared at my side. He said, "Be calm". And, whether it was his presence or the medications, I suddenly became very relaxed. I was certain it would be a boy and in the elevator on the way to surgery, we decided on a name: Jimmy Enrique.

I had an unexpected reaction to the spinal and had to be given a general anesthetic. When I awoke, I heard a faint whimper and the doctor said, "The baby is fine, but we have to give him oxygen." A usual procedure in the high altitude. The little bundle wrapped in blue was whisked away. Isabel Siles had been waiting outside with Enrique and in her concern, she promptly phoned the top pediatrician in the country. He came immediately to examine Jimmy and reported, "He is a little agitated, but he will be just fine. They will have to monitor his oxygen."

The next morning my doctor stopped in early and as soon as I saw her face, I knew. Before she could say anything, I said, "We lost him, didn't we?" She nodded and said she didn't know what happened and left. At that moment Enrique arrived with a radio and some fruit. He already knew, since he had first stopped at the nursery window. We speculated about the medication the doctor had given me a few days earlier "just in case," but with no real need. Enrique called our good friend, Dr. Carlos Calvo, who had literally begged to deliver the baby and now vowed to find out what happened.

My doctor ordered an extended hospital stay for me allowing for a steady stream of friends and co-workers to come by with kind words of support. Mid-week, a transportation strike paralyzed the city and that day no one, not even Enrique, was able to come. I was alone and I cried hours of uninterrupted tears of grief.

After the strike, the visitors returned. Another day I got dressed and sneaked out of the hospital to buy stationery. The rest of the week, I wrote letters and read. The hospital had a huge collection of Readers Digests in English. Filled with pallid jokes and trivial "Americana" articles, they were totally irrelevant and disorienting. Their only saving grace was that they did not require much effort or concentration, so I poured over them until I finally swore I would never pick up another as long as I lived.

In the meantime, Enrique bought a small coffin from a carpenter, whose newly opened workshop was located a couple of blocks from our house. I remembered how I had felt a twinge of anxiety the day I saw the artisan hang small white coffins in the doorway with a sign that read, "specializing in *cajones infantiles*" (infants' coffins). I could only imagine how Enrique's heart must have ached as he arranged for a niche and burial. At home, he thoughtfully put away all of the things we had prepared for the baby's arrival.

Carlos Calvo reviewed the hospital records and told us that there were indications of negligence on the part of the doctor and staff. Although I thought we had chosen a good hospital, I did not know until it was too late that it did not have modern incubators. He told us that the nurse, who was supposed to monitor the oxygen for Jimmy, had left him alone to go out for supper.

Friends urged us to sue the doctor and/or the hospital, but the truth was that I could not handle another strong emotion. Adding bitterness to our grief would be overwhelming. The loss was more than enough for us to handle.

After a week, I returned to Achachicala and Enrique said that during my absence, Pastor refused to leave the house. He must have sensed that something was wrong because for the next few weeks, he wouldn't let me out of his sight, watching intently from his small throw rug by the door.

By Bolivian law, I was given three-months of paid leave from work and that provided space for sadness. But even at that, much of our dealing with the heartbreak was done in bits and snatches because we had two important projects that demanded our attention: the hospital in Achachicala and a presidential campaign.

CHAPTER 53

POLITICAL GAIN

When Enrique wasn't traveling with the Siles campaign, he was hassling with red tape at customs. Bread for the World had accepted our proposal for the hospital and shipped medicines, medical equipment, and even a VW bus to be used as an ambulance. Neither of us had driven a car in a number of years, so learning to drive again was a challenge for both of us. We entered into a kind of competition to see who could make the other more nervous. Once we took Pastor along for the ride, but he was a very unhappy passenger. He yelped and howled the whole time Enrique was driving. Strangely, when I took the wheel, he let out a few final whimpers and calmed down completely. I had passed the driver's test! But Enrique renewed his threat to expatriate poor Pastor!

This campaign was different because for the first time in Bolivia's recent history, freedom of expression was guaranteed and there were no political prisoners and no exiles. Democracy was sweet to the taste, but the economy was on the brink of disaster. Nowhere was that more evident than in the mines where the cost of living had increased by 500% during the Banzer years, while during that same period, income grew by only 80%. Although the price of tin soared, the purchasing power of a miner's salary was 75% less than it was before Banzer came into power. But they did have television! Even Rome had bread with their circus.

We had come through a long dark tunnel of repression and a gruelingly disappointing electoral experience. Now in two short weeks, Bolivians would go to the polls again. This time the two top contenders were Siles Zuazo and Paz Estenssoro, two seasoned old friends and leaders of the 1952 revolution. We knew it would be close.

Enrique returned from campaigning and applied for a special credential for us to circulate as political party representatives. So on July 1, 1979 Bolivians again forgot about the rest of the world for one day - no news, no transportation, no stores, no market, no movies, no *telenovelas* - nothing. We used the hospital ambulance to tour the city to see how the voting was coming along. Everything was quiet. Except for a few cars with official election observers and the usual assortment of stray dogs and an occasional chicken pecking into the dust, the streets were empty. People bustled along the sides of the roads, on their way to the polls.

We checked on several polling places and ended up at John Kennedy, the local grade school in Achachicala where we cast our votes. We then took our seats on the playground to watch the voting. An official committee, made up of a representative from each political party, sat at the table and presided over the process. First, the ballot box was checked to make sure it was empty and then it was properly sealed. Then the committee members made sure there were enough ballots in each stall and that each voter added only one. Later, they directed the voters to register their names in a notebook. One very sick and elderly woman had walked on crutches down the rugged mountainside for an hour just to be able to exercise her democratic right, casting her ballot in a sense of triumph. At the end of an eventful day, filled with barking dogs, children and papaya soda, the box was opened and one-by-one, the votes were read aloud and counted for everyone to see. The party representatives signed the tally sheet, sealed the box again and then took it to the Electoral Court Headquarters in La Paz.

We observed the counting of votes in the two centers in Achachicala. Anyone who wanted to could watch, and the large crowd around the splintered wooden tables on the school playground was a testimony to the intense interest. Enrique copied down the totals and when we got home, he phoned the results in to the radio station. By that time many tallies were coming in and we kept record at home until the reports stopped at midnight.

Exactly as the year before, the UDP was ahead on the national total. Paz and the MNR were running second, but no candidate had the required number of votes of 50% + 1. With so many candidates, it was impossible for anyone to get half the votes. The department of La Paz, the most populace, voted overwhelmingly for the UDP. It was surprising to see that Banzer got so many votes, even in places where he had massacred campesinos. But he was way behind in his own home department of Santa Cruz. Enrique's spot as substitute senator was secure, that is as secure as anything could be in Bolivian politics. There was, however, a great seriousness and maturity in the voting that year. There were no incidents of violence or fraud reported. General Padilla had kept his promise to keep things clean and correct. Given Banzer's history, Padilla could have sent him to the border in his shorts and bare feet, but he took no reprisals. It probably was better to keep the cocky ex-dictator busy campaigning out in the open where he could be watched and would have little time to scheme behind the scenes.

In the Department of La Paz, Siles and the UDP won by a landslide. In Potosí, where Enrique had organized the campaign his party was ahead only by a narrow margin. Paz Estenssoro, who reportedly received money from the U.S. government and gave away sewing machines and typewriters to encourage voters there, ended up in second place and Banzer came in third.

An unexpected outcome was that Marcelo Quiroga Santa Cruz, leader of Socialist Party I ended up in 4th place. He had been the cabinet minister who had spearheaded the nationalization of Gulf Oil in 1969. With no funds for ads or travel or posters, and only by using the free TV and radio time provided by the government, he caught the attention of 10% of the voters. No one was more surprised than the PS-1 representative who was at the table in Achachicala. He nervously chewed on an unlit cigar and choked back shouts of astonishment each time votes for his candidate were announced. Marcelo Quiroga Santa Cruz, the young, brilliant and extremely charismatic leader was the answer to the frequently heard criticism that Bolivia was a "new country with old leaders." There was no doubt that he was the rising star on the left or that he could easily win a future presidential election.

The result of the voting in the 1979 elections was that no presidential candidate received the required majority of votes, and so according to the constitution, it would be up to congress to elect the head of state. On August 6th the new congress was sworn in and their first task was to fill the presidency. Everyone predicted that loyalty ballots would be cast in the first round and that for the second vote, the congressional members would cross party lines and re-align to give the majority of votes to one of the candidates.

Observers were allowed in Congress and the first sessions were so unruly that nothing got done. The newspapers said it was like a soccer game, "only noisier." Eventually, the voting did get underway and international representatives began arriving in La Paz in anticipation of the pending presidential inauguration.

For the first time in Bolivia, the sessions of congress were to be televised. Ironically, Enrique and I were invited to spend the evening in the home of a friend whose entire family had voted for Banzer. We filled our plates buffet style and gathered to watch the voting process on television surrounded by *banzeristas*. For two uncomfortable hours, we politely muffled our cheers every time there was a vote for Siles and cringed at the hearty applause at every mention of Banzer's name.

The first round of votes went as expected and not a single Member of Parliament made a switch. There were no signs of backroom deals. Each and every congressional member stuck with his/her candidate. Surely the "good old boy" negotiations would begin to show their results. Surprisingly, on the second round, the outcome was exactly the same.

A recess was declared and we excused ourselves from the family gathering. We left the house sweating with tension and burst into laughter with relief as soon as the chill air brushed our faces.

We hurried home to continue watching the session: the third vote showed Paz, 68, Siles, 46, Banzer, 22 abstentions. Again, no candidate received the required 73 votes. Not one congressperson had sold out! Not one! That was truly amazing. The voting continued all night long with no variation. At 4 a.m. Congress took a break and scheduled to re-convene at eleven in the morning. Banzer's refusal to give his votes to either candidate meant he was trying to pressure for something he wasn't getting. Enrique claimed that Banzer did, indeed, offer his party's 22 votes to Paz but that in return he was asking for 1) five cabinet posts, 2) money and 3) amnesty for anything he did during his term in office. Paz told him, "I don't need your 22 votes. I only need 5 and if I really wanted to buy them, I could have done it days ago." However, in the corridors, a deal was being made to divide up the cabinet posts 50-50 between the UDP (Siles) and the MNR (Paz Estenssoro.)

The congress would have continued voting through the second night, except that someone spread the rumor that the military was taking over the country, so in Enrique's words as he walked through the front door, "They scattered like scared rabbits." He added that, "The only other place I've seen men that nervous is the maternity ward."

According to the Bolivian Constitution, in the absence of a president, the head of the senate fills the post and has to hold elections within the year. What, again! Congress reconvened the following day and tried at all costs to find a constitutional solution to the stalemate. The rusty wheels of democracy began to hum in the chambers of parliament and after days of around-the-clock deliberations, the exhausted members of congress finally came to a decision: to name as president a man who had not received a single vote. Walter Guevara Arce, the newly elected president of the senate was named President. Guevara had been one of the founders of the MNR, a leader who had split with Paz Estenssoro in the early days to form his own party. He was a venerable figure and by all measures, a technocrat. His mandate was to hold office and conduct elections again in 1980. Respecting the constitutional mandate, both Siles and Paz withdrew from the process and gathered energy for the next presidential campaign, and so did we.

That meant that we, too, had time to work on projects in Achachicala. On weekends, we joined the neighbors in an ambitious project: to put in a new public water spigot. A few Sundays were spent working in "community action" with a big crowd of neighbors: digging a well and ditches, installing pipes and making connections. The pipes ran right past but not into, our house giving us hope that one day we might even have water piped to our house. For the time being we were very happy with a new spigot, even if it would only be open for use from 6 –7 in the morning and from 3 – 4 in the afternoon.

Then, after two years of haggling and negotiating, Bread for the World, a German foundation accepted the barrio's project to remodel and staff the hospital in Achachicala. Enrique and the Doctors Calvo set to work with the barrio representatives and drew up plans. *Albañiles* were contracted and the building started. The barrio junta appointed Enrique as Administrator. The next months were interspersed with getting medicines from Customs, translating shipping lists from German to Spanish, looking for construction material, and supervising the construction workers.

It was then that we got a new addition to our house. Simon Yampara, the security person at the hospital, had a ten-year-old cousin, Lino, who had been abandoned by his mother. Simon brought him to our house and asked if he could stay with us. Needless to say, we took Lino in. He was a bright little boy with a big smile. In spite of his sad experience, he was always very happy and Pastor never got so much attention. Lino was always busy, cleaning something, painting or fixing the dog's house. Truly, he was great company for the whole family. I bought him some books and we worked on his reading skills.

One afternoon, I overheard him making a deal with a neighbor girl who was studying to be a beautician, telling her that she had to do a "good job" on his head. Unfortunately, she didn't, and the more she cut, the worse it got. Finally he ordered her to shave it to the skull. Afterwards, he was too embarrassed to show us what had happened. I saw his shiny bare head at the window, but when I went to open the door, he scurried away. Finally, Enrique's daughter knit him a cap and that was the only way he'd come to supper. When he saw himself in the mirror, he looked like he was about to cry. However, his biggest concern was that the dog wouldn't recognize him. Of course Pastor didn't care, so Lino quietly resigned himself to wait until his hair grew back in.

We enjoyed some months of relatively calm and sunny days with time to finish details in the house. We even planted seeds in little tin cans with Lino and Enrique's youngest daughter, Graciela. Life was good!

In addition, it looked like justice would soon be served with an intense drama unfolding in Congress. Marcelo Quiroga Santa Cruz was reading his famous "Juicio a Banzer," a series of accusations against Banzer and his collaborators.

He described with careful detail the horrendous crimes of the Banzer regime: torture, murder, drug dealing, pillaging and negotiating natural resources, and high treason. The sessions were televised and broadcast. Aware of the historical importance of the event, I taped the hearings from start to finish. Along with most of the country, I was riveted to the radio during three days for the sixteen-hour presentation.. The courage and intelligence of Quiroga Santa Cruz was astounding. Nowhere in Latin America had any citizen ever presented a case against an ex-military dictator. There was hope of vindication, but also fear for what might happen if this new attempt at democracy failed.

CHAPTER 54

THE MOST BIZARRE COUP
IN BOLIVIA'S HISTORY

On November 1, a rare balmy evening in the Altiplano, Lino and I drove down to the Plaza Velasco to meet Juanita who was just passing through on her way to Tarija. We three sat in the van for about an hour watching the passing crowd hurrying home in the night. Juanita and I caught up on recent events in each other's lives and then said another "adios."

As Lino and I drove back up to Achachicala, I thought how the city felt much safer and happier than it had in a long time. And indeed it was. That very night Bolivia was hosting an OAS (Organization of American States) meeting. And at that very moment, the representatives of the Western Hemisphere's nations were toasting the Bolivian government's successful return to constitutional rule. La Paz was basking in the glow of their lavish praise. For the moment, the air was sweet and easy to breathe.

In another part of the city, ominously, a different kind of celebration was under way: General Natusch Busch was guest of honor at an event commemorating the foundation of the rubber-producing department of Beni. Emboldened by a night of heavy drinking, he left the party at 3:00 a.m. and with a small group of soldiers, stormed the government palace.

Reportedly, Natusch made his move to prevent a takeover by General Banzer and with great confusion ensuing: some of the lower level officers carried out orders not knowing for which general. Word reached the OAS delegates, who were just getting in to their hotel rooms from a lively night and they scrambled to quickly change their travel plans, and revisit their opinions of Bolivia, as well.

Early the next morning, the air was again cold. The city awoke and listened with disbelief as the news programs presented a proclamation naming General Natusch Busch president. No one was more surprised than some of the military who thought they had aided in a Banzer coup.

General Natusch Busch appeared on TV in a sinister lighting arrangement, illuminated from below. He cast a large, frightening shadow on the wall behind. His speech seemed harmless enough, for he promised that everything would be the same: labor unions, as well as all student organizations, would continue to function; the universities would remain open; freedom of the press would be guaranteed; and the national congress would convene as usual. There would be no repression, no arrests and no violence.

The first day of the coup, there were no visible changes in the life of the city. Parliament convened and its first order of business was to reject the coup. Labor unions, students, campesinos, foreign governments and organizations of all types issued statements censuring the senseless interruption of the constitutional process. But the most desperate meetings of all were those within the ranks of the military who were trying frantically to untangle the mess.

The next day, we were all very confused, not really able to understand why or what had happened. Although his promises were being kept, no one took General Natusch seriously. After a decade and a half of military dictatorships, Bolivians were not about to be browbeaten back into a repression by the likes of this drunken fascist soldier from the backwater town of Riberalta. The censure of the cup was unanimous. Then there were rumors that Victor Paz Estenssoro was to take over as president once Natusch had things in order. However, if that was true, when Paz saw the negative reaction internationally, he backed out and left his supporters out on a limb.

Enrique received a phone call that morning from opportunistic political leaders who were already jumping on board with Natusch. There would be a high level meeting to help organize the new government. "Would he consider a cabinet post?" "No," he told them. He wouldn't. But he did interview those leaving the meeting and was told that Natusch was claiming he had prevented a brutal coup being planned by Banzer, that he had saved the country from a blood bath.

Some of the civilian leaders were convinced, but the general public was not so easily swayed, and Natusch's position was greatly weakened. The extreme right military faction, of which he was allegedly not a part, moved in to take advantage of his vulnerability and put him under house arrest in the presidential palace. What followed was one of the most bizarre and unfortunate episodes in Bolivia's history.

Natusch spent the following days stone-drunk. The right-wing military were now in charge and they sobered him up only enough to prop him up before the TV cameras to read decrees that they had written.

Then the pendulum swung. A new cabinet was named and its members were sworn in before a shocked and incredulous nation. When Natusch named his cabinet, Panfilo Anave, Enrique's co-senator, accepted a cabinet post!

The former legitimate cabinet and members of congress whipped into action and met clandestinely to work out a plan. Enrique received a coded phone call telling him where and when the meetings would take place.

By the weekend, the people could not be contained and protesting crowds took to the streets. Natusch, no longer in charge of affairs, yielded to pressure and threats from military honchos, ordered the soldiers out of the barracks and into the streets to shoot at anyone caught protesting. Radio stations reported the events of the evening: the riots, the arrests, pillaging of homes and businesses.

On Sunday morning all radio stations signed off one by one, after carefully informing their listeners that they were declaring a national and indefinite strike, and that there would be roadblocks on all routes of transit in the country. All that day, Natusch made frequent TV appearances, piece by piece dismantling the constitutional framework: first, the labor unions would be banned; then, student organizations would be prohibited; later congress was dissolved; the university was be closed; the school year was be ended. Then he began issuing a series of new decrees promulgating repressive measures with: curfew, a state of siege and the lynchpin of repression, martial law. Anyone could be shot and executed for any reason and without any right to protest.

The news blackout enveloped us in sepulchral silence. For three days our only sources of information were the official government radio station, the military radio and the government-run TV channel. Only military vehicles were on the streets – tanks, jeeps and armored cars. A helicopter patrolled overhead.

From our windows we could see the highway that curved its way through the stand of eucalyptus trees on the mountain across the way. We watched children set up roadblocks. They placed rocks on the road and ran into the woods when they heard a tank coming. The tank stopped and the rocks were cleared. As soon as the tank would disappear around the curve, the children would dart out to set up the rocks again. They repeated the operation several times making one think they were playing a game. We picked up the radio frequency from the helicopter, "Watch it! The children are around the next curve. We'll be right there." The helicopter swung around and swooped down, strafing the highway and tanks rounded the curve with deafening blasts. The children scattered. We couldn't tell if they had been hit. We watched in horror as children, unable to see the tanks around the curve, would come out and put rocks on the road.

The massacre lasted for days. At first I tried to keep away from the windows, but in the end, I went right on cooking and carrying on pretty much as usual, until the strafing became especially heavy. I recalled my first revolution sixteen years earlier, on exactly the same date, and remembered Chela, the young cook who had prepared a meal for us in the midst of that heavy strafing and shelling. Here I was doing the very same thing.

By Tuesday evening, the violence had quieted down and there were some efforts to return to work in some critical service areas. However, the great majority of Bolivians remained firmly behind the strike, in silent protest, opposing the military at all costs. We had come this far and there was no giving up now.

The news blackout was especially unnerving. Labor leaders met clandestinely and voted to end the strike because food was running out in many homes and also because the transportation workers were threatening to break the strike and go back to work. The return of public transportation would mean that movement in the cities would return to normal and that would make it hard to maintain the strike. At the same time, the civilian and military leaders were negotiating an agreement whereby President Guevara Arce would be ousted and the naming of a new president would be left to Congress.

The ball was tossed into the congressional court, but the parliamentarians, meeting clandestinely, could not reach an agreement. This delay gave Natusch time to rally more military support. When an alternative was finally presented to him, he felt strengthened and refused to budge. This brought more violence, more roadblocks and revived the strike. Congress did not have a chance to resolve the situation.

Then, as if all that wasn't bizarre enough, Natusch appeared on TV and retracted his decrees of the previous week, one by one: first, he declared, there would be co-government in the university; then, two hours later, labor unions were told they could function freely and two hours later, he announced that yes, there would be freedom of the press. By evening, all constitutional rights had been restored.

After examining various alternatives, Congress opted for the constitutional solution to the stalemate. In the absence of a president and vice president, the president of the senate, Lydia Gueiler Tejada had to take charge of the nation. She was sworn in as president of the republic on November 16, a little more than two weeks after Guevara was ousted. Guevara then returned to his earlier post as president of the senate.

If it hadn't been for a chance bit of lucky timing on the part of the labor leaders, Natusch might have remained in power. The union leaders had already decided to end the general strike but when they arrived to make their announcement to the press, they overheard the president of the congress inform the nation that they had named a woman to the presidency. The labor spokesperson crumpled his notes, put them in his pocket and left the room.

This senseless military fiasco took the lives of more than 400 Bolivians with seventy disappeared and hundreds wounded. After sixteen terror-filled days, with strafing and planes circling during the day, Natusch left the government palace by the side door with, it was claimed, sixteen cases of empty whisky bottles and bags of money "withdrawn" from the *Banco Central*. It was estimated that $18 million disappeared that night. He set a record for stealing the most money in the shortest time in office, and probably for killing the most people. He had been inebriated the whole time.

A few days later, a little boy proudly informed me that he knew the name of the new president. "Who?" I asked. Stretching himself to a confident pose, he recited, "Walter Guevara Arce!" Who could keep up? It has been noted that Bolivia writes its history faster than any other country in the world.

In the end, the political leaders, who had supported Natusch, were considered traitors, at least for the short term. Among them, was the senator for Potosi, Panfilo Anave

Bolivian and other historians will debate for a long time to come what actually motivated the Natusch coup. Some call him a hero and say that he really wanted to save the country from a bloody takeover by Banzer, that the Banzer faction ganged up on him and made him look like a beast. Others paint him as a fascist ogre who in less than two weeks took the lives of hundreds and as a drunken sot who pillaged the national bank.

Lino's mother must have been very worried about him during those days of unrest in La Paz, for as soon as things were calm again, she sent his brother to bring him back to her side. When Lino said good-bye to us, he cried right from the bottom of his heart. I often wondered what kind of person his mother was; in spite of what she had done, I couldn't think harshly of her. I had to believe that she was a good woman and that she must have had a positive influence on him, for he was considerate of others, interested in everything and just a fine little boy.

However historians may interpret the Natusch coup, one thing was certain: the entire nation and we were totally exhausted after sixteen terror-filled days of violence and chaos. The newly sworn-in *Presidenta* Lidia Gueiler promised elections and we, understandably, wondered just where on earth we would find the energy and motivation to go through yet another campaign. We waited and began to gather our strength.

CHAPTER 55

COCAINE AT CENTER STAGE

News from San Francisco had me concerned. My father's health was failing and he was in the hospital. Johnny was at his wits' end. I made a hurried trip stateside to see what, if anything, I could do. After spending a little over a month there, I was delighted that my Father's health improved so much that he was able to return home. On one of my last days in San Francisco, the Spanish language radio station ran an alarming news bulletin: "A Spanish Jesuit priest, Luis Espinal, had been murdered in La Paz!" A phone call to Enrique confirmed the worst.

I returned to La Paz saddened and fearful for what might lie ahead. I could not believe that the always upbeat Luis could have been assassinated. His keen sense of humor had invariably broken the tension at clandestine meetings during the Banzer years and his gentle manner was evidence enough that he was incapable of harming anyone. Luis Espinal was an internationally respected film critic, who used many an opportunity in his newspaper column in <u>Presencia</u> to take sharp jabs at the powerful and ruthless. He had survived arrest and exile, yet that did not make him shrink from speaking out against injustice. For twelve years we had been friends and taught together in the Sociology Department. Since 1971 he had been a source of information about mutual friends in exile, passing on news, greetings and an occasional letter. His brutal murder sent shockwaves through Bolivia and it affected me deeply.

And how brutal it was! On his way home after his weekly viewing of films at the 6 de Agosto Theater, he was kidnapped and taken to the slaughterhouse in Achachicala. There, he was stripped and thrown into the trough used to kill the animals. According to one source, his torture lasted 4 hours and was a "demonstration" class for future torturers. At one point during his torment, Luis managed to escape and hide in the eucalyptus woods behind the building. His torturers followed him, dragged him into a jeep, drove him to the end of the barrio of Achachicala, dumped him on the local garbage heap and riddled him with bullets. The following day campesinos on their way to the city discovered his body.

It was truly the culmination, the confirmation of what had been coming for some time, a new actor in the struggle for political power, a new enemy, unleashed by Banzer, deliberately ignored by the United States and eating into the fabric of Bolivian life. In a word, it was cocaine. Luis Espinal had been working on a series of investigative articles for *Aqui*, the weekly newspaper he had founded a year earlier with a small group of progressive journalists. He had uncovered evidence that members of the military, some cabinet members and other high officials were complicit in the production and smuggling of cocaine. There were warnings; the newspaper's offices had already been bombed. *Aqui* had to be silenced. Luis Espinal had to be silenced. He was dangerous. The truth was dangerous.

The evening I returned from San Francisco, there was a candlelight procession in Luis's memory. Students, religious, priests, workers, teachers and grieving citizens joined together in this, our poor, forgotten barrio, where many in the march may not even have set foot before. I watched from our second floor window, as thousands of mourners traced Luis Espinal's terrible final ride from the slaughterhouse through Achachicala. Songs and chants could be heard in the distance, then a swelling wave of voices in unison, "Viva Mi Patria Bolivia." The endless line passed our house and wound up the dirt road towards the site of the dump where his body had been found. They came and came until the music and flickering candles faded into the darkness. I was too numbed to participate; I could only watch in tears and wonder what or who would be next. Of all the losses, of all the killings, of all the senseless brutality, it was the assassination of Luis Espinal that tore most at my heart. It was both an accumulation of pain and an unbearable sense of defeat. I recalled watching from a window in 1964, while a mob demanded the blood of a henchman. Then, I did not understand their cry for justice, but now I was watching again from a window (not a frenzied mob, but an orderly, peaceful, sorrowful march) and I understood all too well. This was a price too high. This was very personal. The "rules of the game" had changed now. The bestiality had been ratcheted up to a new level.

Soon there were other victims of the cocaine calamity. Carmen, the neighbor who accompanied me to the hospital when I had my baby, tearfully told me that her husband had been murdered. He was a detective, one of the first to be assigned to narcotics investigations. He was found hanging from a post on the same playground where we had assembled with such great euphoria to count votes after the elections. He had been slit from neck to pelvis. The brother-in-law of another friend had his throat slit in the Altiplano for allegedly taking off with drug money. These and other such occurrences terrified me. Until that time, La Paz and Quito, Ecuador were considered two "crime-free" capitols in Latin America. These murders were most extraordinary and uncomfortably close to home. Then a mysterious plane crash in the Altiplano scattered dollars over the area. All of these events meant that political analyses had to be reframed. The U.S. backing of Banzer with a wink-and-nod drug policy had unleashed a nightmare whose full impact was now being felt.

The coca leaf is a millennium-old mild stimulant and an herb with profound spiritual significance. It is as commonplace as chewing gum, and in the decades before the 1980's, most Bolivians were unaware of and certainly unconcerned about its existence as a processed narcotic. After all, it had been used for medicinal purposes in the West for almost two centuries. It was even used in Coca Cola at one time, and Sigmund Freud prescribed it for his mother-in-law on a regular basis. In Bolivia heaps of coca leaves were sold in the open marketplaces, and it was and was not unusual to see a campesino chewing a wad in his or her cheek. Often there was a leaf stuck to the forehead of a cholita – to help ease the pain of a headache. Coca tea (*mate*) was and still can be ordered in any restaurant there. It was and is as much a part of the culture, the heritage and the psyche of Bolivia as coffee in the USA. No one ever doubted its importance or questioned its use.

Well into the 1970's, however, disturbing news related to illegal drug activity had begun filtering through the press, the radio and the events of daily life. Growing incidents of arrests for drug trafficking had also made the news. It was no secret that students in schools for the wealthy Bolivians and the children of foreign diplomats were increasingly involved in illegal drug use. The rules of the game had changed and the stakes were higher now. The anti-Communist policy-makers in Washington would soon use drug smuggling as a new excuse for military aid and enforcement in the area. Bolivia and cocaine would become indelibly linked, especially in the upcoming presidential election.

CHAPTER 56

CLEAN ELECTIONS AT LAST

We began 1980 preparing for another presidential election with restrained enthusiasm. Congress went back to work and began with a debate over the rules of representation. Marcelo Quiroga Santa Cruz led a broader effort to change the electoral law. When members were unable to reach an agreement on the laws, he threatened, "If we can't make up our minds in here, we will have to do it on the streets," and that is just what happened. He and his group of PS-1 parliamentarians marched out of the legislature and gathered a massive crowd demanding electoral reform. Congress quickly capitulated and made three significant decisions.

1. There would be a system of equivalent representation. The number of deputies would depend on the population in each department (geographical state).

2. The president would be elected by a simple majority.

3. Because of the change in the system of representation, the upcoming 1980 elections would be general, meaning that all electoral positions in the country were up for grabs again.

Although there had been a strong and proud tradition of indigenous uprisings in Bolivia, the campesinos became relatively dormant politically after the 1952 agrarian reform. During the Barrientos regime, they enjoyed certain privileges with the signing of a pact with the government, and in 1979 they united in the historic national confederation (CSTMB). This organization became key in the defeat of Natusch Busch. The campesinos were able to discover that their role in the national general strike was extremely effective and significant. Indeed, the Natusch coup signaled a new kind of political awakening among indigenous sectors, and more attention had been given to their problems in two weeks than in the previous four hundred years.

There were two things that had made this possible. First was their organization, for although the Bolivian campo is a sparsely populated area and families live at subsistence levels in isolation from one another, it is actually highly structured. Significantly, the rural area is strictly divided into cantons, towns, villages and communities, each with its local decision-making system.

Second, in spite of being spread so thin over vast, mountainous areas, the campesinos had an effective system of communication. In the nineteen-sixties, when the transistor radio made its way into every campesino hut, there was a demand for programs in Aymara and Quechua. The government gave them use of the radio waves during the worst hours, from 5am until 7 am when every Bolivian with any common sense would be sound asleep. Unwittingly, the officials handed the campesinos just what they needed to mobilize at a minute's notice with the additional advantage of broadcasting in their native languages when no one was listening.

For example during the general strike, word was sent out via radio in the early morning hours and they were able to block the roads, their ponchos moving swiftly in the darkness. They scattered rocks every 20 meters on every road in the country. When the sun rose, they were gone. No one was in sight. No one could be reached for dialogue. The army had to spend the day clearing the roads and the next night the process started all over again. The campesinos had effectively thrown gravel into the machine!

Attempting to make light of the campesinos success, the propaganda mill tried to justify the military takeover by accusing the campesinos of being armed and drunk. They had not been intoxicated nor were they armed.

With all congressional seats open for election again, each political party began to fill its slate with names. When Siles Zuazo needed a candidate for Senator for the department of Potosi, he could not name Panfilo Anave because he had made the unpardonable mistake of accepting a position in reproachable Natusch Busch cabinet. Instead he looked to Enrique to take the number one spot and run for Senator for Potosí and replace the disgraced Anave. Siles realized that Enrique was well known as a civic leader in his home department and that he understood the area as few did. Enrique had seen enough Senate sessions to know that he was fully capable of filling the position. He accepted and his commitment was firm.

One afternoon Isabel Siles invited me to tea with the Siles Family. I was amused by the way they all treated the candidate. Everyone launched a good-natured attack on "Papa" for giving such long speeches. Doña Teresa, his wife, said, "You remind me of the priest who preached at Marcela's (Eldest daughter) First Communion, the one who talked until Marcela fainted from exhaustion." Siles must have heard these barbs so many times that he didn't bother to defend himself. He only sighed and complained that he didn't like being last to speak on the program, because the other speakers say everything and never leave anything for him. That prompted gales of laughter from the table and the last comment, "Even with nothing to say, it takes you too long to say it."

It was then that he asked me if I would help write the education portion of the party platform and his inaugural address. I accepted with some reservations. After all, when no one was paying attention, I was free to speak my mind. Now there was the danger that my ideas would be taken seriously, and that made me a little more cautious. It was one thing to risk making a fool out of myself, but not of the presidential candidate. I began a series of meetings with the UDP platform committee at the Siles residence in the barrio of San Jorge.

Enrique and I were certain that the results of the next election would be a clear win for Siles. The campaign would be shorter but more intense because we were fighting an enemy that would not give up easily. Drug money was involved now, with an enormous amount of coca dollars, even more money than the CIA usually spent to buy votes for the State Department's candidate. To be sure, we were out on a limb, but we could not turn back.

Understandably, after two failed elections and a series of erratic palace coups, we were extremely distrustful of the whole process. There was no doubt that the UDP was the obvious front-runner, but it was also clear that we would have to pay a price for our party affiliation. One night the flashing of headlights from an unmarked military jeep parked right outside our bedroom window startled us awake. The intent was clear when shots were fired into the air. Later, threats on Enrique's life were more explicit and we had to take precautions.

With fear of another coup and a rash of repression and violence, we decided to look for a hideout, a place where we could go in a hurry from our work downtown. In hindsight, this was a mistake. At considerable financial cost, we rented two rooms near the Plaza Uyuni in Miraflores and began a period of confusion and disorder in our lives. To our new neighbors, we had to make it look as if we were living in their patio and so we spent Sundays and some evenings there. The rest of the time we divided between work and Achachicala.

We thought this would be a temporary arrangement and that it would end as soon as things were safe and ,of course, our belongings were never where we needed them. I was particularly torn by this arrangement, since I had to prepare meals and think about dishes, cleaning supplies and toilet paper for our basic needs. Sometimes we got our signals mixed and we ended up passing each other on buses going in opposite directions. It was chaotic and in the atmosphere of tension and fear, nerve-wracking.

In the final weeks of the campaign, each candidate organized his supporters for massive rallies and marches. Enrique went to Potosí to organize the closing campaign event for Siles. I went to the one in La Paz, which counted on a huge UDP following. Thousands crowded into the Plaza San Francisco and the mood was euphoric, but tense. I stayed in the rear near the Obelisk and watched out for anyone who might be causing problems. There was a festive spirit with balloons and songs. After the speeches and entertainment, the march began. I joined in for a few blocks down to the Prado, and then left to head for our hideout, which was within walking distance. At that moment, a loud blast shook the air. A bomb had been set off where I had been just minutes before. Siles's opposition was giving us notice. By the time I reached the rooms, the city was blacked out – a second explosion had taken out the electrical power plant.

I waited alone in the dark for what seemed like hours until the power was restored. News of the blast at the Siles rally filled the airwaves. Four people had been killed, and sixty-three seriously wounded.

Again, a brief moment of glory and triumph was forcibly ended by those directly or indirectly supported by the U.S. State Department.

Enrique continued campaigning with Siles and on June 1 they flew together to Potosí. They returned that afternoon and were to continue on a flight into the interior of the country the following day. However, Siles phoned very early the next morning to say his very dear aunt had passed away and that he would not make the trip. Enrique could rest and the vice presidential candidate would make the trip instead.

I spent the better part of that morning at a community center at the far edge of a barrio called Calacoto, in the lower part of the city. My "Creative Experiences" method was being used there with a group of *campesino* children and the volunteers had asked me to stop in to see how they were doing. The children were easy to work with – unspoiled by television and consumer madness. Probably any method would have been successful. I was satisfied that the volunteers were doing a fine job.

The visit ended with effusive hugs and promises to return *pronto*. Then I boarded microbus "A" that would take me back to Achachicala. It was a pleasant ride at the southern end of the city. Here the streets were paved and the warm sun bathed the interior of the still-new municipal vehicle. Radio

Metropolitana provided soft music and the sweet scent of *retama* blossoms from unseen gardens hidden behind high walls wafted through the open windows. I half dozed in a back seat momentarily oblivious to the fear and uncertainty that gripped the country.

The bus climbed the *Avenida Arce* and as we rounded the *Plaza Isabela la Católica*, radio Metropolitana interrupted its mid-morning concert with a special bulletin. "Minutes ago Hernan Siles's campaign plane exploded as it took off from the airport in El Alto!" I bolted to attention! I was sure Siles was not on the plane. I knew Enrique should have been, but wasn't. For a moment I feared that there had been a last minute change of plans and that there might be a note on the kitchen table telling me he had gone after all. The news continued. "Vice-presidential candidate, Jaime Paz Zamora survived. As the plane exploded in flames, he was thrown from the plunging wreckage. Campesinos have rushed to the scene and wrapped his burning body in their ponchos. An ambulance is on its way to pick him up." The reporters assumed Siles had been killed, but I knew that he (and Enrique) had been saved by the death of a beloved aunt.

There was ample reason to suspect foul play. A bomb had been set off at Jaime Paz's residence the night before and, by all calculations, the presidential candidate, Siles Suazo, should have been on that ill-fated flight. Not surprisingly, later investigations led nowhere.

Jaime Paz was flown to Washington that same day, but his sculpted good looks were gone. His face was badly disfigured with permanent scars that served as another sobering reminder of the price being paid in the fight for democracy in Bolivia.

As Election Day drew closer, the carnival atmosphere of La Paz intensified. The cramped and foul smelling bus rides through the poorer upper part of the city became mini rallies on wheels. Electrified by the political events, we couldn't contain ourselves. A frustrated passenger cursed the inflationary prices and the busload of chronically neglected women and workers echoed the sentiment by attacking Banzer and U.S. imperialism. The political analysis was admirably clear. Everyone knew who the enemy was and no one was afraid to say so. Whether or not they had stared down the barrel of a gun in their lives or had been gassed and/or arrested, they most certainly knew exactly why they were barely scraping out an existence and why they were sweating on that flea-bitten bus. I joined in with the rest and added my two cents. We shouted and swore and complained all the way to the end of the line, which was at our doorstep.

I again received news from San Francisco that my father was not doing well, and so in between classes, political events and research projects, I made several visits to the U.S.Embassy to inquire about a visa for Enrique so he could accompany me to San Francisco if necessary. It would be our first, but not last, bout with the U.S. Immigration and Naturalization Service. I explained that it would probably be an emergency trip, since my father's health was poor. "No," they said, "your husband cannot have a tourist visa. He has to apply for permanent residence and that will take from six months to a year to process." "Yes, I replied, "but what if we need to travel soon?" We went back and forth: I filled out forms; I tried to reason; finally, an exasperated consular officer stamped a visa in Enrique's passport and, then vindictively printed in big letters, "MARRIED TO A U.S. CITIZEN. CAREFUL!"

At last it was Election Day again! By now, along with the rest of the Bolivians of voting age we had had plenty of practice in going to the polls. We repeated the routine of previous elections, including the cigar-chewing Socialist Party (PS-) representative chalking up a surprising number of votes for Marcelo Quiroga Santa Cruz, and eager onlookers making sure the process was honest. As expected, Siles easily received a majority of the votes and Enrique was Senator-elect. The swearing-in ceremony would be in August.

That gave us two weeks to work on the inaugural address and the Parliament began a series of preliminary meetings to get things in order for the big day. But just at that moment, a friend returned from Washington with very unsettling news.

The United States was in a presidential election year and Ronald Reagan was nominated for the Republican Party. Our friend reported that ultra right members of the Bolivian military had met with the "Reagan people," who assured them that if Reagan were elected U.S. President in November, he would do nothing to oppose another military takeover. "If it were to hold back communism", they could count on his "full support."

The Bolivian election went smoothly and this time international observers had only good things to say about the process. The votes were counted and the results were official. But the opposition did not rest. Newspapers carried paid ads denouncing the newly elected officials. Each day the newspapers came out with news of clandestine plots to overthrow the government. At lunch one day we pretended not to be worried when we opened the newspaper to a secret hit list that had been discovered. It had the names of those to be "eliminated" by the military in a proposed "St. Bartholomew's Day Massacre." At the top of the list was the "Senator for Potosí."

The leaders of the UDP coalition knew that these were no empty threats. No time was wasted in preparing for the worst. This time we wanted to be ready for any retaliation on the part of the right. The Pro-democracy Committee (CONADE) was formed. Workers, students, teachers, campesinos and political leaders planned together to react immediately to any attempt to derail the election results. At the first indication of interference from the opposition, the plan was for the leaders to assemble in the Bolivian Workers' Center (Central Obrero Boliviano, COB). They would declare a national general indefinite strike and the campesinos would set up roadblocks. This time we would not be taken by surprise. We would not get caught unprepared. Everyone had marching orders and knew just what to do.

Then there was actually some good news to report. One afternoon when I returned home, I optimistically declared, "things are looking up." The U.S. Aid Office had just delivered 20 new ambulances to the city. I had seen the gleaming white vehicles lined up outside the *transito* (Bolivian for DMV) waiting for papers and license plates. They were beautiful! Unfortunately, my enthusiasm would soon fade.

CHAPTER 57

COCAINE COUP AND EXILE

July 16th was a holiday, La Paz's founding day celebrated with patriotic speeches and activities. It was crowned in the evening with a candlelight parade through the center of the city, followed by drinking and partying until dawn.

The next morning I awoke to a city suffering from a hangover: traffic was light and heads were heavy. I prepared a sumptuous stew to heat up at lunchtime and left it out to cool. My schedule read, "9:00 International Conference on Education, 11:00 UMSA (Sociology of Education), 3:00 Inaugural address committee meeting.

At 9 o'clock sharp I went to a small conference hall on Calle Ingavi, half a block from the Plaza Murillo where I was to attend an educational meeting and give a report on the work done by CEBIAE. The meeting hall was empty. Bolivians are noted for showing up late for everything, but it was most unusual that the representatives from other countries had not begun to arrive. There was something strange about that. I waited in the dim auditorium until an attendant from the center appeared and told me that the event was cancelled, that the international delegates had called to say they would not attend because, "due to current circumstances," their security could not be guaranteed. "What circumstances?" I asked. He wasn't sure.

Having time to spare, I walked to the Plaza Murillo and bought a morning newspaper. At the bottom of the front page of <u>Presencia</u> there was a short article about a barracks scuffle in Trinidad, a jungle outpost town. I took time to phone Enrique to see if he had heard anything, but he wasn't home. I walked down towards the university and stopped at Eli's for a cup of *cafe con leche* and a sweetbread. I reviewed my class notes, then sat back and enjoyed the cozy atmosphere of the sleepy little restaurant until it was time to go to the university.

I lectured on politics and education and when my class ended, I started up the Avenida Villazon with one of my students, Yadira, who also lived in Achachicala. We had often taken the bus home together. The day was calm and sunny and people were hurrying home for lunch. Suddenly the noonday routine was shattered by gunshots. We couldn't tell from which direction they were coming. Then there was complete silence. No panic, no screaming, no music from the shops. Then again, the crack of guns. We picked up our pace as the shots got louder and closer and then we realized that we had headed right into middle of the fracas. Traffic was at a standstill, but there were no horns. There was only the scuffling of feet as people scattered silently in every direction. Yes, a coup had begun that morning and as planned, the major leaders of CONADE had swung into action against it and were already in an emergency meeting in COB, the labor headquarters just across the street from us. To my surprise, several of the new ambulances I had seen the day before were parked in front of the labor headquarters. Ominously, they weren't there to take out the wounded, but instead, to transport the military and para-militaries for the brutal attack on those assembled in the CONADE meeting. As we turned down a side street with a mob of people, we heard more shots ring out from inside the building. Then, more ambulances arrived with more shooting and scuffling of feet.

Yadira and I jammed into a bus that was packed tight as a sausage skin. I don't know how Yadira managed because she was very pregnant. Then, as luck would have it, our bus drove into the Plaza Murillo just as the military were assaulting the presidential palace. It was another terrifying scene, again with the newly donated ambulances being used for a very anti humanitarian mission.

As more shots rang out, I had to make a quick decision. Was it safe to go to Achachicala? Sensing that it was not, I hopped off the bus in the middle of the chaos and the clicking of military boots on the Plaza Murillo and headed on foot to the hideout in Miraflores.

Oh God! Here we go again. I waited alone. I had no idea where Enrique was. Had he gone home? No one, not even Enrique's daughters knew about our hideout, so I couldn't expect anyone to communicate with me. We had no phone. I waited. A couple of times, I nervously walked out to a small plaza a half a block away to look for a phone, or simply to see if anyone was on the street. Already, army trucks were rumbling past. They were filled with prisoners on their way to the *Estado Mayor*, the military headquarters. It looked very serious. In our spartan room, I turned on the radio and the television and there was a general news blackout. I sat at the rough wooden table, head in hands and waited.

Two or three agonizing hours later, Enrique stood solemnly in the doorway. He had an extra edition of, the evening newspaper, _Ultima Hora_ that had managed to get off the press in record time. It was filled with photos of the violence, frantic pictures taken in utter confusion. We sat motionless for what seemed hours until finally, TV broadcasts were resumed. There they were! The new leaders of this tragic country! Decked out in military uniforms, with lighting from below casting long sinister shadows on the wall behind them. Still in combat gear, they announced in somber tones that they had "saved the country from Communism," and that "in the name of God" they would "exterminate all leftist elements." (Whose God was this?) A state of siege, a 7 o'clock curfew and martial law were declared. The constitution was suspended. Anyone out on the streets would be expected to show I.D. at the many checkpoints being set up in the city. General Luis Garcia Mesa was President, the same man who had said a few days earlier, "If Natusch killed 400, I will kill 4000."

Distraught and despondent, we waited until nightfall. I wasn't hungry but Enrique thought we should try to get something to eat. We ventured out onto the empty street and walked to the nearby plaza where there was a small canteen. The shutters were closed, but we knocked on the door and the owner whisked us inside and barricaded the door. He already had several customers and told us he would have to serve us quickly. It was after seven o'clock. He warned that we'd have to leave as soon as possible, so he could turn out the lights. I tried, not too successfully, to swallow some soup. Then we went back to the rooms and to bed. The house we were in was between two streets that led from the military headquarters to the center of town. We listened as heavy vehicles rumbled past on either side of us, then cringed as the shooting began again. This went on all night long.

At 5 a.m. there was some sense of relief. The night of terror was over but the trucks continued to carry prisoners to the Estado Mayor, Bolivia's Pentagon. Judging from the truckloads of detainees we had seen and heard in the night, we concluded that the arrests were massive. In the early morning, we ventured out to the corner. The streets were deserted. There were no newspapers. No one was selling fresh bread on the corner. There were no buses. No one was going to work. The city was paralyzed with terror. Later, a pharmacy opened its doors and we used their phone to try to contact our closest friends. No one was home –or possibly the lines were cut. We called the house in Achachicala and were relieved to learn that the girls were all right. I told them I hoped they had eaten the stew I had prepared the day before, since we wouldn't be coming home just yet. We hoped and even expected that this crisis would pass, as had so many others.

That morning the military chaplains celebrated a mass of thanksgiving that was televised to the whole country. They praised the generals who had saved the country from communism and gave their most solemn blessing to the new dictator, General Garcia Meza. I hung my head in shame and disgust but not surprise, for I had long ago discovered that the Catholic Church could be very complicit with evil. At the same time I had also learned that some of its members could be very courageous and outspoken in the defense of justice.

I saw how U.S. military aid and training were used to repress workers, students and religious personnel, how U.S. foreign policy disregarded and trampled rights - all in the name of some distorted notion of democracy and how violence was perpetrated in the name of God. It used to be that the government of a poor country could be bought at the bargain price of a million dollars, but in this, Bolivia's 1980 cocaine coup, however, the military took a page directly from U.S. State Department and the CIA handbooks. Now awash in coca dollars, the generals and the colonels bought the country for themselves!

There was no hope of dissent or popular uprising in the city. Everything had been crushed. By day's end we knew we had lost. Night and darkness brought out the fleet of military vehicles again with more shooting and arrests. When the generals threatened that the members of the UDP were to be "exterminated," they were not using simple rhetoric, this was already happening.

The next morning, a few people began to trickle out on the streets and we were able to reach a close friend by phone. No, he hadn't seen anyone and he assumed everyone was still "ill after the party," in other words, "in hiding". He mentioned something about the Spaniards and we understood that the Spanish Embassy was accepting exiles.

I remembered a group of Spanish Dominican nuns from my first years in La Paz. In fact, two of them had studied in our novitiate in Racine. Their convent was within walking distance and I thought they just might remember me and help us contact the Spanish Embassy. It had been a long time since I had seen them, but it was worth a try. As soon as it looked like it might be safe to leave our rooms, we set out to find the sisters. The streets were strange; it no longer felt like our city.

I rang the doorbell and the sister who answered the door was understandably alarmed. I explained who we were, that I had been a Dominican and that I was an acquaintance of Sisters Aracely, Cecilia and Corina. No, no one knew who I was. They'd have to see. After a little more conversation and persuasion, they let us in and agreed to contact the Spanish Embassy. We understood the risk they were taking in helping us.

They made a few calls but found out that the only place receiving exiles was the Mexican government, at the residence of the Mexican Ambassador in the barrio of Obrajes, and that the ambassador would wait for us. We thanked the sisters and I sensed their great relief when we left.

We went back to our rented room passing through hostile and empty streets. I reluctantly placed our checkbook and passports in a small purse and with a crushing sense of finality and loss, we closed the door behind us and turned the key in the lock for one last time. Even though it was the middle of winter, the day was warm and sunny, like so many other lazy Saturdays in La Paz. It was a long way to the Mexican Ambassador's residence and there was no means of transportation, so we would have to walk. We took a rough back road down from Miraflores and unfortunately, when had made our plans to hide out, I didn't think about taking walking shoes and the cobblestones and ruts made the trek most uncomfortable. We passed several checkpoints: covered military trucks guarded by machine-gun-toting soldiers who looked at us menacingly and who had orders to stop and search at whim. Enrique tried looking casual and un-senatorial. We joked and laughed nervously, even though we knew we'd be in serious trouble if we were asked to show our I.D.

We understood that the biggest risk would be at the door to the ambassador's residence. At times like these, agents or paramilitary were dispatched to all embassies to check on who was seeking asylum, and would routinely make arrests on the spot. We feared we would surely be seen at the embassy gate. It was a long hike and suddenly, everything that had been so familiar, the houses, the hills, the medical school and the hospitals, all looked strangely distant, as if someone, something had severed us from reality. After about an hour and a half, we rounded that last curve and made a steep descent to the street and the ambassador's residence. Enrique rang the bell at the gate. Immediately, a casually dressed man in his late forties appeared and hurried down the walkway through the yard. It was the Mexican Ambassador himself. I imagined eyes watching us from behind curtains or a gate or from a parked car across the street. The Ambassador was expecting us. "Your wife is a North American?" He asked. And turning to me, "I'm afraid we can't take you in. You have your own embassy and you need to go there. Your husband can stay here, but you cannot."

Crestfallen, we looked at each other. I wanted him to stay where he'd be safe. But he refused. "I can't leave you alone." We turned to leave. "You can come back," the ambassador said to Enrique.

Now, we began the long uphill walk back to Miraflores. It was already late afternoon and our thoughts turned to the curfew. We probably wouldn't make it back before 7 o'clock. As we climbed up to the old back road, the sky began to cloud over just a bit and the winter air had that all too familiar chill. Children were playing in a plaza along the way. Someone recognized me, "*Madrecita!*" For a brief moment, things were almost normal and we stopped to chat. Then, unexpectedly, an old wreck of a bus that had been parked a few yards away started up and creaked over toward us. The driver yelled out if anyone wanted a lift to the city. We knew now we'd beat the curfew.

Sunday morning followed a long, sleepless night. We realized we had no other recourse but to return to the Spanish Dominicans. They were as dismayed to see us back at their doorstep, as we were disappointed to be there. This time they were more concerned about our welfare and immediately invited us inside. They told us we needed to be careful, that the night before government agents were going from door to door in Miraflores arresting members of the UDP.

We explained that the Mexican ambassador advised us to contact the U.S. Embassy. They graciously let me use their telephone. After dialing several numbers, I finally reached a consular officer who read me a long list of questions: "Have you received threats? What were the dates the threats were made? What are the names and addresses of the person(s) who threatened you? What were the exact words used? Why do you think you are in danger?" Halfway through, I refused to give her any more information and said, "Do you understand what has happened in this country? I refuse to say any more over the phone. Come out here and pick me up or tell me where I should go."

"All right. We'll send a jeep." After a long wait, the jeep arrived with the consular officer. For the next four or five hours, she pressed me with the same questions over and over. She didn't believe we were married and suspected that Enrique just wanted to enter the United States illegally. She frequently reminded us that she could make no promises. "Yes" and "No" were not in her vocabulary. I don't know, maybe your husband can come, I'll have to check on that, I have to make more phone calls. Definitely if there had been a "Miss Indecisive" contest, she would have won it hands down. The process lasted hours and the truth was that neither of us, really, wanted to go to the U.S. Embassy. Then finally, with scarcely minutes left before the curfew, she blurted out, "All right, we'll take you, but we can't take your husband."

By now the Dominican sisters, who had listened to the questioning and served us lemonade all afternoon, were convinced of our predicament and were becoming more and more sympathetic. They assured me that they would see to it that Enrique got to the Mexican Embassy safely, that I should go with the consular officer and not worry. Enrique wrote down the American Embassy 's phone number and promised he'd call me from the Mexican Embassy the next day. It was almost 7 o'clock, so Enrique and I hugged each other and I left in the embassy jeep.

When we reached the embassy, located at that time, on *Calle* Colon, I was taken to the top floor, where a very tall, very blond man sat behind a desk with only a lamp lighting the now almost dark room. The first thing he said was, "Why didn't your husband come with you? You know, he could have!" Then he opened a folder and began reading a record of my activities in Bolivia. He knew how long I had been there, where I had been teaching, what I had been doing, and then he asked me if I wanted to use their Teletype machine to send a telegram to my father and brother in San Francisco. I did. He phoned someone and there was some disagreement about where I should stay. It was obvious that I was not a welcome guest. After a considerable discussion, I was shown to the nurse's station, which was near the main offices and just a stone's throw from two U.S. marine guards who were sitting at the reception desk, dressed in full combat gear.

In the nurse's station the outside wall was plate glass from ceiling to floor giving me a beautiful view of the city at night. The calm was shattered as tanks and armored cars rumbled by below, shooting, breaking windows and causing terror. This was state terrorism and it was working. Across the street a young man appeared at the fourth floor window of a hotel, and seeing him, a soldier raised a rifle and shot in his direction. The frightened tourist dove for cover. I stayed in the dark watching, careful not to move or startle the passing military caravan.

Then, my attention turned to the U.S. marines. They were boys, no more than 18 or 19 years old. They were glued to a radio communication device and were receiving reports from all over the country in English. Evidently, the miners were putting up a good fight in several places, as were *campesinos* with roadblocks. Democracy hadn't been crushed completely; a part of CONADE was able to react. To my horror, the youngsters in uniform at the front desk hooted and cheered when they heard that the army had mowed down a crowd of miners. There were high five's and jokes as if they were listening to Michigan State play Wisconsin. I wanted to cry, but was too tense, too angry, too exhausted. I wandered around to the other offices. Everything was dark. One of the marines spotted me and offered me his rations. It was awful stuff, dry and tasteless and I was sure that it was from the Korean War. I thanked the young recruit and tried munching a cracker.

I went back to the cot in the nurse's room, pulled a blanket over myself and eventually, fell asleep.

The next morning, Monday, embassy employees began to show up for work. They had been picked up from their homes by embassy vehicles for security reasons. The marines told me there was a cafeteria I could use. Since I had a few pesos, I checked it out. I sat at a table with a couple of American secretaries. They introduced themselves, "I'm new. Just arrived last week." The other said, "I'm and old-timer. Been here four months!" Indeed, and old-timer. I listened and did not feel like explaining my situation.

I went back to the office area where I saw that most of the employees were Bolivians and felt more at home there. They shared a newspaper with me and let me sit at a desk and use a phone. We exchanged comments and fears. Of course, they did not support the military takeover. How could they? We even had friends in common; after all, La Paz was a small city. They complained that the U.S. government was a miserable employer and that Bolivian employees were looked down upon.

I called the girls at home and reminded them to feed Pastor.

By noon, the consular officer came looking for me. She didn't know what to do with me. She told me that it was completely inappropriate that I was in the office area and that from now on I would have to sit in the waiting room.

The waiting room consisted of three or four chairs next to the elevator with nothing more than a low railing separating me from the receptionist and a counter off to the right where the young marines were standing guard. After a couple of hours, the receptionist, a matronly Bolivian woman in her forties finally asked me why I was sitting there for so long. I told her I was expecting an important phone call from my husband who had sought refuge in the Mexican Ambassador's residence. We struck up a friendly conversation and I discovered that she was related to a friend. After that she became very helpful.

When I got tired of sitting on the hardback chair, I got up to watch from the window overlooking Calle Colon. Suddenly, on the street below, army jeeps pulled up and there were shouts and scuffling as the soldiers raided the bank on the first floor. They routed the employees out of the building with hands on their heads and shoved them into the vehicles. The presence of the jeeps sent the marine guards into panic mode. They stopped the elevator, stood at alert, guns raised, ready to shoot anyone who moved. (At that time 100 Americans were still being held hostage in Iran after the storming of the U.S. embassy there. This surely made the marines especially nervous.) They warned me to get away from the window and I grumbled, "You've got to be kidding. Can't you see they're arresting the unionized bank employees?" The crisis passed and I pitied the poor labor leaders who had just been pulled out of the bank below.

By afternoon a few people filtered in for visas, mostly Bolivians who were anxious to leave the country. As a political refugee, I'm certain that I should not have been allowed to sit in a public area and much less have access to phones and visitors, but whatever the violation of protocol may have been, the arrangement worked to my advantage.

Just then, an old friend of mine got off the elevator and I told her my story. I asked her if the pharmacy down the street was open. It was and she went to buy me a toothbrush and a tube of toothpaste. "Is there anything else I can do, *Madrecita*?" (Still "M*adrecita!*")

I waited all day and there was no call from Enrique. What had happened? I called Rosario at the travel agency across the street and reserved two tickets to Miami. I didn't want to owe the U.S. government for the trip. When another friend came by and offered to help, I asked her to pick up the tickets. "Just ask for Rosario. She knows me and she'll accept a personal check." The transaction went as planned and in good time; minutes later all businesses closed up and the city became deathly silent.

Evening came and all the employees went home. I was alone with the young recruits again. They offered me more K rations and I realized they were really trying to be kind, even though they didn't have a clue about what was happening around them. Then they received a phone call that got them very excited. From their conversation, it sounded like someone important had just arrived at the airport. "Is he coming here?' "Yeah, he's coming now." Then the elevator stopped and out stepped a gringo with yellowish gray hair dressed in a loud sports coat. He did not look very impressive. In fact, he might be more at home taking backroom bets at a racetrack or selling used cars. He was the kind of man who talks too loudly and smells of cheap after-shave lotion.

The marines recognized him immediately and he returned their greeting by bellowing in a grating voice that he had just picked up embassy personnel from the airport. I wondered, "Who is this guy? How could he have access to the Embassy after closing hours? Then in a hushed tone, one of the recruits asked him, "Hey, is it true? Did they really kill Marcelo Quiroga?" His answer shot through me, "You bet! We finally got rid of that son-of-a-bitch!"

According to eyewitness reports, we know today, twenty-five years after the fact, that Marcelo Quiroga was wounded during the assault on the CONADE meeting at labor headquarters. He was taken alive to the military headquarters, tortured and killed. To this day, his body has not been found. How did this swine of a U.S. embassy employee know with certainty only five days after the coup that Marcelo had been killed? No one knew what had happened to him. Though the worst was feared, his disappearance was still open to speculation. In those early days, his wife, his family and Bolivians still held out hope that he was alive and possibly held in some dark cell. To what degree was the United States government complicit in his murder? They hated him for the nationalization of Gulf Oil and they hated him for founding a political party based on socialist principles. Mauricio Aira states in his book, GOTTENBURGO DESTINO FINAL, that in 1981, ex-president, General Ovando Candia told him while exiled in Argentina, ". . . the Americans would never forgive Marcelo and perhaps the explanation of his death is down that road."

By what authority did the United States trash the constitution and destroy dreams and hopes of a people whose only "crime" was to dare to govern themselves, and try to make a better life for their children? By what authority were they destroying my home and my life?

Consumed with sadness, I withdrew to the nurse's quarters and watched again in darkness as the army swept through the city shooting, arresting and terrorizing.

On Tuesday, I spent the day in the waiting area without any contact with the consular officers. They were, in fact, completely unconcerned about my needs, whether I had food, blankets or news of my husband. No one from the Embassy offered to be of help. Of course, neither did anyone bother me. Fortunately, I managed to phone friends and make some new ones while I sat in the waiting area. I called Enrique's daughters and told them I would be leaving for the U.S. and that I wouldn't be returning home. They hadn't heard anything from Enrique. Two days had passed already – 48 leaden hours.

I wrote a letter to Enrique detailing information he might need if or when he might ever get to the United States: my brothers' phone numbers and addresses, how to get in touch with me in San Francisco, and I assured him that I was and would be all right.

As I was finishing the letter, a young American man stepped out of the elevator in a very agitated state. We began to chat and told me he was a Protestant Minister and that his wife had just given birth to a baby boy, only one week ago. He and his wife had just arrived in Bolivia a month ago and they were terrified. They wanted to leave the country immediately, but everything was closed, even the travel agency across the street. Rosario had opened the agency briefly the day I bought tickets, but just as many other business owners in La Paz; she later closed the shutters and went home. The young man was frantic. I gave him the name and phone number of a Spanish acquaintance who ran a travel agency out of his home part time. I made the call for him to the agency, and it turned out that my friend would be very happy for the business. "No problem. Send him over."

By another stroke of luck, the minister's church was right across the street from the Mexican Ambassador's residence and within walking distance from the in-home travel agent. He thanked me and almost as an afterthought, asked, "What are you doing here? Do you work here?" I did not relish that idea, but I explained that I was under the protection of the Embassy while waiting to travel to the U.S. and that my husband was supposed to be in the Mexican ambassador's residence. I told him that I hadn't heard from him and that I was very worried. We wished each other well and he left considerably calmer than when he arrived.

That evening the two young military guards sat glued to the radio again, listening to a play-by-play account of clashes between miners and the Bolivian army. The reports came through in English with detailed descriptions of what was happening and where. The young marines' cheers echoed through the empty embassy offices as they continued rooting for the Bolivian soldiers who were massacring their brothers and sisters.

For the third night, I slept in my clothes.

Wednesday morning the indecisive consular official came out to the reception area and announced that someone would take me to the airport in about an hour. I sat up in my straight back chair and protested, "In an hour? I have to wait for my husband. I have a flight for a later date."

She assured me that changing my flight was no problem, that, in fact, the embassy had already booked a flight for me on Lufthansa. Of course, how could it be a problem for the most powerful nation in the world? Obviously, they felt a great urgency to be rid of me.

"But I haven't heard from my husband yet! I have his passport and his ticket to Miami." The consul took them both and put them and my letter in an envelope. I wrote his name on it. I tried in vain to persuade her to let me stay another day. She was unmoved. I had no choice and was helplessly crestfallen.

At eleven o'clock I was escorted down the elevator to a car with a diplomatic license. The consular official sat in front with the driver and I sat in the back flanked on both sides by men in suits, very tall gringos in very fine suits. We sat in silence and I wondered if they were supposed to be my bodyguards.

When we arrived at the airport, one of my "suits" got out and told me I was on my own from there. I said, no, I wasn't and that I expected their protection until I passed through immigration. The consular official and escorts then reluctantly accompanied me to the airport and once again tried to leave me at the door. Again, I made it clear that they needed to go inside with me and make sure I got through immigration. As I finally walked through to the departure gate, there was no exchange of words, only an icy silence. My escorts left hurriedly and with obvious relief.

Once in line to board the plane, I finally broke down and sobbed. I looked at the other travelers. Had these Bolivians not been affected by the coup? Were they from another world untouched by the repression convulsing the country? Was their world still intact? The woman next to me was on her way to a tourism convention in Germany as if nothing had changed.

We made the short flight to Peru and when we landed, I discovered that the Embassy had not booked me through to the United States. It was clear that they had just wanted to get me out of La Paz and had sent me on my way without money and with a ticket only to Lima. Luckily, I still had my original ticket but my flight from Lima to Miami wasn't scheduled to leave until the following night. As a passenger in transit, I was restricted to the area designated for that purpose. To make a change to an earlier flight, I needed to go to the main airport, and to do that, I would have to pay a hefty tax. That was out of the question because the only money I had amounted to less than a dollar in Bolivian pesos. I resigned myself to spending the day, the night and the following day waiting in traveler's limbo.

By evening, damp air from the Pacific Ocean penetrated the transit area and the light cotton skirt and blouse I was wearing offered no protection from the cold. For several hours, I tried sleeping but kept waking up shivering. Finally, in desperation, I climbed a flight of stairs to a darkened, empty cafeteria where I hoped it wouldn't be as drafty. A stocky waiter with a white dress jacket approached the table where I was sitting and asked, "Would you like something?" I told him that I didn't have any money and that I was just trying to keep warm. I must have looked very sad, for in a few minutes he returned with a big smile and a cup of piping hot coffee, for which I thanked him profusely. He told me was a Quechua Indian from the Peruvian Sierra.

His kindness was in sharp contrast to the treatment I had received at the U.S. embassy in La Paz. Except for the Bolivian employees and the marines, who offered me their rations, I was left totally on my own until the moment of my departure. I had eaten only one sandwich and a few crackers during those three memorable days. Warmed as much by the waiter's kindness as by the coffee, I went back downstairs and tried to sleep again.

I managed to doze and in the middle of the night, an announcement: broke through my hazy half conscious state. A flight was leaving for Miami at gate #5! I jumped to my feet and ran full speed to the gate. Ticket in hand, I asked if I could switch flights. "No problem," I was told. With the cold, damp night air of Lima behind me, I soon fell sound asleep.

I awoke the next morning to a blood red sunrise spilling over the clouds below and with the plane already beginning its descent into Miami. I had missed breakfast. In customs, I had nothing to declare and that aroused suspicion. You've been out of the country for a prolonged period and you have no luggage? I answered with a casual, "No."

Finally, inside the airport, I had to decide what to do next. I had no cash and had never even heard of a credit card. Besides my passport, the only I.D. I had with me was a Bolivian Permanent Resident card. I had a checkbook from the Bank of America, which at that time had a branch in La Paz but my account did not have quite enough money to buy a ticket to San Francisco.

I made the rounds of airlines to see what I could afford and was met with looks of disdain. No one would accept a personal check and without a credit card, I was a bad risk. I must have walked the whole terminal several times before I finally found an understanding ticket agent, a gray-haired gentleman who surely remembered the days when people trusted each other. He believed my story and said that he was risking his job by selling me a ticket to San Francisco. I wrote out a check hoping it wouldn't get deposited until I had a chance to borrow some money and deposit it in my account. While waiting for my flight, I went to all the stores to see what the newspapers said about the coup in Bolivia. There was hardly a mention, but that wasn't surprising. With the news blackout in Bolivia, no one knew what was happening there either. Only the voices on the radio in the American Embassy had an inside view.

The flight to San Francisco was uneventful. I finally had something to eat but food wasn't my greatest concern. My heart, my thoughts were back in La Paz, flitting from Achachicala to the university and through the streets I had come to know so well. Where was Enrique? Was he all right? What had happened to my students, to my co-workers, to our friends and all those who were struggling to throw off this unjust and oppressive system? What would happen next?

Bolivia was my home; it was where I had matured spiritually, professionally and politically. It had become so much more to me than the subject of a doctoral thesis. I had set out to study Bolivian cultural values but I ended up learning much more about my own values. I learned to question what I stood for, what my country stood for. Not surprisingly, returning to what I had come to consider "the belly of the imperialist beast" was extremely distasteful.

When I arrived in San Francisco, I needed to call my brother John so he could pick me up but all I had in my change purse were a few Bolivian coins. I got in line at a Bank of America desk to change them for two quarters. I stumbled over English words and the bank teller laughed and shook his head in disbelief when I asked him to change my handful of coins. A lady behind me overheard the conversation and asked, "Where did you come from?" "Bolivia," I answered. "Where's that?" she asked condescendingly and gave me a quarter to make my call. Was she concerned about my plight or just upset because I was holding up the line?

John answered the phone immediately and I told him I was at the airport.

"What airport?" he asked. He and my Dad had received the cable from the U.S. Embassy on Monday and knew that I would be leaving La Paz. John was right. I could have been calling from anywhere. He and Pop were grinning with relief when they pulled up to the airport curb in the Datsun.

The following day I contacted the Mexican consulate in San Francisco and two weeks later, I received a phone call from the Minister of Foreign Affairs in Mexico City. He confirmed that Enrique was, indeed, in the Mexican ambassador's residence and that the Mexican government was negotiating his exile to Mexico; he would probably be flying out in a few weeks. Enrique had made it safely to the ambassador's residence as planned, but was under strict restraints, not allowed to communicate with anyone outside.

My chance meeting with the anxious protestant minister in the American embassy was most fortunate. He was able to visit Enrique at the Mexican Ambassador's residence and tell him that he had seen me. After I had left for the United States, he returned to the American embassy to bring me news of Enrique. The indifferent and indecisive consul told him that I had been escorted out of the country, and the young minister had the presence of mind to ask if I had left anything for my husband. The officer said, "No", but the minister insisted that she check just to be sure. She reluctantly opened the bottom drawer of her desk and there buried beneath some papers, she found an envelope with Enrique's name on it. It was the one I had given her the day I left.

On September 21 Enrique arrived in San Francisco and we resolutely took our place in the community of those who denounced and challenged a corrupt and oppressive system The struggle for democracy in Bolivia was not over. It would just take a little more time.

Newly arrived in La Paz – 1964

Children carrying home cans of water 1967

La Paz – 1967

The Convent in Achachicala 1967

Our first visitors in our new house 1967

Children on their way to school – 1968

The first Creative Experiences class

We move to the birdhouse – 1970

Helen opens the children's library in Achachicala

The author with the Sankayuri community

The rural community of Sankayuri 1976

Community action in Achachicala

Community water project in Achachicala 1977

Building a new house in Achachicala 1978

Enrique inspects the hospital remodeling project

Exterior of hospital in Achachicala

The hospital is completed and has an ambulance 1979

The view from the house in Achachicala 1979

The hospital in Achachicala 2008

Enrique

ADDENDUM

BOLIVIA: THREE DECADES LATER

The seeds of democracy that were planted in that season of turmoil did not whither under the violent repression of the 1980 Luis Garcia Meza dictatorship. The brutality of the regime - imprisonment, torture, exiles and executions became international news, and world response was one of indignation and rejection. So blatant was the regime's involvement with cocaine production and trafficking that the eyes of the world were fixed in disbelief on Bolivia. All sources of foreign aid were withdrawn, and, ironically, the only country to give official recognition to the anti-communist military dictatorship was the Soviet Union. Bolivia had been brought to its knees by a cocaine revolution that was allowed to happen by the U.S. and characterized by a friend of mine as, "the U.S. State Department overriding the Pentagon."

Understandably, the Bolivian on the street chose to turn a blind eye to the cocaine problem, hoping that the influx of coca dollars, as they were called, would save the country's economy. Indeed, several infamous drug dealers did shell out money for sewing machines, clinics and other social benefits for their local communities, and the economy may even have been propped up temporarily. More than anything else, the Garcia Meza coup had brought shame, suffering and economic isolation to Bolivia. Again, within the country itself, terror reigned and the labor unions, student organizations and political parties were forced underground and their leaders into exile.

In 1981 a three-man military junta ousted Garcia Meza. Early in 1982, they turned the reins of government over to General Guido Vildoso who in an unprecedented move, called for the return from exile of Hernan Siles Zuazo and the UDP government that had been democratically elected in 1980. This ushered in an uninterrupted period of democratic civilian government, but one that has had its own great upheavals.

Siles and his left-of-center government returned to a country severely traumatized by nearly two decades of repression; a country with problems inherited from previous dictatorial governments: an economy in a shambles, cocaine corruption and a huge foreign debt. In addition, Siles's inclusion of the Bolivian socialist and communist parties into his coalition government did not win him favor in Washington or with the international lending agencies with which he had to deal. The IMF continually pressured for "economic restructuring" and the payment of Bolivia's foreign debt, which Siles believed were the result of illegitimate loans, made to illegitimate regimes. When he declared a moratorium on payments in 1984, he incurred further wrath from the North, and this resulted in the denial of foreign aid.

An especially sore spot with the U.S. was the out of control coca leaf production. In 1982, the colony of Amazamas in the El Chapare region of Cochabamba was one unpaved block long and its 150 families lived in bamboo shacks. One year later, as Siles was about to be sworn in, it had grown to fourteen square blocks with two-story mansions. It boasted of nightclubs for tourists and 2,000 cottage industries, all producing cocaine. The U.S. Drug Enforcement Agency was relentless in its criticism of the Siles government for not doing enough to eradicate the problem. Senator Paula Hawkins from Florida proposed the cancellation of all aid to Bolivia with the words, "If they are hungry, let them chew coca leaves."

Soon, the once popular Siles was being blamed for all of the country's ills. Fueling the discontent were the shortage of cooking oil and food staples, hyperinflation, continuous labor strikes, roadblocks and student protests. So numerous were protests that <u>Presencia</u>, a daily newspaper, even began publishing an "Agenda of Strikes, Protests and Ultimatums" along with TV, radio and movie listings. Nevertheless, Siles confided to his closest advisors that he would not use violence to quell the unrest, a promise he kept to the very end.

He governed under constant threats and rumors of a military takeover. He was even kidnapped by sixty armed men, allegedly belonging to the "Leopards," an elite anti drug force trained by the U.S. Oscar Bonifaz, Minister of Finance, negotiated his release, but attributed the success of his mediation to Siles's promise to allow his captors safe passage out of the country.

Not surprisingly, therefore, the beleaguered Siles cut his term short and called for new elections in 1985, only three years after assuming the presidency. According to Canadian authors, Farthing and Kohl, he was persuaded to do so by officials of the Roman Catholic Church.

In August of 1985, true to the frequently made observation at that time, i.e., "Bolivia is a young country with old leaders," Victor Paz Estenssoro was sworn in as president for the fourth time. Paz was the president who had nationalized the mines and brought a measure of land reform to Bolivia after the 1952 revolution, who later began to backtrack from his own revolutionary position and was finally ousted by *a military coup in 1964. He had chipped away at his own achievements, and now during this new period in office, struck the final blow to the reforms he and the MNR had implemented after the 1952 revolution.*

In 1986, world tin prices declined sharply, plunging Bolivia's mineral-dependent economy even deeper into the red and giving rise to the displaced miners' desperate "March for Life" from the mines to the capital city. Toward the end of his term in office, Paz's Minister of Finance invited a young Harvard economist to help work on an economic reform package for Bolivia. Jeffrey Sachs was convinced that he could solve Bolivia's economic woes and was to return later to try doing so.

Before that could happen, however, in 1989 Jaime Paz Zamora, the badly burned survivor of the mysterious plane crash during the 1980 campaign was elected to the presidency. Unfortunately, in spite of his left-of-center beginnings, Paz Zamora continued the neo-liberal policies and the implementation of the War on Drugs. Then, in 1993, long-time U.S. resident Gonzalo Sanchez de Lozada (Goni), was elected in spite of his gringo accent and mannerisms. Shortly after being inaugurated, he remembered the young American economist who had impressed him so favorably a few years earlier. He invited him to return to Bolivia, and Jeffrey Sachs set out for La Paz with a blueprint for reform in hand.

Sachs describes his glowing admiration for Goni, as they sat at his kitchen table drafting a plan to pull Bolivia out of its downward spiral into financial ruin. Together they crafted Decree #21060 that did, in fact, instantly halt the nation's inflation and devaluation however, it set the stage for an even more disastrous radical economic transformation of Bolivia.

In those years, neo-liberal economists hailed Bolivia as an "economic miracle," but those not so inclined preferred to call the 80's and 90's the "lost" decades. It was a period marked by a frenzy of privatization: first, the national mining company was privatized, then the factories, the railways and finally, the national airline. In addition, large stretches of Bolivian territory were sold or leased to foreign governments for the exploitation of natural resources.

The handful of Bolivian businessmen who invested in Wall Street prospered, but for the majority of their countrymen, the 80's and 90's were indeed lost. They were followed by plant closings and the failure of most of the newly privatized companies, record unemployment and the weakening of the once powerful national labor movement. Passenger trains became a distant memory and even the national airline folded its wings. The "miracle" was no more than sleight-of-hand economics – "Now you see me; now you don't." True, in this new economic order a very few did become extremely wealthy, but most Bolivians were left behind in the dust.

The Sachs/Goni neo-liberal model was an economic policy of the kind described by Gregorio Iriarte in and Execlub online Newsletter: , one without a moral compass for, "devoid of ethical standards, it could only serve to legitimize theft, exploitation and *injustice."* We have seen that Bolivians do not accept injustice quietly, and, here again in true form, they relentlessly, took their frustrations to the streets and the plazas.*

At no time was this more dramatic than in the year 2000, when the people of the city of Cochabamba waged a "water war" with the rich and mighty and won. Even more significantly, it was a victory that launched a popular movement that could not be turned back or contained. In this lovely city in the valley of Cochabamba, an international consortium headed by one of the U.S.'s national interests, the Bechtel Corporation of San Francisco, California, had flown into town with a project to privatize the water supply. They would make improvements and manage water distribution -- all for a hefty price to be paid by the Cochabambinos. When the townspeople received their first bills from the new company, they were outraged and it was time to react. They poured into the streets, coming from outlying areas as well as the city, in a massive spontaneous protest, rejecting the plans of a foreign company attempting to rake in huge profits from their water. Bechtel withdrew only days after, and Cochabamba understood the power of popular pressure as never before. Later, Bechtel tried unsuccessfully to sue Bolivia for $50 million in losses. In the end, after broad international support, the embittered company withdrew its case, settling for the unbelievable amount of 30 cents!

After this unprecedented victory, the indigenous population was fully aware of its strength and clamored for a fair voice in the country's decision-making process. In COCHABAMBA! WATER WAR IN BOLIVIA, Oscar Olivera, a shoe factory employee and labor leader, who had been a key leader of the Cochabamba water movement, writes about important lessons learned from this experience:

> *For the poor in the city and the countryside, the future did not lie in running after city councilors and congress people who have privatized and gambled away the public's wealth.*

> *The future instead came to consist of communal self-government based on assemblies, and town meetings in which all of us are empowered . . .*

During the 80's and the 90's another popular movement was beginning to rear its head in Cochabamba, a movement that would soon sweep through all of Bolivia. The cocaleros were coca growers, a new labor group in the lush mountain jungle of El Chapare. They were ex miners and peasants who had been forced to move from their homes in the altiplano after the tin crash of 1986, or after fighting a losing battle with years of drought. Now they had settled in El Chapare, where they found a new way of earning a livelihood: filling the new demand for coca, both for legal and illegal use.

In the 1980's when Washington began in earnest to train Bolivian military and para-military, as combatants in the War on Drugs, the cocaleros became a prime target. Many had come to the lowlands to work temporarily stamping barefooted on the coca leaves in vats of kerosene and ether as part of the process of making a paste that would later be turned into cocaine. They dreamed of making enough money to return home and build a house and buy a truck, but too often they absorbed the chemicals through their cracked feet did not survive. Others had their crops burned along with their humble shacks and lean-tos. Many, many were arrested, beaten and murdered. In a relentless pursuit of the coca leaf producer, the army swept through the mountain jungles eliminating small operators and leaving the major competitors to produce with impunity. The jungles were dotted with hundreds of hidden landing fields where private aircraft took off to carry the paste to Colombia for it was processed for U.S. and European drug dealers. Bolivian drug kingpins such as Roberto Suarez, made billions of dollars and bankrolled unbelievably lavish lifestyles for themselves, so outrageous that they could make the common garden-variety multi-millionaire blush with shame.

The cocaleros organized a labor union in order to protect their property and lives, as well as the legal production of the coca leaf and the four thousand-year-old traditions behind it. To their credit, they did not bend to these brutal tactics of the anti drug warriors. They fiercely protested the U.S.-orchestrated raids, the assaults on property and life and the rampant human rights violations.

The key leader emerging from the ranks of the cocaleros was Evo Morales. Under his leadership the Movement for Socialism, MAS was formed in 1997, and literally marched into the pages of Bolivian history as a powerful indigenous force.

That same year, Morales stepped forward and entered the presidential elections as candidate. He lost to ex-dictator Hugo Banzer Suarez, turned silver-haired grandfatherly figure but having received an impressive 10% of the votes, he secured a seat in congress and gave an official political voice to the cocaleros.

Before finishing his term, Banzer was diagnosed with cancer. He resigned from office and shortly after died at Walter Reed military hospital in Maryland. His vice-president, Antonio "Tuto" Quiroga, a graduate of U.S. universities, stepped in to finish Banzer's term and his wife, a Texan, became Bolivia's first lady.

Gonzalo Sanchez de Lozada was again elected to the presidency in 2003. Early in his second presidential term the epidemic of turmoil and unrest continued to plague the country. Poverty, unemployment, crime and corruption, which were festering in the national skin, had long since grown intolerable for most Bolivians and finally erupted into full-scale rebellion with protest marches and labor strikes fueling chaos and discontent at every level of society.

The final blow came in October of 2003 when the Sanchez de Lozada government announced that it would sell Bolivia's natural gas reserves to Chile. Bolivians did not want to sell this valuable natural resource to anyone, but making a deal with Chile, was absolutely the worst case scenario, adding insult to injury. Bolivia lost its seacoast to Chile in the War of the Pacific in 1879 and for more than 125 years relations between the two countries had been strained, when not outright hostile.

Immediately after Sanchez de Lozada's announcement, the population of El Alto, a city of one million inhabitants high above La Paz, in a massive protest blocked the passage of gas distribution trucks. The government was quick to order the army to retaliate. The soldiers shot into the crowds at random and killed 60 protesters and innocent bystanders. Infuriated, but undeterred by the massacre, the people returned in even greater numbers and marched down into the city of La Paz, demanding Goni's resignation. The U.S. ambassador sent a helicopter to transport him and a few of his cabinet members to the airport where they boarded a plane to Washington.

Vice-President Carlos Mesa took the helm of a very unsteady ship of state and managed to keep it from capsizing through elections in 2005. Mesa called for a referendum on what to do with the gas reserves, and. as would be expected, the Bolivians declared the gas was theirs and not for sale to foreign companies or countries!

By the time the 2005 elections were held, Evo Morales's popularity had risen to rock star proportions among the indigenous population, or more than two-thirds of the Bolivians. His promises to nationalize the hydrocarbons and rewrite the constitution to bring his indigenous brothers into the governing process won him 53% of the votes, and he became the first indigenous president ever elected in Latin America. His simplicity and humble demeanor won him admiration and support internationally. At home, reactions from his supporters ranged from exuberance to restrained skepticism. Many felt he deserved a chance to prove himself and his enemies awaited his first mistake.

Even though the campesinos strongly support Morales, they are no longer shy about demanding their rights. Protesters still block city streets and country roads almost every day. Traffic snarls, bus detours and the difficulty of goods not getting to the markets have all contributed to the frustrations of supporters as well as his critics. There is no miracle cure for Bolivia but, nevertheless, that is just what the populace is looking for.

Evo Morales' first term in office was riddled with crises, including threats of secession on the part of four resource-rich departments (states.) He succeeded in pushing through a new indigenous-conscious "pluricultural" Constitution and many social reforms. He has weathered almost continuous unrest and chaos so much so that it has appeared from time to time that this simple peasant who has never even owned a necktie, was teetering on the brink but his popularity among the campesino majority has not diminished. He was reelected in 2009 by an even wider margin of approval.

It is hard to say whether the continual civil unrest that plagues Bolivia is only chaos or if it is in reality the sign of a people who take their democracy very seriously. Bolivians are impatient for results and they prefer to take their complaints directly to the street. To what extent is the United States meddling in Bolivian affairs? True, Bolivians do not need a lot of help in destabilizing their government; they do quite well, thank you, on their own. But a few dollars stirred into the pot can always make it boil a bit faster.

Relations with the United States have been, at best strained, at their worst, openly hostile. Morales has ousted the American ambassador, the U.S. Drug Enforcement Agency and has sent warnings to a number of others who meddle in Bolivia's internal affairs and try to destabilize Bolivia's democracy.

In recent years, Bolivia has emerged as an international leader in the defense of the environment, declaring the obligation the industrial nations have to compensate the poorer countries of the world for the destruction and wasting of natural resources. Bolivia has spelled out the part wealthy nations have had in climate change and the resulting crises in poorer nations where the effects are felt most severely.

As 2011 draws to a close, Evo Morales has dodged the proverbial bullet in another crisis. This came when his approval of the construction of a road through TIPNIS, a natural reserve, outraged the indigenous people in the area. They set out on a two-month march to the capital city of La Paz. Along the way, local police assaulted them brutally and, popular opinion overwhelmingly condemned the act. Evo's absence and silence during the crisis left many of his supporters perplexed. In the end, the tribes arrived in La Paz to streets filled with cheering crowds and an historic show of national unity. Evo agreed to halt the construction and the parliament approved his proposal. The affair has become more complicated as new revelations come to light regarding foreign interests that are already developing the area for tourism and are exploiting its resources. There is also concern over murky reports of cocaine production in the area.

So far, Bolivia's path to democracy has been difficult. As treacherous as the crude roads that are hacked into the granite sides of its massive mountains. And if it is true that the past will cast a shadow over the future, Bolivia will still have a rough road ahead. It will also be true, that it will plot its own route and on its own terms.

BIBLIOGRAPHY

ACETO, O.P. Lois, JOURNEYING TOWARD JUSTICE, Racine, WI, 2008.

AGEE, Philip, CIA DIARY, INSIDE THE COMPANY, Penguin, 1975.

AIRA, Mauricio, GOTTENBURGO DESTINO FINAL, Diario de un Exiliado Boliviano, Invandrarforlget, Voras, Suecia, 2004.

CAMACHO, Guillermo, BOLIVIAN FOREVER, Authorhous, \ Bloomington, Indiana, 2011.

COOPER, Linda and HODGE, James, DISTURBING THE PEACE, Orbis Books,

BLUM, William, THE CIA: A FORGOTTEN HISTORY: US GLOBAL INTERVENTIONS SINCE WORLD WAR 2, Zed Books, New Jersey, 1986.

DUNKERLY, JAMES, REBELLION IN THE VEINS, Political Struggle in Bolivia 2952-1982, The Thetford Press, Thetford, Norfolk, 1984.

EDER, George Jackson, "Inflation and Development in Latin America, a Case History of Inflation and Stabilization in Bolivia", Ann Arbor, Program in International Business, Graduate School of Business Administration, University of Michigan, 1968.

FARTHING, Linda and KOHL, Benjamin, IMPASSE IN BOLIVIA, Zed Books, 2006